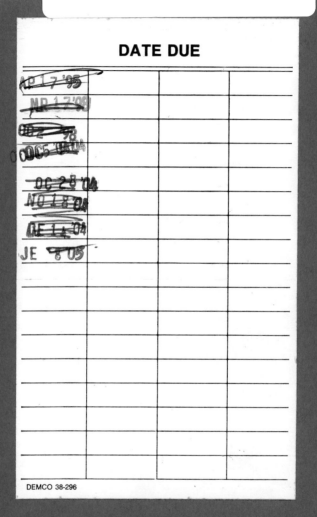

DATE DUE

AP 17 '95			
MR 1 7'09			
OC 2 '98			
OOC5 '98			
OC 2 8 '04			
NO 18 04			
DE 1 '04			
JE 8 05			

DEMCO 38-296

QUIET

ODYSSEY

A PIONEER

KOREAN WOMAN

IN AMERICA

Mary Paik Lee

Q U I E T

A Pioneer Korean Woman in America

O D Y S S E Y

Edited with an Introduction by Sucheng Chan

A SAMUEL AND ALTHEA STROUM BOOK

University of Washington Press ❀ *Seattle & London*

This book is published with the assistance of a grant from the Stroum Book Fund, established through the generosity of Samuel and Althea Stroum.

The paper used in this publication meets the minimum requirements of the American National Standard for Information Sciences — Permanence of Paper for Printed Library Materials, ANSI Z39.48-1984. ∞

Library of Congress Cataloging-in-Publication Data
Lee, Mary Paik, 1900–
   Quiet odyssey : a pioneer Korean woman in America / Mary Paik Lee ; edited, with an introduction by Sucheng Chan.
      p.   cm.
   Includes bibliographical references (p.).
   ISBN 0-295-96946-6 (alk. paper)
   1. Lee, Mary Paik, 1900–   .
2. Korean Americans — Biography.
3. Korean American women — Biography.   4. Immigrants — United States — Biography.   5. United States — Emigration and immigration — History — 20th century.   6. Korea — Emigration and immigration — History — 20th century.   I. Chan, Sucheng.   II. Title.
E184.K6L445   1990
973.00495702 — dc20
[B]   89-28077
                                            CIP

In loving memory of

the Reverend and

Mrs. Paik Sin Koo

CONTENTS

I L L U S T R A T I O N S

PREFACE

I met Mary Paik Lee by sheer good fortune. In November 1986, the Santa Cruz *Sentinel* ran a story about my decision to resign from my administrative position at the University of California, Santa Cruz, noting that I desired more time for research. Because many of the early Asian immigrants were getting old and dying by the day, I felt that I and others should record their stories while we could. My words struck a resonant chord in Allan Lee, a local businessman. He asked if I would like to meet his (then) eighty-six-year-old mother, who had come from Korea at the age of five and had recently written an autobiography—a 65-page, copyrighted typescript (Library of Congress Catalog Card Number TXU–169–794, 1984).

Since I was extremely busy at the time, months passed before I could leaf through Mrs. Lee's account. As soon as I read it, I realized that hers is exactly the sort of story I have wished were available for my courses in Asian American history. While students learn a great deal from history written in the third person (in the case of Asian immigrants, usually a faceless, nameless "they"), they become far more engaged in what they read when the information is presented through individual voices. Unfortunately, few Asian Americans have written autobiographies.

Mrs. Lee's autobiography is compelling—a story of hardships told with grace. When I interviewed Mrs. Lee for the first time in her San Francisco apartment, where she was living alone, I told her I was amazed by her crystal-clear memory. She said, "Oh, I am so old now that I often forget what I did last week. But these things I've written down, what I'm telling you now, I remember them because they made me *suffer so*." Suffering, however, is not her only theme. Side by side with her recollection of hard times are memories of kind gestures: she is ever mindful of people's ability to rise above meanness and hate. She has also been extraordinarily observant of her surroundings. Her obvious love of nature — which she now expresses through oil painting, a hobby she took up at age seventy-six — suffuses her narrative with a visual, almost tactile, quality that enables her readers to feel, hear, and see the world through her eyes. But this book is more than the life story of an old woman. For several reasons, it is a unique contribution to the study of immigrants, ethnic minorities, women, and poor working people.

Most important, Mrs. Lee is a rare specimen. The Population Research Bureau, a private research organization specializing in demographic projections, has estimated that, of the 700,000 persons of Korean ancestry in the United States today (in mid-1988), the vast majority have arrived only in the last twenty years. Korean immigration history, however, began at the turn of the century. Mrs. Lee is one of the last survivors of the seven thousand or so pioneers who traveled to Hawaii between December 1902 and May 1905, when emigration ended suddenly, for reasons that will be discussed in the Introduction. Compared with the Hawaii-bound contingent, the number of Koreans who journeyed to the continental United States directly from their homeland before 1905 was very small — fewer than a hundred students and ginseng merchants. Eventually, about a thousand of the workers in Hawaii returned to Korea, while another thousand remigrated to the Pacific Coast. Between 1905 and 1910, slightly more than two hundred additional Koreans arrived in Hawaii and California combined. After 1910, the only Koreans who could come were women and political exiles — the two groups together numbered about one thousand six hundred. Thus, fewer than nine thousand Koreans landed on United States territory before the passage of the 1924 Immigration Law, which reduced immigration from central, eastern, and southern Europe and virtually ended all Asian immigration. (Most Chinese, Japanese, and Asian Indians had already been barred by legislation and executive agreements.)

Among the Koreans who entered before mid-1905 were some six hundred women. Between 1905 and 1910, another forty females came. Then from 1910 to 1924, more than a thousand "picture

brides" arrived—women who had gone through marriage ceremonies in Korea (with the grooms absent) before sailing to join
their husbands in Hawaii and on the Pacific Coast. Arranged marriages were the norm in most traditional Asian societies; what gave
these transoceanic arrangements their nomenclature was that the
matchmakers showed photographs of the prospective partners to
their interested families. Nine-tenths of the picture brides went to
Hawaii and one-tenth to the continental United States. Though
few in number, these women made possible a continuing Korean
presence in Hawaii and the American West.

Approximately six hundred Korean children, two-thirds of them
boys, accompanied their parents to Hawaii, and almost all of
them remained in the islands. Fewer than thirty remigrated with
their families to California. Of the Koreans who went directly
to the mainland, only a handful took their children with them.
Ahn Chang-ho, an important expatriate leader, was one who did;
his son Philip was one of Mrs. Lee's playmates in Riverside. Al-
together, no more than three dozen Korean-born children resided
along the Pacific Coast during the first decade of this century.
Mary Paik Lee, born Paik Kuang Sun, was one of the girls; she is
the only one who has written her life story.

Mrs. Lee's autobiography is also significant because very few
book-length autobiographies of Asian immigrant women and
American-born women of Asian ancestry have been published in
English. The earliest account, *A Daughter of the Samurai* (1926), by
Etsu Inagaki Sugimoto portrays the author's life in Japan and the
United States, spiced with her observations of differences between
the two cultures. *Fifth Chinese Daughter* (1945) by Jade Snow Wong
and *Nisei Daughter* (1953) by Monica Sone, two well-known classics, focus on their American-born authors' childhood and youth,
and end as the protagonists reach adulthood. *Life Is for a Long
Time* (1979) by Li Ling Ai is the chronicle of a Chinese immigrant family in Hawaii. *Through Harsh Winters: The Life of a Japanese Immigrant Woman* (1981), the biography of Michiko Tanaka
[pseudonym], recorded by her daughter, anthropologist Akemi
Kikumura, covers mainly the years after Mrs. Tanaka immigrated
to the United States as an adult. The much-acclaimed *The Woman*

Warrior: Memoirs of a Girlhood Among Ghosts (1975), by Maxine Hong Kingston, is not an autobiography per se, mixing as it does biography with legend and history. Ruthanne Lum McCunn has produced *Thousand Pieces of Gold: A Biographical Novel* (1981), a novelistic embellishment of snippets of information about a Chinese woman who came to be known as Polly Bemis. *Clay Walls* (1986; paperback edition, 1990), by Kim Ronyoung, is the first novel about a Korean immigrant family in America, but we do not yet have any autobiographies, biographies, or even fictionalized biographies of Filipino or Asian Indian women in early twentieth-century America. Given the minuscule number of life histories of Asian American women available, Mrs. Lee's would have been a valuable addition, even if it had had no literary merit.

Fortunately, it is a well-told tale. This is the first full statement we have of the experiences of an Asian American woman from childhood through old age. Mrs. Lee's life has covered a lot of ground — geographically, culturally, and socially. Born into a secluded traditional society being pried open by foreigners in the late nineteenth century, she traveled with her family first to Hawaii and then to California — the site of countless social experiments — where she grew up and spent her entire adult life. Her natal family partook of the comforts enjoyed by relatively well-to-do Koreans, but her parents, after emigration, shared the poverty-stricken existence endured by thousands and thousands of Asian immigrants in early twentieth-century America.

Her narrative is at once singular and representative: though there were few Korean girls and women in the United States — a fact that makes her account unique — there were thousands of immigrant females from other Asian countries who lived in circumstances similar to hers, whose stories, because they were unrecorded, have been lost to history. Her autobiography is more representative than those of Jade Snow Wong (whose father was a merchant in San Francisco) and Monica Sone (whose father ran a boardinghouse in Seattle), because, though merchants controlled their communities, they comprised a far smaller percentage of the Asian immigrant population than did farmers, produce sellers, cooks, launderers, and common laborers. Mrs. Lee's parents, her father Paik Sin Koo and her mother Song Kuang Do, were educated people, but they had to support their family in America by cooking, farming, and washing clothes; subsequently, Mrs. Lee and her husband farmed, sold produce, and managed apartment buildings. Such occupations were the main ones open to Asian Americans — immigrants and American-born alike — in nineteenth- and early twentieth-century America.

To set Mrs. Lee's life in its global context, I explore in my introduction the complex circumstances that impelled not only her parents but also thousands of other Koreans to come to the United States and to remain here against overwhelming odds. In Appendix A, I discuss the values I hold as a scholar, because these influenced the way I edited Mrs. Lee's text, and I detail the kinds of research needed to turn the story of an unknown woman into a historical document. Appendixes B and C record the history of Korean American farming in California. The Bibliographic Essay lists available English-language sources on selected aspects of Korean history and on the Korean American experience.

During our last interview, I invited Mrs. Lee to suggest a special message for her readers. She has written her book, she says, because she wants young people to know the hardships that Asian immigrants have faced, so that they can appreciate their blessings today. She urges them all to acquire a good education because she believes, as her father told her so long ago, that what one has learned — unlike material possessions — can never be taken away by others. She is not pleased that some of the books she has read depict Asian men as uncaring husbands and authoritarian fathers. She wants people to know her marriage was a happy one, and that both her own father and her husband were loving parents.

"Anything else?" I asked.

"Certainly there are other things I remember, but I'd rather not tell about them," she replied.

"Why not?" I persisted.

"Because," she smiled, "they might hurt others, and I don't want to do that."

Her desire not to hurt others is clear: she does not name the individuals about whom she has negative recollections, whereas those whom she remembers fondly are clearly identified. I feel privileged to make Mary Paik Lee's memoir available to a wider audience, and I envy her for the peace she has made with herself and with the world.

Sucheng Chan
Santa Cruz

ACKNOWLEDGMENTS

I thank the Ethnic Studies Committee of the University of California, Santa Cruz, for a small grant that enabled me to hire Jenni Currie to enter Mary Paik Lee's manuscript into a computer and to do the first round of editing on the text. I appreciate the intelligent manner in which Jenni, who has an M.A. in the teaching of English as a second language, approached this task. Frances Trujillo of the San Benito County Office of Education, Hollister; Beverly Rianda, registrar of San Benito High School, Hollister; Nancy Pedro of the Willows Unified School District, Willows; and Karen Pearson of the Office of the County Recorder, Willows; made documents available to me, while workers in the Office of the County Recorder in Oroville, Butte County; Colusa, Colusa County; Willows, Glenn County; Yuba City, Sutter County; and Marysville, Yuba County, graciously allowed me to spend days looking through their records. I thank them all most heartily. I am grateful as well to the two colleagues who reviewed the manuscript for the University of Washington Press and to Naomi Pascal, Julidta Tarver, and Gretchen Van Meter of the University of Washington Press, who made many improvements in the manuscript.

The wonderful academic and public libraries in northern California are among the region's greatest cultural treasures. The resources of the Bancroft Library, the Government Documents Library, the Doe Library, and the Asian American Studies Library at the University of California, Berkeley; the Flora Lamson Hewlett Library at the Graduate Theological Union, Berkeley; the Dean McHenry Library at the University of California, Santa Cruz; the Willows Public Library in Glenn County; and the Hollister Public Library in San Benito County made doing research for this book a pleasure. Finally, knowing Mary Paik Lee has truly been a privilege.

INTRODUCTION

Mary Paik Lee was born in Korea in 1905 and was baptized by an American Presbyterian missionary. When she was five years old, she emigrated with her family to Hawaii; a year and a half later, they moved to California. Her national origins, her religion, her minority status in the United States, and her gender have together defined her identity. A brief review of Korea's long tradition of fending off invaders, how it became a pawn in the struggle among imperialist powers, how Christianity served as a counterweight to Japanese colonialism, and how the lives of Korean women were changed by Christianity and the anti-Japanese struggle will elucidate why religion and politics — along with efforts to earn a living — absorbed so many Korean immigrants in the United States. This was as true of female immigrants as it was of male, because Korean women who settled in America made crucial contributions not only to the survival of their families but also to the nationalist struggle. Such responsibilities elevated their position in the immigrant community and transformed their consciousness. By discussing the major social and political forces that affected the lives of Korean immigrants in the early decades of this century, I hope to place Mary Paik Lee's life history in its global context.

Koreans, almost without exception, are extremely proud of their long history, which they claim dates back four millennia to a mythical ruler. The country's peninsular setting has shaped this history. Contiguous to the northeastern corner of China and surrounded by Russia, China, and Japan, Korea has served historically as a conduit for people, artifacts, and ideas, but it maintained ongoing intercourse with only one nation, China, until the nineteenth century. Its strategic location, however, has repeatedly subjected Korea to invasion by its neighbors. Toyotomi Hideyoshi, a Japanese feudal lord, invaded the country in 1592 with 150,000 men — an action that caused China to send troops to the peninsula

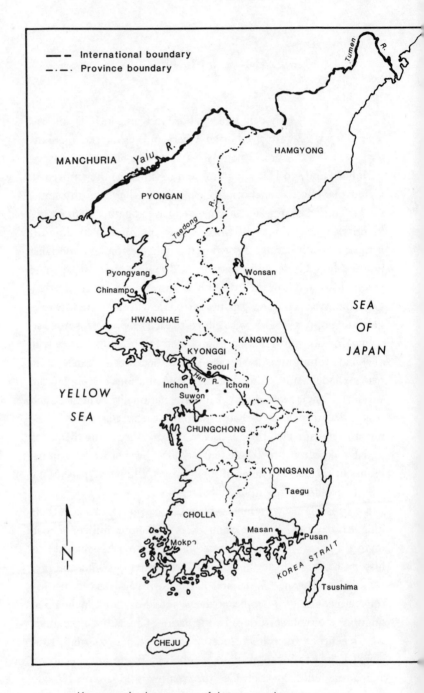

Korea at the beginning of the twentieth century.

to maintain its suzerainty there. After two years of fighting, both sides withdrew, but when a peace settlement was not reached by 1597, Japanese and Chinese troops fought again on Korean soil, devastating much of the south. A quarter century later, invading Manchu armies ravaged northwestern Korea. In response to these fearsome events, Korea sealed itself off from the outside world for the next two and a half centuries, which led Westerners to dub it the Hermit Kingdom.

Revolts have also disrupted life within the country itself. The largest revolt was the Tonghak Rebellion of the early 1890s. *Tonghak* (Eastern learning) was a syncretist religion that first appeared in the 1860s. Even though the government had captured and executed its founder in 1864, the sect expanded greatly in the late 1880s, when poverty became widespread and disgruntled farmers joined its ranks. When the first uprising occurred in 1892, the government tried to suppress it, but that only caused the revolt to spread like wildfire. Unable to put down the rebellion with his own troops, King Kojong appealed to the Chinese for help in 1894. By so doing, he unwittingly opened the door to forces that ultimately dismembered his kingdom.

The chain of events that set modern Korean history on its tragic course began some two decades before the Tonghak Rebellion. For centuries, despite repeated invasions, Korea had managed to fend off complete domination by foreign powers. Western ships began to appear in Korean waters in the 1860s, but Korean shore batteries drove off seven French warships in 1866, five American vessels in 1871, and one Japanese ship in 1875. The following year, however, the Japanese returned to demand reparations; the result was the Treaty of Kanghwa (1876), Korea's first modern treaty with a foreign nation. Modeled after the documents that Western nations had imposed on China and Japan, the Treaty of Kanghwa required Korea to open, in addition to Pusan in the south (where Korean and Japanese merchants had traded with each other sporadically since the fifteenth century), two more ports to foreign trade. These were Chemulpo (Inchon) on the west coast and Wonsan on the east coast. The treaty also allowed Japan to survey the Korean coast and granted Japanese citizens extraterritoriality, virtual monopolistic control of the import-export trade in Korea, and the right to lend money and to open pawn shops. Most important, to undermine traditional Chinese suzerainty, the Japanese insisted that Korea declare itself an independent state. Japan established a permanent diplomatic mission in Korea in 1880, and thereafter its sway over the peninsula increased.

The United States was the second nation to secure a treaty with Korea in 1882, with the connivance and aid of Li Hung-chang, governor-general of the Chinese province of Chihli and for decades the key figure in Chinese diplomacy. Li, concerned with the decline of Chinese control over Korea, urged it to sign a treaty with the United States in order to counter growing Japanese influence. Next came treaties with Great Britain and Germany (1883), Russia and Italy (1884), and France (1886). Each gave the signatory power the right to trade and to import goods into Korea at low tariff rates, to operate under conditions of extraterritoriality, and to enjoy most-favored-nation status. Upon the heels of the treaties came merchants, missionaries, and diplomats, all of whom not only vied with one another for power and influence but also quickly became involved in domestic Korean politics.

As was the case in China and Japan, the entry of foreigners and the concessions they wrested led to intense factional struggles within Korea's ruling class. King Kojong, who had ascended the throne in 1864 at the tender age of twelve and who ruled until he was forced to abdicate in 1907, had to contend with both his father, the former regent, who was called the *Taewongun* (Prince of the Great Court), and his own wife, the clever and willful Queen Min, each of whom headed a faction. Throughout his reign, Kojong tried to balance the contending forces around him, but he did not always succeed.

Besides scheming royal relatives and courtiers, Kojong also had to deal with members of the Independence Club — reform-minded politicians who favored the Japanese path to modernity. The group attempted a coup on the evening of December 4, 1884, with the goal of removing the pro-Chinese faction of Queen Min. Several high-ranking officials were killed, but Horace N. Allen, an American medical missionary summoned to the scene, saved the life of Min Yong-ik, the queen's cousin and the most influential member of her clique. The conspirators placed the royal couple under Japanese "protective custody" and proclaimed a new government, but it fell within three days, when Yuan Shih-kai, the Chinese resident-general in Korea, stormed the royal palace with 1,500 Chinese troops and restored Kojong and his ministers to power. Two of the plotters died, and the rest escaped to Japan. This incident — called the "Kapsin Coup" by Korean historians and the "émeute of 1884" by Western writers — was settled by two treaties signed in 1885. The Treaty of Seoul required Korea to pay an indemnity and other reparations to Japan for the loss of Japanese lives and property. The Treaty of Tianjin required China and Japan to withdraw their soldiers from the peninsula, to refrain from supporting the Korean army, and to give each other prior notice should either country deem it necessary to send troops to Korea in the future. During the next few years, the Chinese and Queen Min's faction were paramount in palace politics.

The outbreak of the Tonghak Rebellion gave China and Japan a pretext to renew their contest for the control of Korea. In response to King Kojong's appeal for help in 1894, China eagerly sent troops to the peninsula. Japan reacted by sending an even larger contingent, even though Korea had not requested its aid. At midnight on July 23, 1894, Japanese soldiers broke into the palace, took King Kojong hostage, and demanded that he recall his father to power. Open hostilities broke out between Chinese and Japanese troops stationed on Korean soil two days later, marking the beginning of the Sino-Japanese War. The Japanese swiftly routed the Chinese, and while the war was still in progress, they forced Korea to sign agreements that opened all southern Korean ports to them and gave them many other rights. Dismayed by the unexpected turn of events, Tonghak leaders led hundreds of thousands of farmers in yet another uprising, this time against the Japanese, but the latter soon overpowered them. Japanese soldiers massacred Tonghak rebels everywhere. They also defeated the remaining Chinese forces, driving them completely out of Korea.

The war ended in April 1895 with the Treaty of Shimonoseki, which awarded to Japan the Liaodong peninsula and Weihaiwei on the Shandong peninsula (both on the Chinese mainland) and the island of Taiwan. Russia, France, and Germany, however, jointly protested the terms of the settlement and forced Japan to relinquish the Liaodong peninsula. The three nations then proceeded to acquire for themselves what they had denied to Japan: Russia leased Port Arthur and Dairen at the tip of the Liaodong peninsula in 1897; Germany moved into Shandong the same year; and France obtained rights in Henan in 1896 and leased Guangzhouwan along the South China coast in 1899. Cheated out of the fruits of its victory, Japan smoldered with resentment.

Meanwhile, Japan tightened its control over hapless Korea by promulgating new laws, changing the administrative and judicial systems, abolishing the old Korean class structure, building railroads and telegraph lines, and introducing capitalist features into the Korean economy. Viewing Queen Min as the chief obstacle to their plans, they instigated a clash between some soldiers and the palace guards to create a cover under which they forced their way into the royal chambers on the night of October 8, 1895. They wounded the queen, poured kerosene on her, and set her afire. The king escaped, disguised as a female servant. The heavy-handed actions of the Japanese led to armed uprisings all over the country.

Then, in February 1896, the Russians entered the fray. They spirited King Kojong to the Russian legation and offered him sanctuary, which he gladly accepted. He lived in the Russian legation for more than a year. When he felt sufficiently safe to leave, he returned, not to the palace where he had lived formerly, but to another one near the compounds of the foreign diplomatic corps. During this period of turmoil, several Americans whom he trusted took turns staying overnight with him and bringing him food to make sure he would not be poisoned. While under the protection of the Russians, he issued decrees that disbanded the pro-Japanese government and installed a pro-Russian one in its place. Following Russian advice, he also changed his own title from "king" to "emperor" in 1897, in order to assert his equality with the rulers of China and Japan, who, as the Russians pointed out, were emperors and not kings.

In the midst of these power struggles, foreigners scrambled to gain numerous concessions to exploit Korea's natural resources; to build roads, railroads, telegraph lines, power plants, and oil storage facilities; and to establish banks and to process loans. When some of the investments did not prove particularly lucrative to their American and European investors, the Japanese bought them up, as part of their efforts to exercise greater political and economic control over Korea. Some former members of the Independence Club, concerned over the exploitation of their country, led mass rallies to demand that the natural resources be returned to Korean control. But instead of listening to them, the government arrested them — imprisoning some and deporting others — and banned their organization.

Events in China soon brought Russian-Japanese rivalry to a head in Northeast Asia. In 1900, Russia, Great Britain, Germany, France, Austria, Italy, the United States, and Japan jointly sent forces to China to quell the Boxer Rebellion. Using this expedition as a pretext, the Russians occupied Manchuria, from whence they refused to withdraw after the troubles in China proper were over. By 1903, they had moved into northern Korea, buying up land, cutting timber, and building roads. Japan, meanwhile, had concluded an alliance with Great Britain the year before. Bolstered by this treaty, the Japanese demanded that the Russians withdraw from Manchuria. When the latter did not comply, Japanese warships struck the Russian fleet at Port Arthur without warning in February 1904.

This was the beginning of the Russo-Japanese War. Though Korea immediately declared its neutrality, Japanese troops landed at Inchon and marched to Seoul. They forced Emperor Kojong to let them traverse Korean territory unhindered. As Japan won one victory after another, it expropriated all the concessions Russia had gained in Korea. The important city of Mukden in Manchuria fell to Japanese forces in March 1905, while the Russian Baltic fleet (which had to sail around the Cape of Good Hope because the British, as allies of the Japanese, denied the ships passage through the Suez Canal) was sunk by the Japanese navy virtually upon its arrival in the Korea Strait. The war ended in July 1905 with the Treaty of Portsmouth. U.S. President Theodore Roosevelt, greatly impressed by Japan's new military prowess, played a broker's role during the peace negotiations. Japan took over all the Russian interests in Manchuria; Russia also ceded the southern half of Sakhalin island to the victor. To ensure that the other powers would not interfere this time, Japanese Prime Minister Katsura Taro reached an understanding with U.S. Secretary of War William Howard Taft, whereby the United States agreed to honor Japan's hegemony in the Korean peninsula in return for Japan's noninterference in American interests in the Philippines — a Spanish colony that the United States had acquired at the close of the Spanish-American War a few years earlier.

To signal to the world its newly won preeminence in Korea, Japan declared a protectorate over the country, though Korea remained technically independent and Kojong continued to sit on his throne. But Ito Hirobumi, the Japanese resident-general in Korea, became the country's *de facto* ruler. Additional changes were made in the legal and monetary systems to facilitate Japanese land purchases and Japanese import-export trade. For the first time, Japanese began to settle in Korea in large numbers. Japan's farmers arrived as agricultural colonists; its businessmen bought up more firms, mines, and timberland; its fishermen laid claim to more and more fishing grounds; and its investors won concessions to build public works. The new administration also disbanded the Korean army, restricted the number of weapons — including kitchen knives — that Koreans could possess, and limited the size of public gatherings. When Emperor Kojong sent three emissaries in 1907 to the Second International Peace Conference at The Hague to plead Korea's cause, the Japanese, with the aid of pro-Japanese members of the Korean cabinet, forced him to abdicate and placed his son on the throne.

Thereafter, the Japanese took over every aspect of internal administration. In 1910, they gave up all pretense and annexed Korea, which remained a Japanese colony until 1945. In the post-1910 period, countless Koreans lost their landholdings, lived in constant fear of the Japanese secret police, and seethed with repressed anger and resentment against their alien overlords. To undermine Korean culture and to suppress nationalism, Japan sent thousands of Japanese to replace Korean teachers and made the Japanese language the medium of instruction in Korean schools. The rules against public gatherings were further tightened so that assemblies of more than three persons became illegal. The Japanese also closed down newspapers and passed laws to control Buddhist temples and Christian churches, lest they become centers of resistance.

Such draconian measures notwithstanding, Koreans did resist, both inside and outside of their colonized country. After forty centuries of sovereignty, they would not accept their subjugation without protest. A number of individuals were so fired with hatred against their oppressors that they took drastic steps. In March 1908, in San Francisco, Chang In-hwan assassinated Durham W. Stevens, an American whom the Japanese had foisted on the Korean government as an advisor in diplomatic affairs and who had publicly stated that he thought Japanese rule was for the Koreans' own good. In October of the same year, in Seoul, Yi Chae-myung, who had worked in Hawaii and California before returning to his native land in 1906, stabbed and seriously wounded the pro-Japanese Korean prime minister, Yi Wan-yong. The following year, in Harbin, Manchuria, An Chung-gun assassinated Resident-General Ito Hirobumi. All three assailants have since been honored as Korean national heroes.

Far more significant than these acts of violence by individuals was the March First (1919) Movement, also called the *Samil* ("three-one," for the month and day it began) or the *Mansei* (ten thousand years, i.e., "long live") Uprising. At the end of World War I, Koreans, like people from other subjugated nations, looked to U.S. President Woodrow Wilson for deliverance. One of Wilson's famous "Fourteen Points" had concerned the reestablishment of independent nations in colonized lands. Expatriate Koreans sent delegates to the Paris Peace Conference to argue Korea's case, but their petition was rebuffed because Japan, which had fought on the side of the Allies, strenuously objected to any consideration of the Korean question. (Irish and Indian nationalists were similarly disappointed, because the United States also refused to interfere with how Great Britain, its chief ally during the war, chose to deal with its colonies.) Apparently Wilson intended national self-determination only for the former colonies of the defeated Austro-Hungarian and German empires. Before Wilson's stance became clear, however, Koreans secretly planned massive, nonviolent demonstrations to call the world's attention to their plight. The death of former Emperor Kojong in January 1919 gave them the occasion they needed.

Although not all Koreans loved Kojong, whom many blamed for the loss of their country's independence, he nevertheless had remained the most nostalgic symbol of Korean national identity. It was expected that millions would pour into Seoul to pay him last respects. The date for his funeral was set for March 3, 1919. Planners of the national demonstration decided to proclaim Korea's independence on March 1. Thirty-three individuals from all walks of life, sixteen (some accounts say fifteen) of them Christians, signed a document modeled after the U.S. Declaration of Independence. The organizers then printed thousands of copies of this declaration and sewed thousands of (banned) Korean flags, which couriers distributed to towns and villages throughout the country. Christian leaders — such as the Reverend Hyun Soon, national superintendent of Methodist Sunday Schools in Korea — under cover of their religious responsibilities, traveled far and wide to organize the event. Members of the *Chondogyo* (the name the Tonghaks had given their sect after their 1894 rebellion), who were deeply entrenched in the countryside, likewise played a crucial role in spreading the word and coordinating plans. The *Chondogyo* also bore the major financial burden for the undertaking. All the planning took place under such utter secrecy that the Japanese police, vigilant though they were, got no wind of it.

On the fateful day, masses of people streaming into Seoul for Kojong's funeral gathered at Pagoda Park in front of one of the royal palaces. As a young man began to read the declaration of independence, the crowds thundered: *"Mansei! Mansei!"* ("Long live Korea! Long live Korea!") The Japanese police, totally unprepared, evidenced no coordinated reaction. March 2 was a Sunday. The Christians insisted that the sabbath be observed, so no demonstrations took place. March 3 was devoted to Kojong's funeral. But on March 4 large groups of people, including many schoolboys and girls, started marching through the streets again. This time, the police were ready. They fired into the crowds, while mounted marines summoned to the scene charged into the throng, standing in their stirrups as they swung their sabers right and left, felling all those in their path. Such harsh reaction galvanized Koreans everywhere. By April, an estimated one million people — five percent of the country's total population — became involved in the movement.

During March and April, demonstrators participated in more than eight hundred disturbances in over six hundred localities, during which they attacked and damaged forty-seven township offices, three military police stations, twenty-eight regular police stations, and seventy-one other public buildings, including post offices, schools, and customs houses. The Japanese retaliated with brutality and seemed to single out Korean Christians for punishment. In one village, the Japanese authorities told Christians to gather in their church, and as soon as they had all entered, the police bolted shut the doors and set the building on fire. They shot dead all those who tried to rush out. Everyone who remained inside the church was consumed by the flames. In the cities, the police and the military searched neighborhoods, rounded up people, and killed many on sight. Even conservative Japanese sources have admitted that several thousand Koreans perished. Two hundred Japanese also died. Almost 20,000 persons, including some 500 women, were arrested. Some 10,000 — 186 women among them — were prosecuted. The captors inflicted incredible torture on their prisoners, kicking and beating men and women, old and young alike, occasionally tearing limbs from their sockets, slicing flesh with knives, jabbing all parts of the body with bayonets, and suspending people by their thumbs. Thousands who survived the torture were summarily executed. What outraged Koreans most of all was that women captives were often stripped and raped. In this manner, what began as a peaceful, nonviolent demonstration was crushed.

Though the movement failed, the fire of nationalism was not

extinguished. It burned on, ever more fiercely. Korean expatriates formed a provisional government-in-exile in Shanghai at the end of April 1919 to carry on the struggle. Meanwhile, the Japanese realized that physical coercion was not the most effective means to govern. Under the glare of international criticism, Japanese Premier Hara Kei installed a new governor-general, Saito Makoto, in Korea and admitted that the Japanese police had abused its powers. The new colonial administration was instructed to use more cultural forms of domination.

The fact that Christians played such a prominent role in the March First Movement was not a coincidence, because in Korea the spread of Christianity converged with the emergence of modern nationalism. Not only did missionary schools introduce the idea of democracy, but since one of Korea's *Asian* neighbors, Japan, rather than a European power, became its colonizer, Koreans did not equate Christianity with Western imperialism — a connection that hindered missionary efforts in other lands. Despite the fact that the Protestant missions, as institutions, maintained neutrality vis-à-vis the Japanese colonial administration, during the harshest years of Japanese rule individual American missionaries were among the few foreigners who spoke out against the regime. They also harbored anti-Japanese activists and on occasion even protected the king. When the Japanese authorities singled out Christians for retribution during the March First Movement, some missionaries felt compelled to send eyewitness reports to their church headquarters in the United States to tell the world about the horrors they had seen. (They managed to evade Japanese censorship by using the diplomatic pouch.) Some of their reports were read into the U.S. *Congressional Record*.

American missionaries were in every part of Korea to witness the events of 1919. This was because, compared with the Catholic priests who preceded them, as well as with missionaries elsewhere, the Protestant proselytizers who entered Korea from 1884 onward were enormously successful in their efforts — so much so that, for a century now, Korea has been called the best mission field in Asia and perhaps even in the world. But Korea had not always been hospitable to Christianity. Catholicism came to Korea via China.

The first Korean to become a Catholic was the son of a *yang-ban* (aristocrat). He was baptized in 1783 while in China on a tributary mission. Upon his return, he converted several hundred people, but they, along with a Chinese Catholic missionary who had entered Korea in 1795, were executed by government officials in 1801. French priests began slipping into the country in the 1830s, but some of them also were executed. The largest number of Catholics were persecuted in 1839 and 1866. An estimated two thousand believers perished during the latter year.

In contrast to the sorry fate of the French priests and their Korean followers, American Protestant missionaries had a relatively easy time. The Methodists were the first denomination to consider opening a mission in Korea, but before they could send anyone, Horace N. Allen, a Presbyterian and a medical doctor, entered the country in 1884. Allen had first gone to China, but, unable to get along with his peers there, he had requested a transfer to Korea. Allen secured entry not as a missionary but as physician to the American legation, which had been established in Seoul in 1883. By an unexpected turn of events three months after his arrival, Allen gained the confidence of King Kojong and Queen Min when he saved the life of Min Yong-ik. In gratitude, King Kojong conferred a royal title on Allen, which allowed him to visit the palace without prior summons — a privilege accorded only the most important courtiers — while Queen Min showered lavish gifts upon Mrs. Allen. By February 1885 Allen had opened a hospital under His Majesty's patronage, and Koreans, as well as members of the various foreign embassies, flocked there for medical treatment.

Two months later, Horace G. Underwood joined Allen as the second Presbyterian missionary in Korea. On the same boat that brought Underwood were the Methodist missionaries Reverend and Mrs. Henry G. Appenzeller. Next came Methodists William F. Scranton, M.D., his wife, and his mother, Mary F. Scranton — the latter was the first woman appointed by the Women's Missionary Society to serve in Korea. Another medical missionary, John W. Heron, M.D., and his wife arrived in June. After Presbyterians and Methodists "opened" Korea, Baptists and other denominations soon sent representatives. In the 1890s, missionaries supported by British, Australian, and Canadian churches also appeared, but Americans continued to dominate until Korean Christians took over all of their own churches.

Since the prohibition against Christian proselytization was still in effect in the mid-1880s, the first missionaries could not openly preach the gospel, having to work, instead, as doctors and teachers. From the beginning, the Methodists and the Presbyterians competed with each other for influence. The Methodists set up the first schools, while the Presbyterians focused on providing medical services. With King Kojong's approval, Appenzeller established the Paechae Haktang, a Methodist school for boys, while the older Mrs. Scranton opened the Ewha Haktang, a Methodist school for girls. The Presbyterians, meanwhile, brought the first women medical personnel to the country, in the belief that a nurse or woman doctor might gain access to Queen Min, whose patronage would help them reach out to Korean women. Annie Ellers, a nurse, arrived in July 1886 and established such good rapport with Her Majesty that the latter began summoning her to the palace even when she did not require medical attention. Then, in 1888, Lillias Horton, M.D., came as the first woman doctor. Within the year, she married Horace G. Underwood.

The question of whether they should preach openly became a point of contention among the pioneer missionaries. Allen was opposed to evangelizing (except indirectly), whereas Underwood, who had no profession other than the ministry, argued that preaching the gospel and winning converts, rather than healing people or teaching them modern academic subjects, should be their main activities. Despite the disagreements among themselves, the Protestants made considerable headway in carrying out their mission. Clearly, royal favor helped. Quite apart from the useful services they provided, King Kojong had his own reasons not to hinder their efforts. To break free from Chinese control and to counter the growing Japanese influence, he repeatedly requested American advisors, but the U.S. State Department never sent any. So Kojong began to rely on the American missionaries in

Korea for informal advice, even on issues quite unrelated to their own expertise.

Other factors also account for the Protestant success in Korea. Church historians tend to credit the approach used by the missionaries themselves—their zeal, the "purity" of the gospel they preached, and their tireless travels to spread the Word. Such writers also claim that adoption of the Nevius Plan, developed by John N. Nevius, a missionary in China—which stressed self-support, self-government, and self-propagation in the churches and missions so established, as well as systematic Bible study—was responsible for the early achievements. No doubt, "indigenizing" their efforts was most helpful, for the Koreans could more easily identify with and cherish institutions that "belonged" to them. The Nevius Plan, however, was also used in China and Japan, but without the same results. Conditions peculiar to Korea must therefore be given considerable weight. These include the simultaneous growth of Christianity and Japanese imperialism in Korea (as discussed above), the simplicity of the Korean alphabet, and the impact of conversion to Christianity on the status of Korean women.

The first missionaries decided to translate and print the Bible in *hangul*, a script that King Sejong (reign 1418–50) had tried to propagate in the fifteenth century, but which was despised by the *yangban*. This proved to be a most fortuitous choice. *Hangul*, one of the world's simplest systems of writing, can be learned speedily, and since translations of the Scriptures were among the first written materials to be distributed widely among the common people, studying the Bible became synonymous with acquiring literacy—a skill that hitherto only the *yangban* and the *chungin* (middle people —professionals such as scribes, astrologers, and herbalists) had possessed. Learning the Scriptures thus gave the common people a privilege they had never enjoyed before.

Christian teachings appealed particularly to Korean women, who, to this day, have remained the most stalwart members of churches, both within their country and abroad. Some scholars have argued that Korean women found Christianity emotionally appealing because it resonated with certain features of indigenous shamanistic beliefs and practices. But a social factor was also at work: becoming Christians gave female converts a measure of freedom they had never known, and this, I think, helps to account for the fervor of female converts who, in turn, influenced their husbands and children.

During the Yi dynasty (1392–1910) Korean women led extremely secluded lives. By the late seventeenth century, the rulers had fully incorporated Confucian precepts into both their statecraft and the organization of society. Confucianism was most succinctly expressed in five sets of ideal social relationships, four of which were hierarchical: subjects, sons, younger brothers, and wives were to obey and serve their emperor, fathers, older brothers, and husbands, respectively, while the latter were to give the former benevolent protection. Only the fifth relationship — that between male peers — contained any hint of egalitarianism: men of the same age and socioeconomic standing could be affectionate and comradely towards one another.

The family and society at large were structured according to patrilineal principles. Though females were included in genealogies, only the barest information about them was written down. From birth, girls were considered outsiders, reared only to be given away in marriage. Married women kept their own names, but they were cut off from contact with their natal families, having become members of their husbands' lineages. Women could not inherit property, while widows were forbidden to remarry. The unequal value accorded men and women was expressed in the saying: *namjon; yobi* (men are honored; women are abased).

The primary duties of married women were to serve their mothers-in-law and to bear sons for their husbands. Women who bore only daughters might as well have been childless — they had no social standing whatsoever. Men whose first wives produced no male heirs took concubines; if the latter also failed to give birth to boys, the families resorted to adopting sons, because only men were allowed to perform the rituals of ancestor worship. The filial daughter, the chaste woman, the obedient wife, and the devoted mother were the models of feminine virtue.

Even architectural design reflected the subordinate status of women. The ideal Korean house contained two wings shaped like an L: the outer wing was reserved for men and the inner one for women. Poor peasants who lived in tiny thatched huts nevertheless still kept an *anbang* (inner room) for their women. Men continued to sleep in the male quarters after they were married, visiting their wives only in the dark of night, and, in some cases, only with their parents' permission.

Women were not allowed outdoors in the daytime: they could travel outside their gates, with heavy veils, only after the evening bell had tolled, signifying the beginning of a curfew for men. Slaves and outcastes who did housekeeping work such as washing clothes by the river or by the village well, were the only women who could show their faces in public. Female shamans, known as *mudang*, who performed both divination and healing, and professional female entertainers, called *kisaeng*, also had greater freedom of movement, though the status of both was very low indeed. Paradoxically, *kisaeng* were the only women allowed some education, apart from a handful of *yangban* women taught by private tutors within the confines of their homes. Because *kisaeng* had to be witty and accomplished in order to amuse men, they learned to sing, to play musical instruments, and to compose and recite poetry and the classics.

Recent scholarship has shown that the status of Korean women had not always been so abject. Unlike the situation during the middle and late Yi dynasty, during the Silla (688–935), Koryo (935–1392), and early Yi dynasties women could inherit property — which was equally divided among all the children, regardless of sex, upon a father's death — could participate in ancestor worship, and could continue to relate to their natal families. Before the mid-seventeenth century, male adoption was rare. Widows could remarry, because the patrilineage was not then the basic unit of society. Therefore, what has been called the "traditional" status of Korean women was, in fact, a cultural borrowing, and a relatively late one at that.

War and the coming of missionaries greatly affected the lives of Korean women in the late nineteenth and early twentieth centuries. Invading armies, wherever they march in the world, have always abused women. The armies in Korea were no exception. Korean women who were raped — or worse, gang-raped — usually committed suicide. But the presence of would-be conquerors also allowed women to take part in resistance movements: they hid men with prices on their heads, acted as secret couriers, and succored their own troops by offering them food, washing and mending their clothes, making their sandals, and tending the injured and the sick. It can be argued that, during such periods, Korean women fleetingly entered the public realm.

The changes introduced by the Protestant missionaries had an even more profound impact. Women missionaries and wives of male missionaries made the first efforts to educate and convert Korean women — not so much for the sake of liberating them, but because they thought women held the key to the conversion of Korean families. The women missionaries conducted Bible classes in their own homes, which more and more Korean women began to visit as time passed. The first three female converts were baptized in 1888. Because they had to overcome so many obstacles before they could adopt Christianity — a religion that directly challenged some of the fundamental tenets of Confucianism — those women who became Christians were ardent believers.

The women missionaries also provided new role models for their female converts, some of whom became "Bible women," who not only visited their neighbors but also on occasion traveled outside of their hometowns or villages to proselytize the new faith — a hitherto unheard-of activity for Korean women. Many of the Bible women were widows from lower-class families who welcomed the wages they earned, meager though they were. Perhaps even more important, widows, who were accorded no rights whatsoever in Yi dynasty society, found Christianity appealing because it gave them a place in the new community of believers. Working within the church allowed formerly secluded women to learn to read, to get out of their household prisons, to organize themselves for good works, to travel in the cause of evangelism, and to become valued public persons.

The missionary schools produced the first women professionals and leaders in twentieth-century Korea. This was especially true of girls educated at Ewha Haktang. Esther Pak (née Kim Chomdong), a graduate of Ewha, was the first Korean woman to obtain an M.D. (in 1900) from an American medical school. Upon returning to her native land, she worked tirelessly for eleven years before dying at age thirty-three. Helen Kim, another graduate of Ewha, earned a Ph.D. from Columbia University—the first Korean woman to receive a Ph.D. anywhere—and became the first Korean president of Ewha Woman's University (which grew out of the girls' school). Louise Yim, a fighter for Korean independence, and Induk Pahk, an indefatigable "traveling secretary" for the World Student Christian Movement, were also graduates of Ewha. These four were but the most illustrious among many modern Korean Christian women leaders. According to Mary Paik Lee, her paternal grandmother, Sin Duk Bok, also dedicated her life to educating women after she had become a Christian.

The American presence also had an unintended consequence: Korean emigration to the Western hemisphere. By the turn of the century, several hundred thousand Koreans lived abroad, the majority of them on the Asian mainland—in the maritime provinces of Russia, in Manchuria, and in China proper, south of the Great Wall. These people had sought no government approval for their departure, having simply drifted across the border and settled wherever they found means of livelihood. In addition, a small number of Koreans had gone to Japan as students and workers. Then, between December 1902 and May 1905, more than 7,000 were recruited to work in the sugar plantations of Hawaii, while about 1,000 were spirited out of Korea in May 1905 to labor in the henequen plantations of Mexico.

The emigrants to Hawaii were the first Koreans whose departure was officially sanctioned. As in so many other developments in this period of Korean history, Horace N. Allen had a hand in this endeavor. Unable to get along with his fellow missionaries, Allen had resigned from the Presbyterian Mission in 1887. For the next two years, he served the Korean government as its foreign secretary in the Korean Legation in Washington, D.C. Finding diplomatic work to his liking, he aspired to become the American minister in Seoul, but he realized that being an employee of the Korean government hindered his chances of being chosen. So he left King Kojong's service in 1889, reenlisted as a missionary, and returned to Korea, where he served in Pusan and Inchon for a year.

When he received an appointment as secretary of the United States Legation in Seoul, he resigned once again from the Presbyterian Mission in 1890. Allen remained legation secretary for seven years, all the while acting as a conduit between the American and Korean governments, as well as between American private citizens and Korean authorities. During this period, he successfully obtained several lucrative concessions, including the Unsan gold mines — the most productive mines ever worked in Korea — and various franchises for his friends. Finally, in 1897, Allen secured the post he had most desired, and he served as American minister to Korea for the next eight years.

While in this post, Allen visited the United States in 1902. On his way back to Korea, he stopped in Honolulu, where he met with representatives of the Hawaiian Sugar Planters Association (HSPA) at their request. These men were interested in recruiting Koreans because, by then, Japanese workers, who comprised two-thirds of the total plantation labor force in the islands, had become militant and were engaging in work stoppages and spontaneous strikes. The planters wanted to import other ethnic groups to offset what they called the Japanese "labor monopoly." Allen agreed to help the HSPA, although he arranged to communicate with them thereafter only through intermediaries, in order not to compromise his official status.

One reason Allen was willing to play a clandestine role in the undertaking was that he thought doing so might help him repay a favor. George Nash, governor of Ohio and a friend of President William McKinley, had lobbied on Allen's behalf for the ministerial post. Nash had a stepson, David W. Deshler, who operated a number of enterprises in Japan and in Korea and whom Allen knew. Nash was fond of his stepson, and Allen thought the latter would appreciate the opportunity to expand his business dealings by recruiting laborers for the HSPA.

As soon as he arrived back in Seoul, Allen went to see Emperor Kojong and persuaded him that it would be desirable to allow his subjects to emigrate. Kojong agreed to set up an emigration bureau, partly because famine had stalked in several northern provinces the year before, but also because Allen's argument — that the desire of American employers to hire Korean workers, at a time when they did not welcome Japanese, would give Korea international prestige — appealed to His Majesty. Allen then asked Kojong to grant the "emigration franchise" to his friend David Deshler.

Royal approval having been received, Deshler set up the mechanisms for his venture. He first hired a number of interpreters and assistants to post announcements to attract applicants. Next he opened a bank, in which the HSPA was the sole depositor, to lend money to aspiring emigrants for their passage and for the "show money" they had to have in their possession upon arrival in Hawaii. When Hawaii was annexed by the United States in 1900, American laws became applicable in the islands, including one that prohibited the importation of contract laborers. Recruited Korean laborers had to "prove" they were free immigrants by having money on their persons. The borrowed funds from Deshler served this purpose.

Few Koreans responded to the recruitment efforts, however, until the Reverend George Heber Jones, pastor of the Methodist Mission in Inchon, persuaded members of his congregation that life for them as Christians would be more pleasant in Hawaii, a Christian land. About half of the first shipment that left in December 1902 were members of Jones's church. Other missionaries gave similar advice. As a result of the missionaries' active role, an estimated 40 percent of the emigrants were Christian converts. Not all the missionaries aided the emigration scheme, however. Some, in fact, tried to prevent their followers from leaving, because each one who departed meant the "loss" of a convert.

Unlike Chinese and Japanese emigrants to America, who came from only a limited number of localities, Korean emigrants hailed from many places — particularly from the port cities of Inchon, Mokpo, Pusan, Masan, Wonsan, and Chinampo, as well as from the two largest cities in the country, Seoul and Pyongyang. As for their socioeconomic origins, according to Wayne Patterson and Hyung June Moon, most were laborers, former soldiers, artisans, peasants, and unemployed men. There were also some students and professionals, however, such as Mary Paik Lee's father, who left for political reasons: towards the close of the Russo-Japanese War, the Japanese had commandeered the Paik family's house, along with the houses of their neighbors, for quartering soldiers; uncertain of the future, the Paik family decided that some of their members should leave, in order to ensure the survival of at least one branch of the family. One of the sons, Paik Sin Koo, and his nuclear family were chosen to go.

The emigrants traveled on ships owned by Deshler to Kobe, Japan, where they were medically examined before proceeding to Hawaii. The fact that almost 10 percent of the emigrants were women and about 8 percent were children indicates that quite a number intended to settle overseas. This is corroborated by the fact that only one-seventh of them eventually returned to Korea — a much lower percentage of return migrants than among the Chinese and Japanese. Japan's ever-tightening grip over Korea no doubt also reduced the return migration rate. Between 1903 and 1907, more than a thousand of the Koreans in Hawaii sailed to the continental United States to join the several dozen ginseng merchants and students who had gone there directly.

Emigration ended suddenly in 1905 for two reasons. First, news drifted back to Korea that the workers who had gone to Mexico were being badly mistreated, so the Korean government halted emigration not only to that country but also to Hawaii. Second, Japan pressured Korea to close the emigration office in order to cut off the supply of Korean laborers to the islands, because the sugar plantation owners were using them as scabs against striking Japanese plantation workers. The secondary migration from Hawaii to the mainland also ended when, on March 14, 1907, President Theodore Roosevelt issued Executive Order 589 to prohibit such movement. This was done to mollify anti-Japanese groups in California, which were demanding an end to Japanese immigration.

Though Koreans were not the primary target of the curb, they were nevertheless affected by this order.

Under Japanese colonial rule, which lasted until 1945, the only Koreans allowed to leave legally for the United States were approximately one thousand picture brides, nine-tenths of whom joined husbands in Hawaii, with the rest going to the Pacific Coast. About five hundred students, many of them anti-Japanese activists, also managed to land in the United States without passports. Their entry was first made possible by the efforts of the Reverend David Lee (Yi Tae-wi), a graduate of the missionary-founded Sung Sil Academy in Pyongyang, who had come in 1905 to study in Berkeley, California. He served as minister of the Korean Methodist Church in San Francisco from 1910 until 1928, when he died of tuberculosis. (This is the same man who performed Mary Paik Lee's wedding.) One day, the Reverend Lee heard that thirteen Koreans were being held in the detention barracks of the U.S. Immigration and Naturalization Service on Angel Island and were forbidden to land. He sent a telegram on their behalf to U.S. Secretary of State William Jennings Bryan, arguing that the students should not be sent back to Korea because the Japanese authorities were sure to execute them. Nor, said he, could they be returned to China, from whence they had sailed, because they were not Chinese citizens. Bryan granted the reverend's petition, thus setting a precedent for the admission of Korean refugee students. After the passage of the 1924 Immigration Act, however, which greatly reduced the number of immigrants from eastern and southern Europe and virtually barred all Asian immigrants, Korean students were no longer allowed to remain in the United States after they had completed their studies.

Almost all the Koreans who went to Hawaii initially worked in the sugar plantations, because that was what they had been recruited to do. Starting in 1835, when the first sugar plantation was established, sugar production expanded until it became the very foundation of the Hawaiian economy. The 375 tons produced in 1850 increased to over 9,000 tons in 1870; almost 32,000 tons in 1880; 130,000 tons in 1890; 300,000 tons in 1900; and over half a million tons in 1910. In the latter year, some 44,000 workers labored in the fields, about 10 percent of them Koreans. But plantation labor was onerous, so as soon as some of the workers finished their terms, they moved to Honolulu to open small stores, bathhouses, or boardinghouses.

On the mainland, the early immigrants lived primarily in California, but small numbers were also found in other western states. In the beginning, most toiled in the fields, as they had done in Hawaii. This was not because, as was often assumed, they came from peasant societies and found agricultural work "natural," but because no other work was to be had. Long before any Koreans set foot on American soil, white Americans on the Pacific Coast had already subjugated the native American Indians, the Mexicans, and the Chinese politically, socially, and economically, forcing them onto remote reservations or segregated ghettos, relegating them to the most undesirable and lowest-paid jobs. Around the time that Koreans started entering, some vociferous "anti-Oriental" groups had already begun to look for ways to stop the influx of Japanese, even as other whites — primarily those with land to be cleared and planted — desired their presence as farm laborers.

As in Hawaii, income from agriculture became the basis of California's prosperity. Beginning in the 1870s, landowners in the state turned increasingly from cereal cultivation to the growth of specialty crops — fruits, nuts, and vegetables — which brought far larger returns. Between 1895 and 1945, deciduous fruit and grape production increased eightfold, while nut and citrus output expanded more than twenty times. But specialty crops required irrigation; an efficient, refrigerated transportation system; marketing cooperatives to deal with the complexities of a national — indeed, world — market; and an enormous amount of "stoop-back" hand labor to cultivate, harvest, pack, and ship. Growers could not find enough white workers to do such work at the wages they were willing to pay. Their solution was to import nonwhite workers who did not have the same rights as whites. Korean immigrants, including well-educated people like Mary Paik Lee's father, found seasonal farmwork to be one of the few available occupations. If they wished to remain in America, they had to accept such work to support themselves and their families. Virtually all of them, at one time or another, labored in the fields, orchards, and citrus groves of the western United States — sleeping on the ground in shacks and bunkhouses, cooking their meals over open fires, and moving from one harvest to another.

Only a small number managed to sustain themselves by non-agricultural work as domestic servants, cooks, common laborers, and railroad section hands. But these occupations, like farm work, also required a migratory existence. Those who desired a more settled existence found only two avenues available: tenant farming in the countryside, and selling fresh produce and ethnic merchandise in the towns and cities. The tenant farmers and merchants soon became the most well-off members of the immigrant community, but the educated individuals and political leaders received the most respect.

Like the Chinese and Japanese who had arrived before them, the Koreans engaged in three kinds of tenant farming: truck gardening, fruit growing, and cereal cultivation. Extant records in county offices in California indicate that Asian tenant farmers preferred to pay cash rent, although a small number did become sharecroppers. In a few instances, tenants not only paid a cash rent but also gave the landlords a share of the harvest. Farming is an uncertain source of income, since weather and market conditions are beyond the control of individual farmers. In spite of this, many an Asian immigrant family has been sustained by agriculture, even during very bleak years when others have starved, because they could grow most of the food they needed for family use — a form of "insurance" that urban dwellers did not possess.

Vegetables and small fruits were usually grown on family farms of ten to eighty acres. As described by Mrs. Lee, family members usually performed all the work, except during planting and harvesting seasons, when even very small farms had to hire temporary help. The Paiks and Lees employed Korean men, Sikh men (from India), and Mexican women. (See Appendix B for a description of how the Lees ran their family farm.) Unlike vegetables, which are annual crops, deciduous (tree) fruit does not require yearly planting. The best-known Korean fruit growers were Charles Kim

(Kim Ho) and Harry Kim (Kim Hyung-soon). In 1921 they established the Kim Brothers Company in Reedley, in the San Joaquin Valley of California, where they managed six farms totaling 500 acres. They developed several varieties of hybrid fruit, including a nectarine, with saplings they imported from Korea. They had their own packing sheds, where every harvest season they employed as many as 200 workers. The tenant farmers leasing the largest acreages grew rice in Colusa, Glenn, Butte, Yuba, and Sutter Counties in the northern Sacramento Valley, from the mid-1910s to the early 1920s. Mrs. Lee's father and her husband both partook of the rice boom during World War I. Kim Chong-lim, who leased thousands of acres, was known as "the Korean Rice King." (See Appendix C for a history of Korean rice cultivation in the Sacramento Valley.)

The success enjoyed by Korean immigrant farmers was extraordinary in light of the laws enacted to hinder their efforts. In 1913 California passed an Alien Land Law to prevent persons "ineligible to [sic] citizenship" from buying agricultural land and from leasing it for more than three years. Chinese, Japanese, Korean, and Asian Indian immigrants, however, quickly learned to bypass this law by leasing land through their American-born children and relatives or through white friends. The Lees, for example, rented tracts in southern California in the name of Stanford Paik, Mrs. Lee's American-born younger brother. The law had little effect, partly because county and state officials did not enforce it strenuously and partly because landowners benefited from the good crops raised by Asian tenants. Then, too, the need for increased food production during World War I gave Asian tenant farmers a breathing spell.

After the war was over, however, farm prices declined, and efforts were renewed to eliminate or at least severely limit Asian competition. To plug up the loopholes in the 1913 law, an initiative was placed on the ballot during the 1920 election. It passed by an overwhelming margin, denying "aliens ineligible to citizenship" any rights with respect to real property in California, other than those secured to them by "now existing" treaties between their country and the United States. Both the 1882 treaty between

Korea and the United States and the 1911 treaty between Japan and the United States explicitly granted subjects of the signatories the right to acquire real estate for "domicile" and "business," but no mention was made of agriculture. Omission was thus interpreted as prohibition.

An amendment passed in 1923 made it illegal for Asian tenant farmers to enter into cropping contracts (though such agreements technically conferred no legal interest in the land itself), forbade any corporations in which they owned more than half of the stocks to engage in agriculture, and provided for the escheat of any holdings illegally acquired. The last condition was made retroactive to the date of acquisition, so that even though an original purchaser could bequeath a plot to someone else, the title received by the transferee was invalid.

Arizona in 1917; Washington and Louisiana in 1921; New Mexico in 1922; Idaho, Montana, and Oregon in 1923; and Kansas in 1925 passed similar laws. Two decades later, while World War II was in progress, Utah, Wyoming, and Arkansas also enacted such legislation, fearing that Japanese released from the internment camps might reenter farming in a big way. Since, during this entire period, Koreans were colonial subjects of Japan, whatever obstacles were placed in the way of Japanese immigrants also affected them. But they managed to farm — as Mrs. Lee's family did — by resorting to oral agreements.

To take care of themselves in the new land, Korean immigrants quickly and effectively organized themselves. On the Hawaiian plantations, almost immediately upon their arrival, they formed *tong-hoe* (village councils) in each locality with ten or more Korean families. Every year, the adult males selected a *tong-jang* (head of the council), a sergeant-at-arms, and a few policemen to enforce the rules they had established for their own governance. Koreans in Honolulu created the *Sinmin-hoe* (New People Society) in 1903 to protest Japanese interference in their homeland. In 1907, the various *tong-hoe* united to form the *Hanin Hapsong Hyop-hoe* (United Korean Society), with headquarters in Honolulu. Two years later, that organization joined the *Kongnip Hyop-hoe* (Mutual Assistance Association) of San Francisco, which had been established in 1905, to become the *Taehan Kookmin-hoe* (Korean National Association, or KNA), which thereafter became the most important body representing Koreans throughout North America. The KNA even had chapters in Manchuria and Siberia. Its aims were to promote education, social welfare, and economic development among Koreans abroad, to train them to work together in equality and freedom, and to restore national independence. To disseminate these ideas, the KNA started publishing a weekly newspaper, the *Sinhan Minpo* (*New Korea*), in 1919.

Because so many of the immigrants were Christians who had left their homeland in the wake of Japanese encroachment, churches and political organizations best served their needs. Within half a year of their arrival in Hawaii, they held the first Korean-language church service and set up the Korean Evangelical Society. Although Presbyterians outnumbered Methodists in Korea, the latter denomination became more active among immigrants in the islands, mainly because George Heber Jones, who had encouraged members of his congregation to emigrate, was a Methodist. He had given some of the first emigrants letters of introduction to John Wadman, superintendent of Methodist Missions in Hawaii, who helped the Koreans rent a house for their worship services. Other Korean Christians in the islands formed the Korean Episcopal Church in 1905, holding their dedication ceremony in the St. Andrew Episcopal Church in Honolulu, which rented a classroom in an elementary school for the group's use. A secessionist independent Korean Christian Church under the leadership of Syngman Rhee appeared in 1917. By 1918, there were thirty-three Korean Protestant churches in Hawaii.

On the mainland, Korean Christians started worshipping together at a mission school in Los Angeles in 1904; the following year, individuals in San Francisco established the Korean Methodist Church. The first Korean Presbyterian Church was founded in Los Angeles in 1906 and was supported by the Presbyterian Missionary Extension Board. This group worshipped in a rented house in the Bunker Hill district. The churches were popular because they served more than religious needs. They were the centers of social life among Korean immigrants. People like Mrs. Lee and her husband financially supported the Korean Presbyterian Church in Los Angeles for years, even though, as farmers, they were always too busy on Sundays to attend services. Even non-Christians went to the functions held at the churches. Furthermore, since a number of the Korean pastors were vocal leaders in the nationalist struggle, some immigrant churches served as institutional bases for political activities.

Not only did the church dominate Korean immigrant life generally, but being Christian also affected the way individual Korean immigrants responded to discrimination by white Americans. Paik Sin Koo, upon the family's arrival in San Francisco, urged his young daughter not to worry about the unfriendly reception shown the disembarking Asian passengers. He told her that the first missionaries in Korea had *also* been mistreated, but *they* had overcome the initial hostility, going on to achieve great things. So, said he, must she. It is likely that at least some of the other Christian immigrants shared Paik's attitude, perceiving Americans as benefactors rather than persecutors. Besides, they could not worry too much about discrimination when they had a far larger concern: freeing their homeland from colonial rule.

That homeland politics mattered more to Korean immigrants than did their treatment by American whites can be seen by what most aroused their ire. Because of their small numbers on the mainland, Koreans were never subjected to a separate, organized anti-Korean movement, like the movements against the Chinese and Japanese. Most of the time they were simply lumped together with the other Asians. After 1905, especially, whatever affected the Japanese also affected them. This fact made Koreans more angry than did anything else. The so-called Hemet incident is a case in point. When Korean farmworkers were ousted from that small town in Riverside County in 1913, the southern California branch of the Japanese Association of America reported the incident to the Japanese Consulate in San Francisco, which, in turn, informed the Japanese Embassy in Washington, D.C. After instructing the acting consul-general in San Francisco to investigate the occurrence, the Japanese ambassador filed a protest with the U.S. State Department. Even before he received the formal complaint, however, Secretary of State William Jennings Bryan had already asked the U.S. Department of Justice to make inquiries into the matter. But the concern shown by the Japanese infuriated the Koreans. The Reverend David Lee, who at that time was serving as president of the Korean National Association, sent a telegram to Bryan (the text of which was reprinted in the *Sinhan Minpo* of July 4, 1919), declaring: ". . . We, the Koreans in America, are not Japanese subjects, . . . we will never submit to her as long as the sun remains in the heavens. The intervention of the Japanese Consulate-General in Korean matters is illegal, so I have the honor of requesting you to discontinue the discussion of this case with the Japanese government representatives. . . . We will settle it without Japanese interference." Bryan did not respond directly to the telegram, but he told the Associated Press that the investigation would be "discontinued" and that the United States would henceforth deal directly with the Korean National Association on all matters concerning Koreans.

Given their strong sense of nationalism, Korean immigrants founded many political organizations through which they made far larger financial contributions to the anti-Japanese movement than their numbers warranted. Though their wages were very low by American standards, they were still better off than were their compatriots at home or in Asian mainland settlements. Just as important, political activists in America could not be reached by the Japanese military police, whose agents operated not only in Korea but also on the Asian mainland.

Outside of the western hemisphere, the only sanctuary Koreans found was the French Concession in Shanghai — an area that the Chinese government leased to the French. There were two foreign settlements in Shanghai where extraterritoriality prevailed: the International Settlement, shared by the British, the Americans, and other foreign nationals; and the French Concession occupied exclusively by the French. Korean political leaders were not safe in the International Settlement because the British, who were allies of the Japanese by virtue of the 1902 Anglo-Japanese Treaty, did not hesitate to apprehend Korean agitators and turn them over to the Japanese police. The French, on the other hand, refused to let the Japanese into their enclave. Thus, when Korean expatriates decided to set up a provisional government-in-exile in the aftermath of the 1919 March First Movement, they located themselves in the French Concession in Shanghai. But the leaders confined in that small area had no means of supporting themselves and had to depend on patriots elsewhere — primarily those in Hawaii and the continental United States — to channel funds to them through the international political network set up by Koreans around the world.

The four best-known political leaders within the Korean immigrant community in the United States were So Chae-pil, more commonly known as Philip Jaisohn (1866–1951), Ahn Chang-ho (1878–1938), Park Yong-man (1881–1928), and Syngman Rhee (1875–1965). Each proposed a different strategy to achieve the common end they all desired: Korean independence. Scion of a wealthy *yangban* family, Philip Jaisohn fled Korea after the failure of the 1884 Kapsin Coup, in which he had participated. He went first to Japan and then to the United States, where he worked as a delivery boy in San Francisco before enrolling at a small private college and then at Johns Hopkins Medical School. He became the first Korean to obtain an M.D. degree. He also acquired U.S. citizenship (in the days when it was still possible to do so) and married an American woman. He returned to Korea after the Sino-Japanese War, became an advisor to King Kojong, established a newspaper, the *Independent*, and raised funds to build Independence Arch in Seoul, as a symbol of his aspirations for his country. But when Kojong, at the behest of conservative politicians, disbanded the Independence Club in 1898 and ordered its members arrested, Jaisohn fled again. After returning to the United States, he assumed an elder statesman's role among the immigrants. He convened a Liberty Congress in Independence Hall in Philadelphia in April 1919 to publicize the March First Movement, because, in his words, he wanted "America to realize that Korea is a victim of Japan." From then on, he carried out public relations work on behalf of Korean independence. At the end of World War II, the commander of the American occupation forces in Korea asked Jaisohn to return to Korea to serve as an advisor.

He stayed there until 1948. Three years after coming back to the United States, he died at age eighty-five.

Ahn Chang-ho came to San Francisco in 1899, where he set up the *Chinmok-hoe* (Friendship Society), the first social organization among Koreans in California. He believed that the Korean people had first to "regenerate" themselves before they could regain independence, so he encouraged his fellow immigrants to clean and beautify their homes — as an outward symbol of their moral rectitude — and to engage in honorable labor. Ahn also organized the *Kongnip Hyop-hoe*, which drew all members of the *Chinmok-hoe* into its circle. The new association, headquartered in San Francisco, had branches in Los Angeles and Riverside. It published a newspaper called *Kongnip Sinpo* (*Kongnip News*).

In 1913, Ahn founded the *Hungsa-dan* (Corps for the Advancement of Individuals, also known as the Young Korean Academy), which had a more cultural and ethical focus than the groups he had organized earlier. When the Korean provisional government was set up in Shanghai, he went there to serve as secretary of the interior and then as secretary of labor. He was arrested by the Japanese secret police in 1935 and died in 1938, shortly after he was released from jail, from the effects of the torture he had received. His followers, however, kept the *Hungsa-dan* active long after his death. The organization still exists under the same name today.

Park Yong-man, in yet another approach, thought that military means were necessary to liberate Korea. He had served a prison term before coming to the United States in 1904. According to one source, there were about 700 ex-soldiers among the immigrants, and Park became their leader. After graduating from the University of Nebraska in 1909, he set up a Korean Youth Military Academy in Nebraska, where he trained some two dozen cadets. He next established four other military academies in California, Kansas, and Wyoming, as well as an airplane-pilot training program in Willows, California — the last endeavor financed by Kim Chong-lim, the Korean Rice King. In 1912, the different groups of cadets were consolidated into a single Korean National Brigade, with over three hundred members commanded by Park and headquartered at the Ahumanu Plantation on the island of Oahu in Hawaii.

Right after the outbreak of the March First Movement, Park formed the *Toknip-dan* (Korean Independence Corps) to raise funds for organizing and training an army of liberation. Two months later, he, too, traveled to Shanghai, where he served briefly as minister of foreign affairs. He resigned when Syngman Rhee, with whom he had strong disagreements, arrived to become "chief of executive" of the provisional government. Upon leaving Shanghai, Park went to Manchuria to train Korean exiles there. He believed that the Manchurian Koreans, given their location and numerical strength, should play the key role in the independence movement, with the financial support of those in North America. Park was assassinated in 1928. After his death, his military corps disintegrated, though large numbers of Korean Communist partisans remained active in Manchuria until the end of World War II.

The most long-lived and controversial Korean expatriate leader was Syngman Rhee. Rhee attended the Paechae Methodist School for Boys in Seoul for a number of years and was a member of Philip Jaisohn's Independence Club. In 1898, when the government disbanded the club, Rhee took refuge in the American Methodist Hospital. One day, when he ventured outside, he was arrested. He spent the next seven years in prison. He read the Bible in jail, decided to become a Christian, and requested baptism after his release. He came to the United States in 1905, obtained a B.A. from George Washington University in 1907, an M.A. from Harvard in 1908, and a Ph.D. from Princeton in 1910 — the first Korean to hold a doctorate from an American university. His education was largely financed by contributions from Korean immigrants.

Rhee believed the best course to follow was to cultivate American public opinion and to influence the powerful nations to exert pressure on Japan. In 1919, he went to Washington, D.C., in an effort to obtain American recognition for the provisional government in Shanghai, but he failed in his mission. Then he journeyed to Shanghai in November of the same year to assume the post of "chief of executive." Rhee stayed in Shanghai only seventeen months. After his return to the United States in 1921, he started calling himself "president" of the provisional government. When his comrades in Shanghai chastised him for taking such a title unilaterally, he argued that he needed a title Westerners could understand and respect if he were to be effective in his propaganda efforts. The other members of the provisional government grudgingly acquiesced. But soon they found another reason to object: Rhee issued $250,000 worth of bonds in the name of the provisional government without consulting its other members or the Korean National Association (KNA). Along with the bonds, he circulated a "presidential directive" to all the immigrants in North America, urging them to subscribe to the bonds. He asked them to send their contributions directly to the Korean Commission, which he controlled, rather than to the Korean National Association. Many innocent immigrants bought these bonds, with the understanding they would be redeemed upon the attainment of Korean independence, but this never happened. Rhee's fundraising campaign was not completely successful, however, because of KNA opposition.

Unable to control the whole nationalist movement, Rhee put his energy into several more personal instruments of power that he had established before he became "president." He had founded the Korean Christian Church, the *Tongji-hoe* (Comrade Society), and a magazine, the *Pacific Weekly*, in Hawaii to advance his own viewpoint in 1919; on these he now depended. He did have many ardent supporters, whose contributions kept him and his projects going for several decades. Rhee lobbied various American and European leaders whenever he could; he traveled to Geneva and to Moscow in 1932 to plead his country's cause. He gave lectures, published articles, and wrote two books to promote American sympathy for Korean independence. During most of this period he lived in Hawaii, but in 1939 he moved to Washington, D.C., to intensify his lobbying efforts when developments in East Asia signaled a change in the international balance of power. After World War II ended, he returned to Korea, where he won the 1948 elections to become the first president of the Republic of Korea. He held office until he was ousted by student demonstrators in 1960, whereupon he retired to Hawaii. He died there in 1965.

As charismatic leaders, men like Ahn, Park, and Rhee inspired strong loyalties. But conflict among them also led to intense factionalism within Korean immigrant communities in North America and, indeed, around the world. The provisional government in Shanghai virtually fell apart from sectarian struggles in the early 1920s, and it was kept alive only by the efforts of Kim Ku, chairman of the provisional government and founder of the right-wing Korean Independence Party. Political developments in China also had an impact on the Korean nationalist movement. When Chiang Kai-shek turned against his Communist comrades in 1927, he fractured the so-called United Front between the Chinese Nationalist party and the Chinese Communist party. Since some expatriate Koreans worked within these parties, their relationships with one another also soured. From the late 1920s until the end of World War II, the Korean nationalist movement survived in several settings. Leftists worked primarily within the Chinese Communist party. When the Communists set themselves up in northeastern China after 1936, Koreans in that part of the country, particularly those in Manchuria, gained prominence in the Korean nationalist movement. Then, as the Chinese Nationalists retreated inland to Chungking when the Japanese took over the eastern part of China, Kim Ku went to Chungking with them and set up the new headquarters of the Korean provisional government. A third faction operated underground in Seoul, while a fourth, pro-American faction existed under Rhee's leadership.

Not only did these political conflicts divide the Korean community in America, but they also imposed heavy financial burdens on its members. Bong-Youn Choy has calculated that, for decades, virtually every Korean in America gave the equivalent of one month's wages every year to support the nationalist struggle, despite the fact that many immigrants, like Mary Paik Lee's parents, were working themselves to utter exhaustion and living from hand to mouth through countless lean years. Yet they contributed willingly, because they felt a special responsibility to do so, living as they did in "freedom" away from their colonized homeland. Though the Japanese censored all news coming out of Korea, and though emigration to the United States had long ceased, the immigrants who were already here remained aware of the situation at home because, from time to time, a few refugee students did slip in. Their presence, along with the exhortations of expatriate leaders, helped to keep nationalism alive among the immigrants. Despite the political differences that existed, Koreans in North America had a true community. It was, by and large, endogamous. Sociologist Romanzo Adams found that as late as 1937 in Hawaii, only 104 Koreans had married non-Koreans. In Mary Paik Lee's family, the majority of her siblings who married had *somehow* found Korean spouses.

While all Koreans in America were weighed down with multiple responsibilities, women immigrants bore the heaviest burden of all. They not only did all the housework, and bore and raised the children, but nearly every one of them worked to help provide for their families and to raise funds for the nationalist cause. Their social adaptations were even more mind boggling: imagine the shock of moving from a world where women were confined to "inner rooms" and were forbidden to go outdoors during the day to a situation where, more often than not, only a piece of cloth separated the living quarters of married women from those occupied by dozens of rowdy young bachelors.

The women who came before 1910 and the picture brides who followed them between 1910 and 1924 lived strenuous lives. On the plantations of Hawaii and on the farms of the western United States, Korean women cooked, washed, and cleaned not only for their own families but often also — for a fee — for bachelors or married men who had come without their wives. In many families, such supplemental earnings made the difference between starvation and survival. Those who fed unattached men had to arise several hours before dawn, often at 3 or 4 A.M., to cook breakfast for as many as forty persons and to pack an equal number of lunch boxes in primitive kitchens with no modern conveniences, not even running water. Those with children then had to dress them for school. Others who worked in the fields for wages spent a full day under the sun, sometimes with babies strapped to their backs, before returning home to fix supper. In the evenings, they washed, ironed, and mended until midnight. Women who did laundry for a fee had to lug water from the well or the outdoor faucet, scrub the clothes on washboards, hang them out on lines to dry, and iron them with irons heated on stoves. For years on end, many of the immigrant women survived with no more than four hours of sleep a night. Those who bore children did all this work even while pregnant.

The life of Mary Paik Lee's mother was typical: though Song Kuang Do did not work in the fields in Hawaii—as many other Korean and Japanese women did—after the Paik family arrived on the mainland, her cooking for thirty men sustained her family for the first four years they were in California. From the day she set foot on American soil until her old age, she worked day in and day out alongside her husband to eke out a living. Mary Paik Lee herself began helping out with chores at the age of six and obtained her first paying job through her own efforts when she was eleven. She did not stop working until she was eighty-five. Mrs. Lee, however, unlike many of the women who moved to urban settings, said in retrospect that she had preferred working with the clean earth to cleaning up other people's filth.

Given such a hard life on the plantations and on the farms, it is not surprising that many women exerted great pressure on their spouses to move to the cities. This was especially true among picture brides—many of whom were from more economically secure backgrounds and were better educated than their husbands. Those who did move opened bathhouses, boardinghouses, restaurants, small stores, and produce stands in Honolulu, San Francisco, Los Angeles, and other urban centers. Such work did not necessarily pay better, but it allowed them, through self-exploitation, to work without supervision and to accumulate some capital.

In spite of their arduous labor, some women found time to work for their churches and for secular women's associations. The percentage of Christians among Korean immigrant women increased after they settled in the United States, because those who had already accepted the faith before they left their homeland converted others. In time, women members exceeded men in numbers, though they still are not given leadership positions.

The first women's organization formed outside of the church

was the *Hankuk Puin-hoe* (Korean Women's Association), established in San Francisco in 1908. The *Taehanin Puin-hoe* (Great Korean Women's Association) was set up in Honolulu in 1913. In the wake of the March First Movement, the *Taehan Puin Kuje-hoe* (Korean Women's Relief Society) was organized, with branches in Hawaii and California, to support the Korean independence movement. To inaugurate it, the members put on traditional Korean clothing and marched through the streets of downtown Honolulu, singing patriotic songs. They raised money by selling food and copies of the Korean Declaration of Independence, as well as by working overtime and scrimping at home. They sent the funds they raised to the provisional government in Shanghai, the Korean Commission in Washington, D.C., the Korean Independence Army in Manchuria and China, and to the family members of the thirty-three signers of the Korean Declaration of Independence who had been arrested, imprisoned, or killed. A second organization that grew out of the March First Movement was the *Taehan Yoja Aikuk-dan* (Korean Women's Patriotic Society), with branches in California towns and cities with sizeable Korean populations: Willows, Sacramento, San Francisco, Dinuba, Reedley, and Los Angeles. There were also two branches outside of the United States — in Merida, Mexico, and in Havana, Cuba. These women's political organizations, like the ones formed by the men, became less active in the 1920s as a result of disunity in the Korean nationalist movement, but they revived after 1937 when Japan and China went to war. Women of Korean ancestry — immigrant and American-born alike — eagerly joined their Chinese sisters in America to protest the loading of scrap iron on ships destined for Japan, in an attempt to prevent American resources from benefiting Japan's armament industry.

The kind of life that Korean immigrant women and their American-born daughters led was a far cry from the secluded existence that had bound women in Korea. Even female Christians in the homeland did not have the same freedom of movement and the opportunities for social interaction that immigrant women found in America. To be sure, public exposure was thrust upon them by virtue of what they had to do to ensure family survival, but the fact is, they rose to the challenge and found meaning in so doing. Daughters like Mary Paik Lee had no choice but to help their mothers. In the process, they, too, learned to fend for themselves and to endure. And endurance mattered. Mrs. Lee, for example, admired the fact that her mother, her husband, and her youngest son — each of whom suffered bouts of ill health — "never complained."

Though Korean women in America could function in the public sphere, their lives were isolated in another sense: they seldom interacted with the larger society. Even their American-born children, who spoke English fluently and who went to public schools, lived in a world apart. Korean children did not have to attend segregated schools — as did Chinese children in San Francisco and in some other California localities — but they did not mix much with white children. Mary Paik Lee's first day at school in Riverside was frightening: the other children danced around her and "chopped" her head off. In Colusa in 1911, she and her older brother had to help their parents wash other people's laundry for meager pay; in addition, she found herself a job as a servant girl, working before and after school and on weekends. While her family lived in the mining town of Idria, she earned money cleaning the schoolhouse; during her first year in high school in Hollister, she earned her keep again as a live-in domestic. She obviously had no time for any social life. Even if she did, few white youngsters were willing to be her friend. In her entire autobiography, she recalls only one white schoolmate who was nice to her.

Unlike their parents, for whom Christianity and nationalism were consuming passions — concerns that had inured them somewhat to the cruelties of life in America — the second generation felt keenly the sting of discrimination. Whereas the immigrant generation had no alternative but to cherish their churches and political organizations, because these served as the most visible symbols of their desire for personal salvation and national liberation, the American-born generation could not find solace in the same institutions. Paradoxically, however, Korean American youngsters like Mary Paik Lee seem not to have shared the desperate desire of Chinese and Japanese American children — such as

Pardee Lowe, Jade Snow Wong, or Monica Sone — to "prove" how American they were. Perhaps this was so because their Korean heritage was an embattled one — one that had to be kept alive and treasured, not resented or discarded. Perhaps this enabled Mary Paik Lee to be a true Korean American: she begins and ends her tale by citing Korean history, but, in between, she shares with us what it was like to have grown up poor, Asian, and female in the shadow of the American dream.

QUIET

ODYSSEY

A PIONEER

KOREAN WOMAN

IN AMERICA

1 ✿ ORIGINS

Korea, a small country attached to the northeast of China, had been independent for centuries before 1882. From 1882 to 1905 Korea had diplomatic relations with many important nations of the world; the United States signed a treaty of amity and commerce with Korea in 1882. In 1904 Japan requested the cooperation of Korea in its war with Russia. Japan asked permission for its soldiers to pass through the Korean peninsula and made a solemn promise to guarantee Korea's independence and to withdraw Japanese soldiers after the war was over. Korea, relying upon the word of Japan, allowed the soldiers on its territory, thus contributing to the latter's victory over Russia. But at the conclusion of the Russo-Japanese War, instead of removing its troops as promised, Japan took advantage of the situation and started to take over Korea. The Korean king vigorously opposed Japan's actions, but since Japan had complete military control of the situation, Korea found itself trapped in a hopeless situation. The king was virtually a prisoner in his palace with no authority to do anything. In 1907 he finally abdicated in favor of his son. This tragedy began a long history of aggression against Korea and created the unhappy world in which the Koreans have lived since 1905.

My paternal grandfather was a teacher, but he also raised mulberry bushes on his property and sold the leaves to a nearby silkworm factory. He owned a stall in the village marketplace that sold dried vegetables, mushrooms, and all kinds of dried seaweeds. Grandfather, being a very wise man as well as a scholar, taught Grandmother to read and write, encouraged her to study his books, and gave her knowledge that was not then available to most women. Grandmother, in turn, taught her daughter-in-law, my mother, so she had the advantages of a private tutor. Since paper was a scarce item, Mother scratched the letters with a sharp stick on the earthen floor of her kitchen. Mother told me

Portrait of the Paik family in Korea, 1905. Left to right, front
row: Paik Meung Sun (author's brother), Paik Kuang Sun
(author); middle row: Paik Goon Un (grandfather), Sin
Bok Duk (grandmother), Paik Suk Wha (aunt); back row:
Paik Sin Chil (uncle), Paik Sin Koo (father), Song Kuang Do
(mother), and uncle's wife (name unknown).

that, unlike most mothers-in-law, hers treated her with love and
kindness.

Two of the first American Presbyterian missionaries to come
to Korea were Dr. Moffett and Dr. Underwood; Moffett eventually settled in Pyongyang. My father was one of the Koreans who
taught him to speak Korean. Dr. Moffett also learned the written language, translated the Bible into Korean, and built churches
and hospitals. Our family had all converted to Christianity before I was born. Paik Meung Sun, my older brother, was born on
November 1, 1897, and I, Paik Kuang Sun, was born on August 17,
1900. We were both baptized by Dr. Moffett.

Grandmother was so impressed and motivated after studying
the Bible that she felt the urge to share it with her friends and
neighbors. She spent all of her spare time going from house to
house, teaching the women to read and write so they could study
the Bible with her. As her circle widened, she obtained a donkey
to help her go beyond her village. Then the idea of establishing a

girls' school became her real ambition. She convinced the mothers that their daughters should also be able to enjoy the knowledge that they themselves were acquiring. Due to her strong personality, patience, and perseverance, and to Grandfather's influence in their community—and in spite of much opposition and criticism from the men—she started the first girls' school in Pyongyang in a small thatched hut.

Her life story shows that whenever women get together and work for a good cause, miracles can happen. From a most humble beginning, Grandmother saw her dream grow, bit by bit. Eventually the thatched hut became a very large brick building, with hundreds of female students attending. Many years later, I met several women in Los Angeles who had graduated from her school.

Although I do not remember the faces of my paternal grandparents, two experiences remain in my memory. The first is waiting for my grandfather to come home in the late afternoon. He left home early every morning before I was awake to attend to his business in the village marketplace. I always sat on the front steps, impatiently waiting for his return. As soon as he turned the corner a block away, I would run out to meet him. He would pick me up in his arms, laughing and pretending not to know why I was searching his pockets. He always had *yut* candy and other surprises for me. I can still hear his laughter and jolly voice. I was told many years later that *yut* candy is made from barley sprouts. It is naturally mildly sweet with no added sugar and is pulled like taffy and cut into small pieces. It was children's favorite candy in those days.

The second thing I remember is Grandmother strapping me on her back one morning and saying she wanted me to see her girls at school. As we entered the room, I looked over her shoulder and saw a large room full of girls who rose to sing a song, perhaps in greeting to their teacher. Grandmother spoke for several minutes and then dismissed the class. That is my only remembrance of her, though we received a few pictures and many letters from her and my uncle through the years we lived in America.

My uncle was the principal of the Pyongyang high school for many years; he was also a minister. His six daughters grew up to be schoolteachers. My father had also studied for the ministry and was about to be ordained when suddenly we were forced to leave Korea.

My maternal grandparents lived in Yangwu, a village some distance away. I do not remember them at all. Most people at that time traveled on foot only, so with the exception of very urgent matters, faraway relatives did not just drop by for visits. The marriage between my mother and father had been arranged by a paid matchmaker, as was the practice in those days. My mother's family were poor farmers; perhaps that is why they did not mind her, their only child, moving so far away to marry. Later on, my parents joked that her family had arranged the marriage because Father came from a family of ministers and teachers, so they thought her marrying him would be a step up; little did they realize that as soon as they came to the United States she would have to work on a farm again. Mother was sixteen and Father was twenty-two when they married.

One afternoon in 1905, as I was waiting on the front steps for Grandfather, I saw two men attired in strange-looking clothes walking towards our house. As they stopped at our gate, I ran into the house to call Grandmother. She came out to meet them. After a few minutes she returned, looking very serious, and said that we had to move out right away. This caused much talk and excitement during the evening meal. It turned out that the two strange men were Japanese officers, and they wanted everyone to move out so they could use our home to house their soldiers. As Grandmother told about the Japanese soldiers, my family sat in stunned silence. Although the news was no surprise to them, it must have felt as though the sky had fallen on us. Soon friends came over, asking what should be done. The only choice was to leave that night or to stay and live with the soldiers in our home, which no one wanted to do. I don't remember any of the details of what happened that night. It was so confusing. In the next few days, every evening as our family ate dinner they talked about all the disturbing rumors from other parts of our country. I felt a bit uneasy, but I was too young to realize the significance of these events and soon forgot about them in play. My family must have made a decision about

Passport issued to Paik Sin Koo in 1905.

what to do when the soldiers arrived, but I didn't know about it until later.

The family decided to go to Inchon, the nearest large city with a harbor, to see what we could do for a living there. It took several days and nights of walking with very little rest to reach our destination. We could only bring our bedding, clothes, and food for the journey. Father must have carried me on his back, but I must have slept most of the way because I don't remember anything about the trip. Many of our friends and neighbors came with us. Mother said that God must surely have been guiding us in the right direction.

There happened to be two ships in Inchon harbor, sent by owners of sugar cane plantations in Hawaii to recruit workers. People were told that if a man signed a contract to work for one year, he and his family would be given free passage to Hawaii. After that, he would be free to go wherever he wished. His wages were to be fifty cents per day, working from dawn to dusk. Father signed on, and that was how we went to Hawaii on the S. S. *Siberia*, arriving on May 8, 1905.

Before leaving Korea we had a family picture taken. The hour of parting must have been very sad and tearful, each of them knowing that they would probably never see one another again. Father was thirty-two, Mother was twenty-six, my brother Meung Sun was eight, and I was five when we left Korea. Many of our friends left with us. All I remember about that trip is that Mother never left her berth, and I was also very seasick at first. After a few days, I felt a bit better and managed to find my way up to a deck where Father's friends walked around. They took turns carrying me on their backs and told me it was dangerous for little girls to be walking on deck alone, because it was easy to get swept off by waves when the ship swayed back and forth. When I said that I had not eaten for several days, they took me down to the galley where a Chinese cook gave me a wonderful-tasting bowl of hot noodles. I felt much better after that and forgot about seasickness.

Life in Hawaii was not much different from that in Korea because all the people I came in contact with were Orientals. I don't remember seeing white people, at least not face to face. There was a small group of Koreans in Oahu, where we lived, and a small church. Father preached there sometimes when he was not working on the plantations. He must have done hoeing or weeding: since he had not had any farming experience, he could not do specialized work such as picking. Mother wanted to work as well, but Father would not allow her to. He said, "Even if we have to starve, I don't want you working out in the fields."

When I asked Father years later if we had eaten bananas in Hawaii, he replied that although a big bunch of bananas sold for five cents, he could not afford to buy any. Since we had arrived with only the clothes on our backs and our bedding, we never had enough money left over to buy bananas. We lived in a grass hut, slept on the ground, and had to start from scratch to get every household item. Fortunately, the weather was warm, so we didn't need much clothing, but we never had enough money for a normal way of life.

While we were living in Hawaii, Mother didn't have much housework to do in the grass hut, so she had time to talk to us about why we were the only ones in our family to have left Korea. She told me that I had begged Grandmother to come with us, but she wouldn't leave her school. Grandmother had said that her students were depending on her to teach and guide them. She was certainly a very remarkable woman, with much courage in the face of danger. It is women like her who get things started in spite of opposition, and who accomplish what seem like impossibilities. I'm glad she lived to see her dream come true. She loved all of her students as though they were her own children, and she wouldn't desert them in their time of need. Uncle said the same thing about

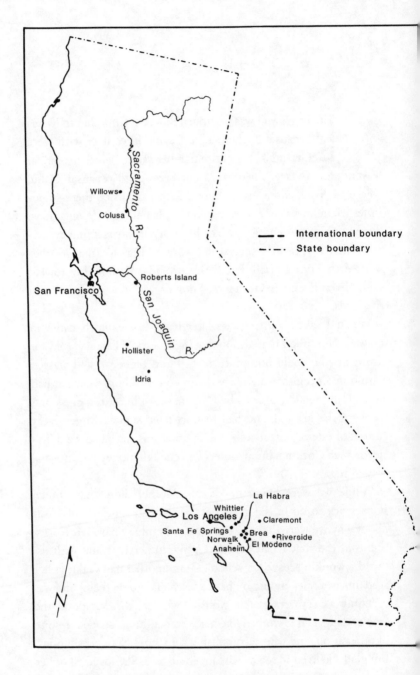

California: locations where Mary Kuang Sun Paik Lee
has lived.

Church on (Ewa?) plantation in Oahu where Korean workers worshipped. Paik Sin Koo is standing, wearing a hat and watch chain, fourth from right.

the young boys in his high school. Also, he had a wife and several children of his own to care for. Of course, Grandfather would not leave without Grandmother. So only my father had no obligations to anyone except his own wife and two children.

Mother told me there had been a lot of discussion for several days before the final decision was made for my parents, my brother, and me to leave Korea to find a better life elsewhere. Father was reluctant to leave, but his parents insisted, saying that his presence would not help them. They knew what would happen to them in the near future. They were prepared to face great hardship or worse, but they wanted at least one member of their family to survive and live a better life somewhere else. Such strong, quiet courage in ordinary people in the face of danger is really something to admire and remember always.

My second brother, Paik Daw Sun, was born on October 6, 1905, in Hawaii. Father was desperate, always writing to friends in other places, trying to find a better place to live. Finally, he heard from friends in Riverside, California, who urged him to join them: they said the prospects for the future were better in America; that a man's wages were ten to fifteen cents an hour for ten hours of work a day. After his year in Hawaii was up, Father borrowed enough money from friends to pay for our passage to America on board the S. S. *China*.

We landed in San Francisco on December 3, 1906. As we walked down the gangplank, a group of young white men were standing around, waiting to see what kind of creatures were disembarking. We must have been a very queer-looking group. They laughed at us and spit in our faces; one man kicked up Mother's skirt and called us names we couldn't understand. Of course, their actions and attitudes left no doubt about their feelings toward us. I was so upset. I asked Father why we had come to a place where we were not wanted. He replied that we deserved what we got because that was the same kind of treatment that Koreans had given to the first American missionaries in Korea: the children had thrown rocks at them, calling them "white devils" because of their blue eyes and yellow or red hair. He explained that anything new and strange causes some fear at first, so ridicule and violence often result. He

Paik Sin Koo in Hawaii, 1905.

said the missionaries just lowered their heads and paid no attention to their tormentors. They showed by their action and good
works that they were just as good as or even better than those who
laughed at them. He said that is exactly what we must try to do
here in America—study hard and learn to show Americans that

we are just as good as they are. That was my first lesson in living, and I have never forgotten it.

Many old friends came with us from Hawaii. Some stayed in San Francisco, others went to Dinuba, near Fresno, but most headed for Los Angeles. We ourselves went straight to the railroad depot nearby and boarded a train for Riverside, where friends would be waiting for us. It was our first experience on a train. We were excited, but we felt lost in such a huge country. When we reached Riverside, we found friends from our village in Korea waiting to greet us.

In those days, Orientals and others were not allowed to live in town with the white people. The Japanese, Chinese, and Mexicans each had their own little settlement outside of town. My first glimpse of what was to be our camp was rows of one-room shacks, with a few water pumps here and there and little sheds for outhouses. We learned later that the shacks had been constructed for the Chinese men who had built the Southern Pacific Railroad in the 1880s.

We had reached Riverside without any plans and with very little money, not knowing what we could do for a living. After much discussion with friends, it was decided that Mother should cook for about thirty single men who worked in the citrus groves. Father did not like her to work, but it seemed to be the only way we could make a living for ourselves. She would make their breakfast at 5 A.M., pack their lunches, and cook them supper at 7 P.M. But my parents did not have the cooking utensils we needed, so Father went to the Chinese settlement and told them of our situation. He could not speak Chinese but he wrote *hanmun*, the character writing that is the same in Korean and Chinese. He asked for credit, promising to make regular payments from time to time. They trusted him and agreed to give us everything we needed to get started: big iron pots and pans, dishes, tin lunch pails, chopsticks, and so forth. They also gave us rice and groceries.

The Korean men went to the dumpyard nearby and found the materials to build a shack large enough for our dining area. They made one long table and two long benches to seat thirty men. Father made a large stove and oven with mud and straw, and he found several large wine barrels to hold the water for drinking and cooking. That was the start of our business. Mother had long, thick black hair that touched the ground. It became a nuisance in her work, so Father cut it short, leaving just enough to coil in a bun on the back of her head. It must have caused her much grief to lose her beautiful hair, but she never complained. We had already lost everything else that meant anything to us.

We lived in a small one-room shack built in the 1880s. The passing of time had made the lumber shrink, so the wind blew through the cracks in the walls. There was no pretense of making it livable — just four walls, one window, and one door — nothing else. We put mud in the cracks to keep the wind out. The water pump served several shacks. We had to heat our bath water in a bucket over an open fire outside, then pour it into a tin tub inside. There was no gas or electricity. We used kerosene lamps, and one of my chores was to trim the wicks, clean the glass tops, and keep the bowls filled with kerosene.

The Chinese men who had lived there in the 1880s must have slept on the floor. Father solved the problem of where we were going to sleep by building shelves along the four walls of our shack. Then he found some hay to put on each shelf. He put a blanket over the hay, rolled up some old clothes for a pillow — and that was a bed for a child. I used a block of wood for my pillow. It became such a habit with me that even to this day I do not like a soft pillow. My parents themselves slept on the floor.

After our shelter was taken care of, I looked around and found that all our immediate neighbors were old friends from Korea. Philip Ahn, who became a movie actor many years later, lived across from us. His father was Mr. Ahn Chang-ho. Mr. Ahn and my father, who had been boyhood friends in Korea, felt like brothers to each other and kept in touch through the years. It was good to see so many familiar faces again, and we felt happy to be there together.

Every day after school and on weekends, my older brother and I had to pile enough firewood up against the kitchen shack to last until the next day. Father found some wheels and boards at the dumpyard to make a long flatbed for carrying the wood, but we had to make several trips each day. An acre of trees grew some distance from us, where we found plenty of broken branches to gather up.

Meung's job was to keep the wine barrels filled with water so Mother could do her work. I cleaned the oil lamps, kept our shack in order, looked after my baby brother, and heated the bath water for the men at 6 P.M. so they could bathe before supper. The workers' bathhouse had just one large tub inside; I heated the water by building a fire under the floor. The men washed themselves with a hose before entering the tub.

Every Saturday Meung and I went to a slaughterhouse some distance away to get the animal organs that the butchers threw out — pork and beef livers, hearts, kidneys, entrails, tripe — all the things they considered unfit for human consumption. We were not alone — Mexican children came there also. They needed those things to survive just as we did. The butchers stood around laughing at us as we scrambled for the choice pieces. When I told Father I didn't want to go there anymore because they were making fun of us, he said we should thank God that they did not know the value of what they threw out; otherwise, we would go hungry.

Meung started school at the Washington Irving School, not far from our settlement. When I was ready to go, Father asked a friend who spoke a little English — a Mr. Song — to take me. My first day at school was a very frightening experience. As we entered the schoolyard, several girls formed a ring around us, singing a song and dancing in a circle. When they stopped, each one came over to me and hit me in the neck, hurting and frightening me. They ran away when a tall woman came towards us. Her bright yellow hair and big blue eyes looking down at me were a fearful sight; it was my first close look at such a person. She was welcoming me to her school, but I was frightened. When she addressed me, I answered in Korean, "I don't understand you." I turned around, ran all the way home, and hid in our shack. Father laughed when he heard about my behavior. He told me there was nothing to be afraid of; now that we were living here in America, where everything is different from Korea, we would have to learn to get along with everyone.

First grade class in Washington Irving School, Riverside, 1907.

The next day when I went to school with my brother, the girls did not dance around us; I guess the teacher must have told them not to do it. I learned later that the song they sang was:

> Ching Chong, Chinaman,
> Sitting on a wall.
> Along came a white man,
> And chopped his head off.

The last line was the signal for each girl to "chop my head off" by giving me a blow on the neck. That must have been the greeting they gave to all the Oriental kids who came to school the first day.

Because our Korean names were too difficult for them to remember, the children at school always said "Hey you!" when they wanted our attention. I told Meung that it was too late to change our names, but we should give American names to our siblings. So we started with Paik Daw Sun, who had been born in Hawaii, by calling him Ernest. When another brother was born in Riverside on August 8, 1908, we named him Stanford.

Meung was only three years older than I, but he was extremely observant and considerate for his age. He told me to stop playing around and to notice how much work our mother had to do. He said that to help her, every day before school he would wash the baby's diapers, and I was to hang them on the line. After school, before going for firewood, I was to take them in, fold them, and put them away. Meanwhile he would fill the wine barrels with water from the pump. We followed this routine from then on. I was always taking care of the babies, bathing them every night, changing their diapers, and feeding them midnight bottles. He heated their bath water in a bucket outside so I could give them baths in the tin tub inside our shack.

There was one large building for community meetings in Riverside, where religious services were held on Sundays. We didn't have a minister, but several persons read the Bible and discussed it. Father preached there whenever he had time. An American lady named Mrs. Stewart, who lived in Upland, used to come to our church on Sundays. She was interested in the Korean people and brought presents for everyone at Christmastime. She gave me the first and only doll I ever had.

Meung and I had a special "gang" consisting of six members about the same age. We ran to school together, ran home for lunch, back to school, and home again. On the way to school there was a large mulberry bush growing in the front lawn of one house. Whenever we passed, we noticed the big black berries that had fallen on the lawn. They looked so tempting that we just had to stop and see what they tasted like. They were so delicious we couldn't stop eating them. After that, every time we passed that house we helped ourselves, but we had an uneasy feeling about whether it was right or wrong to take the fruit. We childishly decided that it was all right because the berries were on the ground and weren't picked off the bush. We had a big argument about it one day. When Meung said it was wrong to take something that belonged to someone else, my girlfriend got so angry she picked up a piece of firewood and hit him on the head. When we told Father about it, he said that the berries belonged to the owner of the bush, whether they were on the bush or on the ground. That settled our arguments. From then on we looked the other way every time we passed that house.

An old Chinese peddler used to come to our place once a week with fruits and vegetables on his wagon. I told Philip Ahn to climb up the front of his wagon and talk to him while I climbed up the back and filled my apron with small potatoes, lima beans, and corn, which we roasted in hot ashes. It was our first taste of such vegetables, and they were so good. But the old man got wise to us after a while, so whenever we approached his wagon, he used the horsewhip on us.

One evening, as I was helping Mother wash the lunch pails the men brought back, I asked her what kind of work the men were doing. She told me they were picking oranges, which gave me an idea, but I didn't dare to tell her about it. After breakfast the next day, as I passed out the lunch pails, I asked some of the men why they never brought me an orange. I said I had never seen or tasted one. That evening as I took in the lunch pails, they felt a bit heavy; when I opened one I saw a beautiful orange for the first time. I was so excited I told Father about it. He must have talked to the men, because there were only a few oranges after that. It helped make the work of washing the lunch pails seem less tiring to find a few. One night some time later, when I took in the lunch pails every single one felt heavy. I got really excited, but to my surprise, each pail had a rock in it. When I asked why, the men said they were afraid I would scold them if they didn't bring something, but there were no more oranges to be picked. Everybody had a good laugh about it.

After the orange season was over, the men picked lemons and grapefruit. In the fall there was work in the walnut groves. The men would shake the walnuts from the trees with long poles, then the women and children would gather them up in sacks, take them to a clearing, and peel off the outer shells [hulls]. They got paid by the sack for their labor. Between the walnut harvest and the time to prune the orange trees, the men got a short rest. When there was no work in the citrus groves, Father worked at the Riverside Cement Company on the edge of town.

Two incidents happened in Riverside that will always remain in my memory. The first was when I told Father I needed a coat to wear to school. He said that he would see what he could do about it. He rode to town on his bicycle to buy some material, and he made a coat for me. Since we did not have a sewing machine, he had to sew it by hand one evening. It was a beautiful red coat; I was so happy to wear it. All the girls at school wanted to know where I had purchased it. They couldn't believe my father had made it himself. When I asked Mother how Father could do such a wonderful thing, she smiled and said that, among other things, Father had been an expert tailor in Korea. He had studied to be a minister and had taught the Korean language to missionaries, but tailoring was how he made a living.

My second memory is equally wondrous. One evening Father woke us up in the middle of the night and said a wonderful thing was happening in the sky. Looking out the window, we saw a big star with a very long sparkling tail that seemed to stretch across the whole sky. The tail was full of small sparkling stars. It was a spectacular, awesome sight, a bit frightening to us children. We didn't understand what was going and couldn't sleep the rest of the night, wondering what it meant and if everything would be all right the next day.

We lived in Riverside for four or five years, but Father became concerned about Mother's health — the work of cooking for thirty men was too much for her. She was a small woman, only four feet eleven inches tall, and she was expecting another baby. So we paid off the Chinese merchants who had helped us get started, paid all our debts to friends, and moved to Claremont, not too far away. It was a quiet college town with many school buildings. We moved into a duplex building, where an old friend, Martha Kim, was living with her parents. It was across the street from the railroad station and a huge citrus-packing house. Those were the days before frozen fruit juices, so after the choice fruit was packed, the culls were piled up in boxes back of the buildings to be taken to the dump once a week. Because of this, we were fortunate that we could enjoy all the discarded fruit.

Our move to Claremont turned out to be our first experience with the American way of living. The new house seemed huge after our little shack. It had several rooms with beds, chairs, and other furniture. The kitchen had a gas stove, electric lights, and a sink with faucets for cold and hot water. But all that was as nothing compared with what we found in the bathroom. There was a big white tub with faucets at one end — I couldn't believe it was the place for taking our baths. And the biggest surprise of all was the toilet. Father flushed it to show us how it operated. He must have seen these wonders before somewhere, because he wasn't surprised at anything. For the first time, I felt glad that we had come to America.

Father found a job as a janitor in the nearby apartment buildings. He told Meung and me to ask the tenants if we could do their laundry, and also to ask our schoolteachers the same thing. On foot, Meung had to pick up the dirty laundry in a big basket and return it later. I helped with the laundry before and after school and with the ironing at night. In Claremont we had our first experience with an electric iron. Before this we had heated the old "sad irons," as they were called in those days, on the wood stove. It was such a relief to use the electric iron. No more going back and forth to the wood stove for a hot iron. No more kerosene lamps, hunting for firewood, and outhouses. Life was getting better. Every Saturday Father bought a beef roast, and every Sunday we had pot roast with mashed potatoes and bread. This was our introduction to American food, and it tasted wonderful. A small group of Koreans lived in Claremont. They came together to worship on Sundays in an old building. There was no minister, so Father preached there several times. Arthur was born in Claremont on December 2, 1910. The memory of our short stay there is a pleasant one.

Unfortunately Father's wages were so low in Claremont that it was difficult to make a living. So, a year later, we moved to Colusa in northern California, hoping to find work there. It turned out we had made a disastrous move. Father could not find any kind of work. There was a depression in 1911, and the situation was so bad the Salvation Army offered a bowl of soup and a piece of bread to each hungry person in town. But when I asked if we could go and get some, Father said no. He didn't want us to be humiliated by asking for help.

The feeling towards Orientals in southern California had not been friendly, but we had been tolerated. In the northern part of the state, we found the situation to be much worse. Although we found a house on the outskirts of town, the townspeople's attitude towards us was chilling. Father told Meung and me to ask our schoolteachers for their laundry. Once again, Meung had to fetch and deliver, carrying a basket on foot. Since we lived on the outskirts of town, it was a hard job for him, but he never complained. But because of the negative feeling towards Orientals in Colusa, we never got enough clothes to launder, and we could not earn enough money to meet our needs.

After paying the rent, light, water, and other bills, we had very little left over for food. Mother would tell me to buy a five-pound sack of flour, a small can of baking powder, salt, and two cans of Carnation milk for the baby. The two cans of milk had to last for one week: it was diluted with so much water, it didn't look like anything nourishing. Mother made tiny biscuits each morning and served one biscuit and a tin cup of water to each of us three times a day. During the time we lived in Colusa, we had no rice, meat, or anything besides biscuits to eat. Nonetheless, when we sat down to eat, Father would pray, thanking God for all our blessings. This used to irritate me. At the age of eleven years, I couldn't think of anything to be thankful for. Once he was sitting out on the porch smoking after dinner, and I asked him what we had to be so thankful for. He said, "Don't you remember why we came here?" I had forgotten that the fate of our family in Korea was much worse than ours. Nevertheless, my stomach ached for lack of food, and I had severe cramps. One evening the pain was so bad I got up to fill myself with water, which helped somewhat. As I neared the kitchen, I saw Father and Mother sitting across from each other at the table holding hands, with tears flowing down their faces. I realized then how much agony they were suffering, and that my own feelings were as nothing compared with theirs. I had been so absorbed in myself that the thought of my parents' suffering had never entered my mind. Seeing them that way made me realize how ignorant I was. It awakened me to the realities of life.

I thought maybe I could get work cleaning someone's home to help out. Since my schoolteacher was the only one I could talk to, I asked her if she knew where I could get housework. She said that the principal lived in a big house, that his wife might need someone to help her. So I went to the principal and asked if his wife needed someone to do the cleaning in his home. He said that he would find out and let me know.

The next day I went to his office and found out that his wife was willing to try me. She said I should work before and after school, and all day Saturdays and Sundays. The wages were to be one dollar a week. In my ignorance, that sounded good to me. I asked where he lived and walked past it on my way home. It was a big, beautiful house, quite far from ours, with a large lawn in front and colorful flowers all around. When I told Father about it, he shook his head and didn't say a word. As if he didn't know it, I said that one dollar would buy twenty loaves of bread, and that it would help feed the younger children who were hungry. Bread cost five cents a loaf then. He said it was too much work for me, but I could try it. Father left the room and went outside to smoke his pipe. Many years later, he told me he had felt humiliated to hear his eleven-year-old daughter tell him that her one-dollar-a-week wages were needed to feed the family. I was too young and ignorant to know how my words had hurt him.

I was totally ignorant of what my employers expected of me, but I was stubborn enough to make the attempt. My secret reason for wanting this job was that I was hoping to get something more than a tiny biscuit and water to eat, but my punishment came in an unexpected way. Before I left home in the morning, Father gave me advice about how I was to behave in my first American home. He showed me how to set a table with napkins, and so forth. He said I should eat in the kitchen, never with the family. I left home at 6 A.M., reached the principal's house before 7 A.M., and was surprised to see his wife. She looked like the pictures of the fat lady in the circus — a huge woman. I also met her son, who was about twenty years old. I helped the woman prepare breakfast and I set the table. Before they sat down to eat, she gave me a cup of black coffee with no sugar, milk, or cream, and she took the trouble to slice a piece of bread so thin that, when I held it up to the light of the window, I could see the outline of the tree outside. That was about the same amount of food I would have had at home. I had to laugh at myself.

After the family finished eating, I cleared the table, washed the dishes, and cleaned up in the kitchen. Then I had to walk to school while the principal drove in his car. His son had a car also. Very few people in town owned cars, so two cars in one home was certainly unusual. When I told Father about it, he said that it *was* surprising, considering the low salaries of teachers. About fifteen years later, as I was passing a newsstand, I saw the principal's name in the headline of a paper. I stopped to read it. The article stated that Mr. So-and-So had been arrested for embezzling school funds. This had apparently been going on for years. No wonder he had a big, beautiful home and two cars in the family.

After school I went back to the principal's house, helped his wife prepare dinner, and set the table. Then I cleaned the other rooms while dinner was being prepared. She gave me a piece of bread and a few spoons of this and that for my meal. When I cleared the table, she put all the leftovers in dishes, covered them tightly, and put them in the ice box. I guess she was afraid I would eat their food. After washing the dishes and cleaning up the kitchen, I was told I could leave.

On Saturdays, I had to wash all the sheets, pillowcases, towels, and clothes in a big washtub, scrubbing them on a washboard in the backyard, rinsing them, hanging them on a line to dry, and taking them into the house after they were dry. There were no washing machines in those days. Everything had to be done by hand. On Sunday mornings, I sprinkled all the clothes that needed ironing and ironed all day. By nightfall, I was so tired I could hardly walk home. I had to admit to myself that the work was too much for me. Finally, summer vacation came. Father said that he was going to Dinuba, near Fresno, to work in the fruit orchards there to try to make some money. Thus, I should stay home and help Mother while he was away. I was really glad to have an excuse to quit my job. After that, I learned to listen to my elders and not to be such a stubborn fool over things I knew nothing about.

One day we heard music outside the house. Looking out the window, we saw a small truck painted in bright colors with a big picture of an ice cream cone filled with white ice cream. All my younger brothers had their faces pressed against the window, wondering what the truck was. We had never tasted ice cream. Seeing so many children, the man thought that surely someone would come out to buy from him. After waiting several minutes, he gave up and left. The children looked around at Father with questions in their eyes, not daring to say a word. That must have been an agonizing moment for my parents. I looked at their sad, desperate faces and felt sorry for them. Father asked all of us to come into the kitchen and sit down at the table. He took out all the money he had and said that we were not earning enough money to buy everything we wanted, and that we had to pay for several things before we could even buy food to eat. Picking up a few coins, he said, "We have to save this much every week in order to pay the rent for this house, otherwise the owner will not let us live here. Then we have to pay so much for the electric lights, gas for the stove, water, and laundering supplies. That is why we cannot buy enough food to eat three times a day. There is nothing left for such things as ice cream cones." It was a lesson in economics that even a five-year-old child could understand. There were five children in the family then, and ice cream cones cost five cents apiece. Twenty-five cents was a lot of money when one did not have it. From then on, the children never looked out the window when the music sounded, and the ice cream man never stopped at our house. The children never asked for anything after that.

When Father left for Dinuba, Mother, Meung, and I tried to keep going as usual, but we could not do any better. We still had just one biscuit with a cup of water three times a day. Father came back from Dinuba in September, looking so sick and tired it was pitiful. We were shocked at his appearance and wished he had not left home. After paying for his room, board, and the train fare home, there was little left over, but he said he had just enough for us to move out of Colusa.

While Father was working in Dinuba, he met a friend, a Mr. Kim, who was looking for someone to help him on a farm that raised potatoes. They made plans to grow Burbank potatoes on Roberts Island, a big island in the Sacramento-San Joaquin Delta. So in 1912 we took the train to Stockton, where we boarded a small motor boat and traveled for several hours to Roberts Island. We didn't have much to take with us, only our bedding and a few kitchen utensils and clothes. It was a relief to leave Colusa, even though we didn't know where we were going. But, as Mother always said, God was surely leading us to the right place. Moving to Roberts Island saved our lives and prevented our starving to death.

The motorboat ride was exciting. We saw many trees but very few houses along the banks of the river. After several hours, the boat stopped, and the crew put up a plank of wood so we could land. As I walked up the plank, I looked at a branch on a nearby tree and saw a green snake staring at me. That was our welcome to the farm, an indication of things to come.

We had never seen a vegetable farm before. It looked like a heavenly paradise to us. Fish jumped up and down in the river, and the banks were full of various vegetables growing wild from seeds scattered by former farmers. We had plenty to eat and to be really thankful for. The farmhouse was an ancient, wooden two-story building, barely standing. There was also a big old barn with some hay in it, a few chickens, rats, and numerous snakes. All of a sudden we were in a new world. We felt alive and eager to see everything. The younger children ran towards the barn, but they stopped suddenly. They just stood there, looking in. I wondered why and went to see for myself. Their noisy approach had startled the creatures living there: rats and snakes of all sizes and kinds were running around trying to avoid one another in their haste to leave the barn. It was our first look at such wildlife. The sight fascinated as well as frightened us. We backed off to join our parents, who were more interested in the old house. They were trying to figure out how to arrange things to make it comfortable for everyone. Father told us children that Mr. Kim would arrive in a day or two with twenty single men to work on the farm and all the groceries we needed for cooking. The kitchen and dining areas took about two-thirds of the ground floor of the house; the rest of the space became our bedroom. We were back to using kerosene lamps, a water pump outside, and outhouses, but the house was about twice the size of our old shack in Riverside.

We were so hungry that we pulled up the vegetables growing on the banks, washed them at the pump, then cooked and ate everything. It felt good to have something solid to chew on. Father found some white butcher string and some old fish hooks. He said he would show us how to catch fish. He cut a long, slim branch from the willow tree, tied the string to the branch's tip, and tied the hook to the other end of the string. Then he dug up enough worms to fill a coffee can and put one of the worms on the hook. An old rowboat belonging to the farm was tied with a long rope to a tree. He told us to sit in the boat and to let the worm fall into the river. In a few seconds there was a pull on the line. We saw a big grey-black catfish coming up at the end of the string. It was our first sight of a live fish — a very exciting moment. Father told Meung to take the fish off the hook and to put another worm on it. A large grey cat living on the farm jumped into the rowboat and sat on the back seat as we were fishing. When Meung pulled up his fish, the cat stood up, trying to grab it. Meung took the fish off the hook and put it in an old bucket that was in the boat. The cat tried to eat it. It must have been very hungry, because although there were plenty of rats around, they were so big and strong the cat was afraid of them and never went near the barn. When Meung took the fish out of the bucket and gave it to the cat, she ate it right away.

The river seemed to be crowded with fish that kept jumping up as though looking for something to eat. I didn't want to put my hand in a can full of worms, so Father made some dough with flour and water. He told me to make a small ball like a marble with it and press it over the hook. The fish didn't seem to care what they ate: they liked my bait just as well as the worms. It didn't take long to catch enough for our supper. Father made an open fire, put a piece of chicken wire over it, and cooked the fish for dinner. We also had lettuce, celery, and carrots that grew along the river banks. What a wonderful experience after our ordeal in Colusa! We all felt happy again.

Though vegetables grew wild on the property, the only trees in the area were the willow trees growing along the river banks, which were too green to use for firewood. Father said he would have to buy wood by the cord. Whenever we ordered wood, a loaded barge came by and threw the logs on the river bank. Then we had to pile them up outside the kitchen door.

Father solved the problem of our beds just as he had in Riverside. He built shelves along the walls, gathered hay from the barn, put blankets over the hay, rolled up some old clothes for pillows — and those became the children's beds. Our parents slept on the floor. We used a big old tin tub on the property for our bathtub. We had to heat the water in a bucket on a fire outside the house. We never had toothbrushes or toothpaste — just a spoonful of salt and our forefinger for a brush. Perhaps because we didn't have sugar in the house, no one ever had toothaches or any other dental problems.

There was no furniture in the house. Upstairs, where the men were going to sleep, there were no beds. Father said twenty men would have just enough room to sleep on the floor with their blankets. After all the excitement of the day, the little children were tired, so we heated the water for their baths and prepared for bed.

As I stretched my legs on my shelf bed, I felt a cold, rough object against my toes. I threw back the blanket and saw a red snake coiled up. It was as surprised as I was and slithered off outside. After that, we always pounded our beds with a long stick before jumping in. Then I woke up one night feeling a sharp pain on my nose and found myself staring at two black, beady eyes. I screamed. Father came running to see what was wrong. A big rat about the size of a baby kitten had tried to eat my nose. No wonder the cat was afraid of the rats.

The morning after we arrived, Meung and I got up early and caught enough catfish for our breakfast. Then we looked into the problem of cooking for twenty men. The house evidently had been occupied by Chinese before we came. There were big cast-iron pots, pans, and a Chinese-style *wok* — all the heavy equipment they had not wanted to take with them. It was our good fortune to find almost everything we needed to get started. Mr. Kim and his friends arrived that afternoon with the supplies we needed for cooking — rice, soy sauce, and so forth. Suddenly there was a crowd. We had so much to do! Everyone helped. We filled all the huge wine barrels with water from the pump so the red clay from the river could settle before we drank it or cooked with it. Some men went fishing so there would be enough to eat for several days; others helped clean up everything around the house and barn and chased all the rats and snakes away; yet others cleaned the outhouse. There were a few chickens, so the men made a place for them to lay their eggs; but we had to watch them and get their eggs before the snakes did. After a while, the big rats and snakes stayed away. Maybe they came back at night, but we seldom saw them during the day. Some men started a garden, planting corn, cucumbers, Chinese cabbage, and watermelons.

To ensure a regular supply of fish, Father made a fish trap with a bushel basket. He put chicken wire around it, made an opening on top, then tied a rope around it and attached it to a tree. He put several fish heads and scraps in the basket, stood in the rowboat, and threw it into the river. I always got up early to pull it out, curious to see what had been caught during the night. There were several other kinds of fish besides catfish, small crabs, and lobsters. On weekends, some of the men took the rowboat somewhere to dig clams. Once, Meung caught a striped bass about a foot long. It tasted better than catfish, but that species rarely came our way.

At harvest time, when more men were needed, the extra help stayed in tents. I remember one man had a guitar; it was the first time we ever had seen such a thing. Father sometimes hired twenty or so Sikhs to help us with the harvest. They would sit around a large pot of melted butter and garlic, dipping into it with tortillas made of flour and water. The children had the job of weeding and irrigating plants in the garden. Mother and I were relieved to find that she would not have to pack lunches for the men. The field was close by, so they could come home for lunch. Plenty of good food helped all of us to recover our strength, and there was much to be thankful for.

Meung and I went to school on the other side of Roberts Island. One teacher taught all eight grades, and the whole school had only about thirty children. The teacher came to school on horseback. She looked very young, about eighteen or twenty years old. We noticed that the boys and some of the girls were barefoot, so we asked Father if we could go barefoot, too. We said our shoes were getting worn out. He told us it was all right if the others were also barefoot. The soft soil on the island, known as peat, didn't have rocks or anything in it to hurt our feet. It felt so good to walk without shoes.

One evening Father woke us up in the middle of the night and told us to hurry, put on our clothes, and come to the river bank. He wanted us to see something wonderful that happened only once a year, in June. We rushed up the bank and looked down at a mass of shining silver glittering in the moonlight. At first we were so startled we couldn't tell what we were looking at. A solid silvery mass completely covered the water. Our cat, who was with us, of course, seemed to know what it was. She went berserk at the sight. She ran down the bank, jumped on top of the silvery mass, and ran back and forth over to the little island in the middle of the river. Then we could see that a mass of very large fish were so jammed together that the water was hidden from view. Father said they were shad coming from the ocean to spawn in the river. He had brought a long pole with a chicken-wire basket that looked like a huge soup ladle tied to one end. The pressure of the fish had pushed our rowboat halfway up the bank. Father stood at the end of the boat and forced the pole into the water. He brought up several huge white fish and dropped them in the boat. He told us to go get some men to help us. He had evidently prepared everything for this occasion. The men laid the fish on a long board, rubbed off their scales and took out the roe, which was large and long. Then they filleted the fish and cut them into pieces about three inches wide. The roe and fish were carefully laid in wine barrels, where Mother salted them. This went on all night until several barrels were filled.

The salted roe is a favorite Korean delicacy, served with a special hot sauce. Before cooking, the fillets are soaked in water to reduce the salt content. Then they are drained dry and cooked over an open fire. They are very delicious, and we enjoyed them all that year on Roberts Island.

One day Ernest, who was six years old, became ill and refused to eat for several days. I knew he would not tell Mother what he wanted, so I asked him when no one else was in the room. He said he would like some canned peaches, which surprised me because we had never eaten such a thing. Mother gave me some money when I told her his desire; she sent me with Meung to a small store on the other side of the island. It took us a long time to find the store, asking people along the way how to get there. We bought a can of peaches and started for home. On the way back, we came to an irrigation ditch with just a narrow board across it. As we crossed, Meung dropped the can of peaches. We were scared stiff. The water was about six feet deep, and neither one of us could swim. We just stood there frozen with fear, staring at the can of peaches on the bottom of the ditch. Meung was fifteen years old then, but he acted like a man. He jumped into the water, grabbed the can of peaches, and struggled to the side, where I helped pull him out. We both gave a big sigh of relief and rested for a while. We did not dare say a word about what had happened, and we were relieved when Mother did not ask why we were so late or why Meung was all wet. She just said she had been worried and left it at that. Ernest was surprised and happy, and he ate the peaches. Maybe that was the medicine he needed, because he felt better the next day and got out of bed.

Another member of our family arrived about then. Ralph was born on Roberts Island on February 16, 1913.

Our potato plants that year were big and healthy looking. Instead of men digging them up with pitchforks, as they used to do, we now had a machine to make the work easier. As the horses pulled the machine, the plants were uprooted. All the potatoes were exposed, so it was easy to pick them up and put them into sacks. Almost as many snakes as potatoes came out of the ground. They were nonpoisonous, but we were afraid of them anyway. The men had to work longer hours at harvest time, so they needed a "snack" between meals. Mother made yeast doughnuts, which Meung and I took out to them with wine.

We had had a big harvest and were expecting a good profit from it, but Mr. Kim took a barge load to Stockton one morning and returned a week later with a sad story. He said the market price had dropped to ten cents for a hundred-pound sack of potatoes. He had not found even one buyer and had had to dump the load in the river. The depression that had caused us to move from Colusa was still in full force. We were so isolated from the rest of the world, we didn't know what was happening outside. No one came to Roberts Island and none of us went outside. Father had never farmed before, so he didn't know about watching the wholesale market prices. It was a heartbreaking situation. Everyone had worked so hard all year, only to find that no one wanted to buy our crop. We learned that just raising a good crop did not mean success.

Father became desperate. He wrote to friends everywhere, trying to find another place where we could make a living. We were sorry to see the men leave; we had all become good friends. A letter soon came from Mr. Byung Joon-lee, who was working for a quicksilver mining company in Idria, San Benito County, California. He said to come quickly, that a few jobs were available. Once again we had nothing to take with us, only our few clothes and blankets. The kitchen things did not belong to us, and we could not take the food. We left them so that whoever should come after us would find everything with which to start farming.

We were told that there were only a few quick-silver mines in the United States, the largest of which was in Idria. On the way to Idria, we had to stop in Sacramento, because Mother became very ill. We stayed at a boardinghouse owned by a Mr. and Mrs. Lee, where another brother, Young Sun, was born February 26, 1914. Mother was so weary and ill she almost died that night giving birth. Young Sun, also named (but never called) Lawrence, was born more dead than alive, a blue baby. Father and I had to place him in hot and cold water alternately and massage him vigorously. It took a long time to get his circulation going.

After a day or two of rest, we continued to Tres Piños, a very small village some distance south of San Jose, to catch a wagon to Idria. It was a big haywagon with benches on both sides, hitched to four large horses, which took us up the mountains. It took half a day to reach the place. We crossed several creeks and stopped to move big rocks that had rolled down the road from the mountain. The scenery was beautiful — tall pine trees and hilly country — with very few houses along the way. Every time we moved, we came to a different kind of world. This was the best so far. The pine trees smelled good, and the cool air made us feel refreshed.

Mr. Lee had found an old house for us. It had four small rooms, and a shack in the back served as a kitchen and dining area. There was a big oven in the shack and a picnic-style board table with benches on both sides. The house had a small wood stove for heat. The mines, the company buildings, the hotel, the store, the houses of a few Caucasian families, and the boardinghouse for Caucasian workers all had electricity, but there was no electricity in the shacks for the rest of the workers — mainly Mexicans, with a few Koreans. We were back to our old way of living, but we felt happy to be in such a beautiful, wild country. Meung and I had to hunt for firewood again. There was a water pump outside the house, and the outhouse was halfway down the hill.

Mr. Lee took Father to the company office and asked if he could work there. He was accepted and was given a card to record the supplies from the company store which we bought on credit. Father bought kerosene lamps, a sack of rice — and a big ham. It was the first time we children had ever seen such a luxury. The ham tasted wonderful, and we enjoyed it very much for several weeks.

Father got a basket and took us up in the hills to see what could be picked for food; he showed us what was good and what to avoid. In a shallow stream, we saw crayfish, which hurried to get under the rocks when they heard us coming, and soft green watercress, which grew on top of the water. All kinds of wild vegetables grew there. They had a light green color. The celery had thin stalks and smelled a bit like the celery we buy in the stores now. The lettuce looked like romaine, the same shape and size, but was soft green in color, with thin and very tender leaves. Little cucumbers on vines climbed on the tall bushes nearby. Also, gooseberries and blackberries took the place of other fruits that did not grow in that location. Nature had provided a great wild vegetable market for all the poor people living there. As we sat around the table for our supper that evening, Father thanked God for leading us to this place.

The short stay on Roberts Island had been a wonderful experience for us children. We learned a lot about all the wild creatures who share this world with us. This new place, Idria, was yet another exciting experience — an interesting new way of life.

Around the house of every Mexican family in Idria were two or three burros, one or two pigs, and some chickens. We found that burros were a necessity of life in those mountains. They were the only means of getting around because of the numerous rattlesnakes. We needed two of them to bring the firewood down from the mountains, so Father and I went to a neighbor who had several and asked if we could buy two. He brought the burros out to us and told them in Spanish that this man was to be their new owner, that they should go with him and should stay at his house and not come back. The burros just blinked their eyes and stood waiting while Father paid for them. The owner patted their backs and told them to go with us. I asked if we should tie them up. He said that was not necessary, that they knew what to do. Also, he said there was no need to feed them, that they would go up the mountains at night to feed on the grass there. I didn't believe him but waited to see what would happen. The burros followed us home. All my brothers were so excited and happy to see them. They brought water for them to drink and played with them all day. I thought the burros would run away at night and not come back, but the next morning I looked out the window and there they were, standing meekly by the kitchen shack. It was a wonderful surprise to see them there.

Meung and I took the burros up the mountains to look for firewood. There was plenty everywhere. We had to chop the wood into shorter lengths so we could pack bundles on both sides of the burros. We first put down a layer of sacks to protect the burros' bodies; then we tied the bundles of firewood tightly. The burros knelt down to let us tie the bundles with ropes around their bodies, but they would not get up when ordered. We were told this might happen, so we just left them there and returned home. They came home later when they felt like it. They must have received harsh treatment from others and expected the same from us. They were showing their feelings in the only way they knew. When they got home, we took off the loads, and the boys brought water for them and petted them. They seemed to enjoy the attention and love shown to them. After this happened a few times, they decided not to be so stubborn. They stood up after the loads were tied and walked home with us. It was a joy to have such cooperation from them. On weekends we made as many trips as possible to gather wood. We had to pile up a lot of wood by August, because our neighbors had told us that the winter might bring snow storms and that sometimes it might be impossible to get wood. We made a shelter for the woodpile so it would not be covered with snow or get soaked with rain.

Father worked in the furnace area of the mining company, stirring the rocks so they would burn evenly. He had to wear a piece of cloth over his nose so he would not breathe the poisonous fumes whenever the lid was opened. It was a hard, nasty job that few men wanted to do, even though the pay was five dollars a day, an unheard of amount in those times. But Father was desperate and felt compelled to take it.

The fumes from the furnace were poisonous not only to humans but to plant life as well. Nothing grew where the fumes went. Because quicksilver was used to make explosives, soldiers guarded the entrance to the mines. When the quicksilver was being shipped out, several soldiers accompanied the cargo to its destination. No one was allowed to walk around the mining areas or furnaces.

One day Mother asked me to see if the store had fresh meat to sell. The clerk said meat was sold at the back. A big hole had been made in the side of a hill and boarded up, just big enough to hang one side of beef and one of pork. An electric bulb was hanging in the back. It was a spooky place; I had to chase a snake away from the entrance. The so-called butcher asked how large a piece I wanted. I told him I wanted a small piece about the size of my fist. He just cut off a section from the side of beef, put it on a piece of paper and gave it to me. I told him to put it on my father's account.

When we were fairly settled, we looked around for the schoolhouse. It was on top of a low hill not far from our place. Meung and I discovered it was another one-room schoolhouse with a teacher who taught all eight grades. We registered and started going to school the next day. There were about thirty Mexican children at that school, mostly little ones, though some were big boys who looked about twelve to sixteen years old. They had never been to school before and spoke very little English. They were so noisy the teacher had a hard time. She didn't have time for Meung and me. She was forced to tell the boys to go home, but they couldn't understand what she said. I had picked up a few words of Spanish, so I told them what she had said. They were so startled to hear me speak Spanish that they got up and left. After that, the rest of us could learn our lessons.

There was a wood stove in the middle of the schoolroom. The

teacher built a fire at noon and heated something in a small pot which smelled so good I asked her what it was. She said it was a can of Campbell's soup that she had bought at the store. That was my first introduction to Campbell's soups. I told Mother about the soup, and she bought one can at the store. She said it was good but that we couldn't afford to buy enough for the whole family.

I noticed that there was no one to sweep out the schoolroom, so I went to the company office and talked to the supervisor. He was a kindly man who listened to my story. I told him that I wanted to earn enough money to buy my books when I got to high school. He decided to hire me. My job was to clean the blackboards, sweep out the room, chop the wood for the stove, keep the outhouse clean, and ring the school bell at 8:30 A.M. so the children would know it was time for school. He would pay me twenty-five cents a day.

I had also been helping in the boardinghouse kitchen every evening. A couple there cooked and served about forty men every day. The wife paid me twenty-five cents every night and gave me leftover roast meat and rolls, which my family enjoyed. One evening while we were all busy in the kitchen, the couple started to argue about something. The wife said something that made her husband so angry he picked up a small can of lard and threw it at her. She screamed and fell to the floor. I was so frightened, I dropped everything and ran home. Father told me not to go there anymore.

Instead, he wanted me to do something for him. He told me to look for two stones of a certain size and thickness. He said he wanted to make a millstone to grind beans, so we could make our kind of food to eat. There were lots of big boulders around, but very few small ones of the size he wanted. It took me several days to find the right kind. When I did, I loaded them on the burros and brought them home. Every day after work, Father would chip away at the stones with a hammer and chisel. He made a beautiful two-piece mill. The top stone had a small oblong hole on one side and a handle inserted on the other side. On its bottom was a small hole, exactly in the middle. The bottom stone had a metal bolt, which fitted into the hole of the top stone. When the two stones were put together and the beans were put into the hole, the upper stone was turned around. It ground the beans into powder — a very ingenious machine. It must have been invented by someone like my father in the ancient days. He was always thinking up ways to improve our living conditions, always making things out of materials other people had discarded. We never had much, but he always tried to make our lives as comfortable as possible — even though harsh circumstances made that difficult most of the time.

Life in Idria was exciting; we had something new to learn every day. In the fall, when the cones on the pine trees were large and ripe, the boys climbed up with hatchets and cut them down. They buried them in hot ashes. The cones opened up in the heat, exposing the big nuts. They tasted better than peanuts and were very delicious. Then the bright red holly berries and small trees made everything look like Christmas. We cut lots of berries and pine tree branches to decorate the schoolroom and make it smell good. Meung cut a small tree for our house, and I went to the company store and bought bright tinsel and decorations for the tree with the money I had earned as a janitor. What a difference from our last Christmas in Colusa!

About two weeks after Christmas, Meung and I walked through the alleys in town to select the best tree that had been put out for the trash man. We picked out one that had some tinsel on it. We took it home and decorated it with strips of colored crepe paper. Our little brothers were happy to see it. Our parents never said a word; they just looked at us with sad faces. I was too young at that time to realize how they must have felt to see such a pitiful sight. On Roberts Island we had decorated a tall bush outside our house and had pretended it was a Christmas tree. The little children were happy with anything we did to pretend it was a special occasion.

In Idria the snowfall was heavy that winter. We couldn't open the front door and had to crawl out the window to shovel the snow away from the door. In the spring, after the snow had melted away, the sun brought all the beautiful flowers to life. The mountains were covered with different flowers and were full of color. It was a wonderful sight. Their fragrance filled the air. Every week-

The Paik family in Idria, 1915. Left to right, Ernest, Meung
Sun, Mrs. Paik, Ralph (in front of mother), Kuang Sun,
Stanford, Young (in father's arms), Mr. Paik, and Arthur.

end people from San Francisco, Berkeley, and San Jose drove up
to enjoy the scenery and to get some flowers. All the children
came out to pick flowers, which we sold for twenty-five cents a
bunch. We used to look forward to making a little money. The
people were afraid to get out of their cars because of the numerous snakes, especially the rattlesnakes. But somehow, none of the
children ever got bitten, perhaps because we always made enough
noise to scare the snakes away.

We saw tarantulas for the first time in Idria — giant spiders with
big, round, black velvety bodies about two inches in diameter,
eight long hairy legs, and piercing eyes. They are scary but very
fascinating creatures. They dig holes in the ground and camou-
flage the openings so cleverly that it's easy to pass by and not
see them. We were told that their bite is poisonous, so we always
carried a long stick with a sharp point. Whenever they heard any
sound approaching their hole, they would lift the cover a bit and
peek out. We just stood and watched them.

There were also ugly little horned toads in the mountains which
were born fighters. The Mexican boys would put two together in a

box. The toads would squirt blood from their eyes and tear at each other until one was dead. That was about the only amusement the boys had; they bet on their favorites and had as much fun as watching a cockfight.

One hot July afternoon as I was walking in the hills, I noticed a strong, peculiar odor that was very unpleasant. It seemed to get stronger as I climbed higher. I found a big pile of rocks with an opening in the middle, and when I climbed up and looked down the opening I saw a curious, frightening event in progress. A huge gathering of snakes was entwined and entangled, just moving around in one huge mass. A heavy silence in the air made me shiver, so I quickly walked away.

I asked the teacher if there were large wild animals in the higher mountains. She said that mountain lions and red foxes had been seen, but the Mexican men did not go hunting because they did not have hunting rifles.

Whenever it rained on a school day, all the mothers of the Mexican children in school got together and made big tamales with everything good stuffed in them. One apiece was enough for each person. The Mexican families were so generous — they always remembered to make extra ones for Meung and me. They didn't have much, but they were willing to share with others. Their generosity turned rainy days into picnics.

I saw a motion picture for the first time in 1914. Some film company showed a cowboy movie in front of the hotel. It was a free preview to advertise the real picture at the dance hall that night. The movie showed cowboys drinking in a saloon. They were staggering out, laughing and firing their pistols. When they saw an old Chinese man walking home on the other side of the road, they said they wanted to see if he could dance. They started firing at his feet, and they laughed as he kept jumping to avoid being hit. Of course, their aim was not accurate, and he fell wounded. That made them laugh louder. They told him to get up. When he could not, they kept shooting until he was dead. Then they walked away, laughing as though it were a big joke. I was so shocked, I vowed I would never go to see the pictures again. That movie reflected the attitude toward Orientals in those days. Our Mexican friends didn't like it, either. They remembered the days when their people were also treated that way. They had bitter memories of how their country lost California.

During our stay in Idria, Mother had time to sit down and talk to us once in a while. We wanted to know how our grandparents and uncle were getting along in Korea. So for the first time, we learned about the tragic events that had taken place since we had left in 1905. After Japan took possession of Korea, the Korean people were treated like second-class citizens. They were not allowed to possess any kind of weapon to protect themselves; they could have only one kitchen knife to a family. They were deprived of all their property and had no rights under the new Japanese laws. Names of towns, streets, and persons were changed to Japanese; the teachers in all the schools had to speak Japanese and teach from Japanese textbooks. All Korean books and Korean flags were destroyed. It was the complete humiliation of an entire nation. Since all letters leaving Korea were censored, the tragedy was unknown to the rest of the world. But there were letters from people who had escaped to China or elsewhere. We could not do anything to help our loved ones; we had only the agony of hoping and praying. Life was just one crisis after another.

Meung and I graduated from the school in Idria. The teacher said that we were the only students to have ever graduated there. She told us on the last day of school that we had passed the state tests and were now eligible to go to high school. So Meung and I talked about going to high school. We were so absorbed in our own plans, we had not noticed what was happening to Father. When we told him of our hopes, he said he was very sorry that he not only could not help us but also that he needed Meung to help him support the family. He had become quite ill and was unable to do much work. The effects of inhaling the poisonous quicksilver fumes had caused his teeth to turn dark, and they were so loose he could not chew his food. He had been losing a lot of weight, all of which we had not noticed because he never complained or talked about it. He said that he was unable to care for the family by himself and that he had been forced to give up his job in the furnace area to take a different job with half the pay. He said that there was work for Meung, repairing roads and cleaning up the work areas. That was what all the Mexican boys of his age were doing. Because Meung had such a generous nature, he could not refuse. He consented to go to work.

After Father had left that day, I looked all over for Meung. Finally I found him behind the kitchen shack, crying. I said I was very sorry, that I would stay and help, too, but there was nothing I could do in Idria. Meung had always dreamed of going to high school; not being able to go was a very bitter disappointment for him. That's why, later in life, he tried to educate himself by reading books as much as possible. Time and circumstances beyond our control were always against us poor people. Of course, he could have left home and made his own way, but his love and consideration for our family made him stay. He was that kind of man, even at that early age.

I had been planning to go to Hollister, the nearest town, about sixty miles away in the valley. During my year as janitor of the schoolhouse, I had saved some money to buy the books I needed. There wasn't much left to buy the other necessities, but I was determined to start school anyway. I asked my teacher what I should do. She said to get a "schoolgirl" job. That meant room and board in exchange for working before and after school and on weekends, with no pay. It sounded good to me because it was the only way I could ever go to high school. I ordered two dresses from the Sears Roebuck catalog, one for work and one for school. I didn't have a sweater, coat, or umbrella. My undergarments were made from the sacks for rice and flour. I was naive enough to think that would be enough. I bought a pair of shoes at the company store and two pairs of stockings, and I packed everything in a little old suitcase we had at home. Father tried to discourage me from going. He said it would be too difficult to work so much while studying. He said I would not last more than three months before being forced to come back home. I made a bet with him that I would not come home until the end of the school year. My argument was that the children were all old enough to take care of themselves, and that Mother did not need me to help at home. I guess he was too sick to say any more.

Before I left, he gave me some advice about how I was to conduct myself in an American home. He said that I should eat in the kitchen and always watch the wife's reaction to whatever happened and try to please her. He also told me to go to a Presbyterian church on Sundays, if possible. Up to that time, none of us had gone to an American church, knowing that we would not be welcomed there. He gave one piece of advice I have never forgotten: although girls and women were supposed to be soft and obedient, they should also learn to think like men and make correct judgments. He told me to speak up when the occasion demanded and to stand up for what is right. That advice gave me strength in later life.

Charlotte was born in Idria on September 6, 1915, the day before I had planned to leave for Hollister. After six brothers, I was happy to see a sister join our family. I bathed her and gave her a bottle of milk. I didn't know what to do, but Mother said it was all right for me to leave as planned. So I left feeling worried and sad that I had not thought about Mother's condition. It made me realize what a selfish plan I had made. At fifteen years of age, I should have noticed what was happening. My going to Hollister should have been a happy day for me, but I felt guilty and regretted my hasty departure. But it was too late to remedy the situation.*

After a long ride on an old hay wagon, we reached Hollister. I went straight to the newspaper office to advertise for a "schoolgirl" job. Luckily for me, the man I talked to at the newspaper office said his wife was hoping to find someone to help in their home. He said to wait a while and he would take me to his house. After a short wait, he drove me to a house not far away. His wife took one surprised look at me and pulled her husband aside and whispered to him. It was evident that she was not pleased with the queer-looking creature he had brought home. He must have told her there was no harm in trying me out for a few days, because, though she was angry, she gave in. She showed me a small room with a pile of boxes on one side and a cot on the other.

I left my suitcase there and followed her into the kitchen, where dinner was being prepared. I set the table for two in the dining room. When her husband came in, he wanted to know where I was going to eat. My reply was that my place was in the kitchen. He said, "You should sit at the table with us." I glanced at his wife, who was looking daggers at him, trying to signal no. She was so furious she got red in the face and could hardly eat dinner. I was nervous and uncomfortable and didn't feel like eating, either. After dinner, I washed the dishes and cleaned up everything in the kitchen. I could see that I was not wanted.

The next morning she gave me a long list of what I was expected to do before and after school and on weekends. I had to do all the housework and the yardwork as well. I didn't mind the work, but the atmosphere was so unfriendly, I decided to look for another job. After several weeks, I found a place not far from the

*See Appendix A for a discussion of the problems concerning this anecdote. *Editor*

high school. It was the home of Mr. and Mrs. Jenkins. They had three boys, ages five, eight, and ten. The children made me feel at home, but I went through the same scene at their house the first day. As usual, I set the table for the family and helped Mrs. Jenkins prepare dinner. She didn't say anything about my place, evidently taking it for granted that I would eat in the kitchen. She was friendly in a way, but dubious about my ability to help her. Mr. Jenkins, a plumber, came home at 6 P.M. — a big, heavyset man with a happy smile. I liked him on first sight. He shook hands with me and said I was welcome in his home. Then he looked in the dining room and asked why my place was not set. One look at his wife told me she was very annoyed with him for asking. When I told him why, he said, "Not in my house. You bring your plate right here next to me." His wife was furious. The children watched this scene with open-mouthed interest. He served me first, which further annoyed his wife. It was a very uncomfortable meal.

After dinner, while the family was in the living room, I could hear them talking about the situation, and I wondered what would happen to me then. I was shown the room where I was to stay. It had a single bed, where all the unused household articles were stored. There was a bureau with a large mirror on top. My first look at myself in the mirror was shocking. I had never seen a full view of myself before. At home, Mother had a very small pocket mirror that didn't show more than a few inches of our faces. I didn't even know what I looked like, and I had to admit I was a strange-looking thing. Our family's main goal was to earn enough money to buy food to feed all of us. There was never any left over to do anything about our appearance. The first night when I sat on the bed in the Jenkins's house, the springs were so loose it felt like a hammock. Sleeping on that bed gave me a backache. Having slept on hard surfaces all my life, it was unbearable, so I pulled the mattress onto the floor and slept there.

One morning Mrs. Jenkins asked why I was sleeping on the floor. She must have come into my room to get something when I was asleep. When Mr. Jenkins heard about it, he said, "Why didn't you say something before? I'll fix it when I get home tonight." He was such a thoughtful man; he made me feel welcome as a member of his household. His garage was in the back alley across from his house. It used to be a barn where he had kept his horse and buggy in the old days. He said he had boards that could be placed on top of the bed springs, and he fixed the bed that night.

Because I proved to be of a great help to her, Mrs. Jenkins and I eventually became friends, and my stay there became a very pleasant one. For example, one evening while I was studying in my room, I heard Mr. Jenkins's angry voice in the living room. When I asked what was wrong, he said it was his lodge night, but his wife had forgotten to get his suit pressed. Showing me his wrinkled pants, he said, "How can I go in this?" I said I could fix it in a few minutes. I got the ironing board and electric iron, asked for a long piece of cloth, which I dampened slightly, and then pressed the suit. He was so surprised and relieved when I finished. He asked how a fifteen-year-old kid knew how to do that.

One evening, out of curiosity, I looked into one of the big boxes in my room and saw perfectly good clothes with rips here and there, buttonholes that needed to be enlarged, and other such simple mending problems. I asked Mrs. Jenkins about the clothes. She said that she didn't know how to fix them but hated to throw them away, so they were piled up in the box. I told her I could mend them, and she was glad to have me do the job. After they were mended, I washed and ironed them. They looked like new, and she was pleased.

I had to get up at 5 A.M. to make breakfast for Mr. Jenkins and fix his lunch. He had his own business, which was very successful, so he was quite busy. He had a large propane gas tank in his garage and, being a plumber, he had laid down long pipes to pump the gas into the kitchen stove for cooking. It took about fifteen minutes to pump the gas into the stove, but it made cooking easy. They also had a large water tank on the back porch. I saw my first washing machine on that back porch. It had to be operated by hand. A long upright handle on one side of the tub had to be thrust back and forth to stir the clothes around in the tub, but it was better than rubbing the clothes on the washboard and was certainly easier on one's hands.

Every day after Mr. Jenkins left for work, I cleaned the house a bit, cooked breakfast for the rest of the family, and made lunch for the two older boys. Since nothing was said about my lunch, I didn't dare take anything to school. A little after eight, I walked to school, which was about twenty blocks away.

The books I had bought were not enough, but I didn't have the money to buy any more, so I would copy the next day's lesson from a friend's book during the lunch hour. The principal happened to pass by one time while I was doing this. He said that students were not allowed to stay in the room during lunch hour, and he wanted to know why I was not eating my lunch. When I explained that I had no lunch, he told me to come to his office. He said that I was the first Oriental student in his school and he was very curious about my nationality. Of course, he had never heard of Korea. I gave him a brief summary of the kind of life all Oriental people had to live. He was amazed and shocked and said he had never heard of such conditions. He said he would talk to Mrs. Jenkins about me. I asked him not to do so and told him it would be difficult for me to find another place at this late date. He said not to worry, that he might be able to help me somehow. On the way home, my mind was troubled. I wondered what Mrs. Jenkins's reaction would be. As I entered the house, she acted friendly and said the principal had been there. She did not mention what he had said, but she told me in the future to take whatever I wanted for lunch.

She also gave me an umbrella and an old sweater of hers, as the result of another incident in school. One morning when it rained, I used a layer of newspapers to cover my head. Of course, that kind of protection didn't last too long, and I was very wet by the time I reached school. So, I went down to the basement to dry out near the furnace. The principal saw me and asked why I didn't wear a raincoat and use an umbrella. I had to tell him the facts of my life again.

During my early life, I had the very good fortune to meet kind people who helped me in times of dire need. When my family came here in 1906, the feeling towards all Orientals was hostile and cruel. "For Whites Only" signs were everywhere. We could not go to restrooms, theaters, swimming pools, barber shops, and

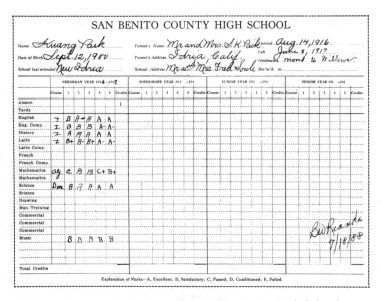

Transcript for Kuang Paik from San Benito High School, Hollister, 1916–17.

so forth. But in the midst of all this, there were also kind and courageous persons, like the principal, who helped me in spite of their friends' disapproval. That was a wonderful experience.

The two older Jenkins boys, Billy and Milton, were very friendly to me, but Paul, the youngest, did not like me, perhaps because of his mother's attitude at first. But something happened one day to change his mind, and we became good friends afterwards. There was no kindergarten in those days, so he was always home. One afternoon, as I came home from school, he was in the back yard crying. I asked where his mother was, and he said she was visiting a friend. When I asked why he was crying, he said he had had an "accident," pointing to his pants, the odor of which was very noticeable. I told him to take off his shoes and socks and to go stand in the bathtub. Then I took off his clothes and put them in a bucket of water, just in case his mother came home early. I cleaned him, gave him a hot soapy bath, and put clean clothes on him. He asked me not to tell his mother about this. I said, "It will be a secret between us two." And we shook hands on it. He was so relieved and thankful, he went into the living room and fell asleep on the sofa. I hurried to clean up the mess, washing his clothes just in time before his mother returned. Seeing the clothes on the line, she asked why they were there. I said they were dirty, so I washed them, and that was that. I have to laugh every time I think of this incident.

I found out that Mrs. Jenkins went to the Presbyterian church every Sunday, so I went with her but did not sit with her. I thought it might embarrass her if I did. The minister was friendly. He said he wanted to speak with me one Sunday and took me to his study. He was curious about my background and was very surprised when I told him that I had been baptized by Dr. Moffett in Korea. Every Presbyterian minister knows the history of Drs. Moffett and Underwood. He wanted me to join his church. I told him that his congregation might not like it. He evidently did not know about the hostile feelings in the world outside of his church. I had to tell him about the kind of world I lived in. He was surprised but stood his ground. He said a minister is the head of his church, so what he says "goes." He insisted for several weeks, and he asked if I would answer the questions that new members were required to answer. I hated to keep refusing him, so I agreed to do so. He was surprised when I answered everything correctly, and he wanted to know where I had learned so much about the Bible. I told him my father was a Presbyterian minister and an authority on Bible history. He then pressed me again to join his church. I had to fall back on the old female excuse of not having anything to wear for the occasion, which for me was really true. He must have spoken to Mrs. Jenkins, because she surprised me with a new dress, a simple one-piece dress that was much better than my old one. I couldn't refuse after that, so I became a member of the Hollister Presbyterian Church in 1916.

The minister insisted that I teach a Sunday School class of teen-agers, about twenty boys and girls. They stared at me as though I were something from Mars. That occasion was their first look at an Asian. I said, since it was our first meeting, they were free to ask questions. One boy stood up and asked, "Are you really a human being like us?" My answer was, "I have two eyes, a nose, a mouth, two ears, two arms, two legs — just like all of you. The only difference is the color of my skin and hair. I have black hair and dark skin. Do you know that there are more colored people in this world than there are white people? Some are black, brown, yellow, or red. They are all human beings. They speak their own languages, of course, but they love, fight, and hate — just like you. When you grow older and are able to travel to other countries, you will see that America is not the only country in the world." By the time the class and I were getting to know each other, it was time for me to go home.

One Sunday Mr. Jenkins said that he had to see someone in the countryside, and he asked if I would like to go for a ride. I was happy to see something besides school and church. Outside of town, the land I saw was mostly planted with hay and alfalfa. But we also rode past acres and acres of sweet peas in bloom. The flowers were of every shade, one mass of color after another. The air was heavy with their fragrance, a most beautiful sight. The C. C. Morse Seed Company was then famous for its sweet pea flower seeds. There were Japanese women with babies strapped to their backs picking the seed pods in some fields. There were very few automobiles in town. One never saw more than a dozen at any time.

Near the end of the school year, I learned that Father was planning to move to Willows, Glenn County, California. World War I was still in progress, and all grain products were in great demand. Many Koreans were going to Willows to cultivate rice, in order to take advantage of the high market prices. Another brother, Edward, was born on March 21, 1917.

I managed to stay in Hollister until the end of the school year. I was glad that I had stuck it out and had won my bet with Father, but I felt weak and sick. I was very tired and weighed only ninety-eight pounds. I wanted to get back home before I collapsed. Mr. Jenkins was kind enough to buy my train ticket to Willows. I fell asleep as soon as I sat in a seat, and I don't remember anything about the train ride. I didn't wake up until the train was almost there. Father was waiting for me at the station. I found to my surprise that I couldn't remember the greeting in Korean, but the words all came back to me later.

was surprised and shocked to see how much my father had aged during the short time I had been away. I guess he was just as surprised at my forlorn appearance. We just looked at each other without words. It was impossible to express our feelings then. We walked home in silence. Mother took one look at me and led me to a bed in a small room, where I fell asleep, relieved and thankful to be home again. It took days to relate all my experiences in Hollister. Father said that I had paid dearly for my education and that he was sorry he was unable to help me.

The day after I arrived in Willows, I went outside to see where our family was living. We were about a block from the railroad tracks outside the town limits. There were three old wooden buildings on one side of the dirt road. A sign on our building read "Chinese Food." A half block away were two other old buildings on one side. My family was living in a long building with one long hallway in the middle and several small rooms on each side. There was no bathroom and no hot water tank. A toilet was attached to the house outside the back door. The building had one small kitchen with a gas stove and a small dining area with benches and small tables. There was electricity for lights.

We were living in the so-called red light district. An old Chinese man owned the cafe and the buildings. He sold liquor and opium, which we could smell at night. Father said that it didn't matter where we lived, as long as we maintained our own way of life and tried to get along with everyone. We were in no position to judge what others did.

A large irrigation canal about half a block away brought water from the river to irrigate the rice fields and provided plenty of fish for us to catch. Willows was a small town with just a few stores, one of each kind. The attitude towards Orientals was rough and tough, a "take it or leave it" kind of treatment. Father and Meung worked in the rice fields.

Charlotte was two years old and Eddie was three months old at that time. Charlotte was afraid of me, this stranger who came to live in her house. When I resumed my old job of taking care of the younger children, she resented my supervision and thought of me as an outsider. That feeling persisted through the years. We never had the opportunity to get acquainted with each other.

On Sundays, about seven Korean families came to our house for services. We sang hymns, without music. Father preached a short sermon, then Mother served lunch. Everyone stayed and visited. We had a pleasant time together. It was good to see old friends again. No matter where we lived, Father always invited people to come to our house for a brief time of worship. He never asked for an offering, and Mother served whatever food we had for lunch. One Sunday, as Father was praying, I noticed that the little children were sneaking out. I followed them and found them eating whatever food they could find. The children could not help themselves; those were "hungry years" for all of us. Wages were low and work was hard to find. It was the custom among us to take some food as a gift whenever we went to visit friends. Father laughed when I told him not to make his prayers so long because the children would eat up everything in the kitchen.

My parents did not believe in whipping the children. I don't remember Father ever striking anyone, and Mother never raised her voice at us. She always spoke in a soft, calm voice, explaining why we should do this or that. She insisted that we keep our house clean, even if it was an old shack. Each child had a box for his personal things and a few clothes. We kept an orderly home no matter what the circumstances.

Since Father was a minister, friends always came to him for advice on different matters. He could not speak English, so he told me to interpret for them, and he told me what to say and how to say it. That's how I got started helping people with their problems. Mother gave me good advice about what my conduct should be in doing this. She said never to talk about a person's problems or sickness to anyone else, unless they were matters to be discussed with families. Each person's problems should be kept secret. Listening to my parents' philosophy has been a very interesting part of my life; I have learned a great deal about human beings and their peculiar notions. I learned early in life about all the ills of the older generation, which has helped me as I grew older. No matter how modern the world gets, human nature remains the same.

Mrs. Jenkins wrote twice asking me to come back to Hollister. She said she would pay me regular wages, but Father said no, it was too much for me. I started my second year of high school in Willows. The atmosphere in school was chilling: none of the students except one spoke to me, but my good luck was working for me again. The girl who sat across the aisle from me in several classes was very friendly and eager to talk to me. Her name was Margaret Finch. Strangely enough, although there were many Chinese, Japanese, and Koreans cultivating rice in Willows at that time, there were no Oriental students in the school, so I was an object of curiosity. During lunch and after school, Margaret always talked to me and we became friends.

One day she asked if I would like to go to her church with her. She said she went to the Presbyterian church, which was not far from our house. I asked Father about it. He said, "Why not? Maybe times are changing." He told me to go and find out. He was always the optimist. I told Margaret I would meet her at church the following Sunday. Something told me to go early and find out what kind of person the minister was, so I took three of my brothers and started out. As we neared the church, we saw a man standing in the doorway. As we were walking up the steps, he placed his arm across the door and said, "I don't want dirty Japs in my church." My reply was, "Would it make any difference if I told you we are not Japanese but Korean?" He said, "What the hell's the difference? You all look alike to me." He just glared at us with hatred in his eyes and told us to "go to hell." So we came back home and told Father about it. He just shook his head and didn't say a word.

Margaret was very annoyed with me for not meeting her at church. I told her what had happened. She said, "I don't believe it." I shrugged my shoulders and replied, "Well, it's the truth." The next day at school she said, "My father wants to talk to you after school." She led the way to the Glenn County Courthouse, which was a few blocks from school. At the end of a long hallway, she stopped. I looked up over the door from force of habit and saw a sign that read "Superior Judge Finch." As she opened the door, I saw a middle-aged man sitting behind a large desk. Margaret said, "Father, this is the girl I was telling you about." He told me to sit down and to tell him exactly what the minister had said to me that Sunday. He listened very intently, told me to go to church the next Sunday, and he guaranteed that I would be welcomed there. I said, "Thank you very much." We left his office and Margaret said, "You'd better not forget. I'll be there to meet you." Father was pleased when he heard. He said it often takes someone of courage and position to turn things around.

The following Sunday I went by myself, wondering what would happen. The minister was evidently waiting for me. He ran down the steps, shook my hand, and said, "You are welcome in this church." He was like a different person; he went out of his way to introduce me to a surprised congregation. The minister in Hollister was right; the congregation follows the leader whether they like it or not. In time they all became friendly and discovered that we, too, were human beings.

I have to match this story with another that involved Margaret's mother, the Judge's wife. Sometime after I started going to the church, Margaret said she had had a birthday party and had received a lot of presents that she wanted to show me. Father had told me a long time ago that I was not to enter my American friends' homes unless the mothers had invited me in. Margaret's house was a few blocks from school. As we entered the backyard, we saw her mother washing clothes in a tub on the washboard. She glared at me. I remembered my father's advice and asked Margaret to bring her presents outside. After Margaret went into the house, her mother turned to me and said in a very angry voice, "Don't you dare go into my house. I don't want dirty Japs walking around in my home." I felt a chill running down my back. What a difference between her and her husband!

My stay in school was a constant battle of wits. My English teacher was an old lady with a sour face. It was a common practice to give the nonwhite students lower grades than the whites, but one day she was so unfair, I protested. Her eyes were blazing with hatred as she said, "If you don't like it, get the hell out of here. We don't want you here anyway."

My history teacher was something else. He was a young man in his thirties, a "good looker" and a "smart aleck." When we came to the pages about China and Japan, he referred to them as the lands of "stinking Chinks and dirty Japs." Looking straight at me in a taunting manner, he said that Korea was a wild, savage country that had been civilized by the "Japs." That was the last straw. I was furious. I waited until the bell rang and all the students had left. I walked up to him and said, "Where did you learn Asian history? You don't know a thing about the subject. If you ever say such things again, I am going to stand up in class and in assembly meeting on Friday and tell everybody in school where you go every Friday and Saturday night." His face turned white, red, and purple, and he fell back in his chair. He finally managed to say, "What are you talking about?" I replied, "My family lives in an old building across the road from the Chinese place where you always go every weekend. I recognized the two girls with you, as one is from this class. I can ask them if you wish." His mouth fell open, he was speechless for a while, and then he asked, "What are *you* doing there?" I said, "My family and I are forced to live there because damned hypocrites like you think we are not fit to live in town. We are forced to live there, but what about you? You go there because you like it. That's the difference between us!" After that, he just turned past the pages about Asia; the class never learned about the subject.

Something happened that would change everything. Ernest started high school at eleven years of age, which was very unusual. The Willows newspaper ran a front-page item about him. It said that he was the youngest student ever to enter high school there. I kept the newspaper clipping and the old pictures, but I lost them in a fire two years later. I had taught him at home to the third grade level. When he started school, the teachers gave him tests to determine his ability. They were satisfied that he could start at the third grade; then, he skipped a grade or two later.

Our family had to save and sacrifice to get him a suit, white shirts, ties, and shoes for school. There was a rule in high school that all boys had to wear dark suits. The girls had to wear simple dresses, no fancy party dresses. Ernest was the object of great curiosity and hatred the first week of school. I was waiting for him in front of school a few days later, but he didn't show up. I went around to the back of the building and found him crying. What a sight he was. He had been sprayed with water and sprinkled with flour. As we walked home, I was furious. But I felt helpless, wondering what I could do. Then I remembered Judge Finch and how kind he had been to me. I hastened back to town to the courthouse, went to his office, and asked if I could speak to him. He was kind enough to listen to my story. I told him my parents were unable to buy my brother a new suit, and his had shrunk up when it got wet. The judge told me not to worry but to take my brother to school next day in whatever clothes we had at home. He said he would talk to the principal, and there would be no more trouble for us in the future. I was so thankful and relieved. It sure pays to have friends in high places.

I can imagine all the talking that must have transpired during the night between the principal and the teachers. It was unusually quiet in school the next day: word must have passed down even to the students. No one said anything; even the teachers were subdued. The judge had really worked a miracle for us again.

In the late summer of 1918, influenza came to the United States. Called the "Spanish flu," it was said to have originated in Spain and spread all over Europe. Almost every family had someone ill, and there were many deaths. Father and several friends dug graves, and Father conducted the brief funeral services. The family across the road from us lost a member. Mother and I were with a woman who lived close by when she died. She asked us to take care of her daughter, who was five years old. We took the girl home with us; she slept with me for several weeks. Father helped with her

mother's burial. Her father went to Stockton to find a place to
live, came back for his daughter, and left Willows. It was a very
sad time for all of us.

My parents did not get the flu, but the rest of us were in bed. I
was the only one in danger, however. I had a high fever and was
unconscious most of the time for a month. One day I awoke to
complete darkness; I couldn't see at all. Father said he was going to
get a doctor. I told him to get Dr. Walker, the one to whom I had
been taking Korean women who were ill. Dr. Walker said I had
severe malnutrition and that I should eat nourishing food, such
as milk, eggs, and orange juice. I laughed and said my family had
never had such things in the house. He also said my eyes needed
a complete rest, that I was to stay out of school for one year at
least, that two years would be better, and I was not to read even
a newspaper. That meant the end of my hopes for a high school
diploma.

While we were living in Willows, Mother told me why Father
had taken the job working in the furnace in Idria, knowing how
dangerous it was and what it would do to his health. She said
they had wanted to save enough to send Grandmother Sin Bok
Duk three hundred dollars to help celebrate her sixtieth birthday,
which is called *Han Gop* in Korean. The amount would be a small
fortune when exchanged for Korean money. In Oriental countries,
the sixtieth birthday is considered the most important of all and
must be celebrated accordingly. It is considered the duty of sons
to make a big celebration possible, although daughters also help.
Father knew that Uncle could not do it alone, so he felt compelled
to help, no matter what the consequences. His desperate sacrifice ruined his health, but he felt relieved to have done his duty.
Grandmother's letter expressing her love and happy thanks made
Father feel that his privations had been worth the effort. She said
that everyone in town celebrated her *Han Gop* — all her students,
as well as old and new friends. It was a very happy occasion to be
remembered by everyone.

My parents were constantly fearful of what might happen to
their loved ones back home. Their fears tragically came true.
Through the years, news of what was happening in Korea came

Members of the Paik family left behind in Korea:
grandparents, uncle and his wife, their children, and an
unmarried aunt, ca. 1917.

out only in bits from persons who had escaped to China and other
places. Letters leaving Korea were severely censored, so there
was no mention of conditions, just family news. The Japanese, in
trying to control twenty million people against their will, executed those whom they suspected might influence others to rebel;
countless others were jailed, beaten, and tortured for rebelling or
for complaining about the numerous restrictions. Free speech and
the free press were abolished.

My parents told us that in 1895, when Japan was first trying to
gain a foothold in Korea, Queen Min, who had much influence
and power in the country, was considered the first obstacle to be
removed. Japanese soldiers murdered her in the palace, soaked her
body in kerosene, and burned it. Her three ladies-in-waiting were
also murdered. The king was taken away where he would have no
contact with his people, and the crown prince was taken to Japan,
where he was forced to marry a Japanese girl years later. As long as
their king was alive, however, Koreans held their actions in check,
hoping against hope that he might somehow manage to help them.
But when, in February 1919, the Japanese government announced

the death of the king, claiming the cause to be apoplexy, Koreans everywhere were convinced that he had been poisoned. The news of his death seemed to release all their pent-up emotions, and they abandoned their previous restraints.

March 3, 1919, was the date set for the king's funeral, and there was to be a rehearsal on March 1. Although the Koreans had appeared to cower and submit to the superior force of Japan, they were secretly preparing to take action when the appropriate moment arrived. It took plenty of patient planning to obtain the cooperation of millions of persons to rally to one cause. It was done in such a manner that even the Japanese police were not aware of anything unusual occurring. There were countless details to be considered and made known to everyone, mostly by word of mouth. It is a tribute to everyone involved that such a gigantic plan worked out successfully, especially when the people knew that their lives would be in danger if they were caught.

After much deliberation and many meetings in secret places, thirty-three patriotic men wrote and signed a Korean Declaration of Independence, patterned after the American Declaration of Independence, knowing full well that it meant their death sentence. Copies were printed secretly, along with directions on where to gather for the parade on March 1, 1919. The information was circulated to every Korean home, and Korean flags were distributed by various persons, sometimes by Boy Scouts and Girl Scouts. None of the Koreans were armed with any kind of weapon — it was to be a peaceful demonstration for all the world to witness.

The Japanese rulers were indeed taken by surprise. In their haste to quell the crowds, they used all kinds of harsh measures. Just firing into a crowd did not accomplish anything, so they concentrated on all persons of influence in their communities, such as schoolteachers, ministers, doctors, and lawyers. Dr. Underwood* wrote a letter to his friends in the United States, telling how the Japanese soldiers had rounded up as many men as they could find, had herded them into a church, and had shot them to death. Similar events were going on all over Korea. In Pyongyang, where my

---

*Son of the pioneer missionary, Horace Grant Underwood. *Editor*

Paik family lived, my grandparents, uncle, and relatives were all dragged off to camps where they were beaten and tortured to force them to admit that they had influenced their students to rebel and join the parade. My grandmother was blinded. When my relatives were no longer able to stand up, their friends were allowed to take them home. Japan did not want it reported that such people had died in the prison camps.

As a result of so many tragic events and human sacrifices, however, the nationalist movement got organized. The Constitution of the Republic of Korea was promulgated, and representatives of a provisional Korean government were elected. They assembled on April 23, 1919, and elected Dr. Syngman Rhee as president, even though he was in Washington, D.C., when all this took place. The constitution was carved by hand on blocks of wood, and millions of copies were printed by presses located in caves or in secluded graveyards.

We felt sad and troubled by all the tragic news from Korea, but we had to carry on and do the best we could with our lives.

A young Korean man named Hung Man Lee served as foreman of a large rice farm in Willows. He came into town once a week to buy supplies for his men and to visit friends who lived across the road from us. He and I became acquainted through a mutual friend, and he asked if I would go to see a movie with him one evening. I asked my father, who gave his permission. That was the first time I had ever been to a movie theater. The only movie I had seen was that terrible cowboy picture in Idria. We sat down in the front middle section, where we could get a good view. A minute later, a man rushed over, tapped my friend on his shoulder, and said, "What the hell are you doing here? You belong over there!" pointing to a corner way in the back of the room. I said, "We can't see the picture very well from there." The man replied, "What the hell do I care?" We got up and left. We didn't want to make a scene, so we didn't ask for our money back. After that we spent our time together enjoying nature, riding around, and eating ice cream cones, which I had never had in my childhood days. Cars were still a novelty in 1916, and we liked visiting other towns. That was the beginning of the friendship between Hung Man and me, which slowly developed into serious plans for the future. Perhaps because he had left Korea at an early age, as I had, we found that we had much in common.

Although his name was Hung Man Lee, all his friends called him H.M., a habit I adopted easily. He had left Korea in 1905, the same year as my family, but he had gone to Mexico instead of Hawaii. He was born in Seoul, Korea, on January 14, 1892. His mother had died giving birth to him. His father then found a woman who had plenty of breast milk to sell, and he was taken to her every day for feeding.

H.M.'s grandfather was Lee Kwong Kun, who was famous for his skill in archery and was the head of the Archery Society. He

Hung Man Lee at age twenty-two, Mexico City, 1914.

had a workshop at home where he made bows and arrows. Young men came from all over to learn the art from him. Every so often, all the experts in Korea came to Seoul to compete for the grand prize in archery. H.M.'s grandfather always won. He could shoot the farthest to hit a small dot placed above the city gate.

H.M.'s father was Lee Juhn Kew, who was born in Seoul and who worked for Dr. Gale, helping to publish a Christian newspaper. Dr. Gale and Dr. Appenzeller were two of the first American Protestant missionaries to settle in Korea. American missionaries established the famous Severance Hospital, a university for women, and several churches. H.M. played with Dr. Gale's children, with whom he became good friends and from whom he learned English. When H.M.'s father remarried, H.M.'s home life became difficult because his stepmother resented his presence. Whenever his grandfather brought him toys, she tried to hide or destroy them. One time she threw them into the outhouse. When that happened, he began to think of running away from home.

The family had a friend named Chun Sung Chil, who lived on his father's property in a separate house with his family. One day H.M. heard the Chuns talking about going to another country to find work and a better way of life. They were saying that there was a ship in the harbor waiting to take workers to Mexico, a far-off country.

The Chamber of Commerce and Agriculture of the Yucatán, Mexico, had sent a ship to recruit people to work in hemp plantations. Hemp is a tough plant with coarse fibers from which the famous hemp ropes are made. When his stepmother sent him on an errand one day, H.M. decided to escape on that ship. He boarded the ship, telling the person at the gate that his uncle and family were coming later, and he hid below. After the ship had sailed several hours out of port, he went on deck to look for Mr. Chun and his family. They were surprised to see him and were worried that his family would blame them for taking him along. But it was too late to do anything about it. He was twelve years old then. The Koreans on board were among the more than 1,000 who left for Mexico in 1905, the same year that our family went to Hawaii.

Since he was too young to work in the fields, the patron in Mexico sent H.M. to school and named him Antonio Eduardo Lee. He graduated from high school in Mexico City. As soon as he had learned enough Spanish, the patron used him as an interpreter. He also worked for the Korean National Association (KNA) as an interpreter, finding work for Koreans and negotiating with the Mexican government to improve the workers' conditions, as well as working as a sanitary inspector in Mexico City.

The Koreans who settled in Mexico did something wonderful. Their living conditions were worse and their wages much lower than what we received in the United States, yet they got together and started a Korean language school that also taught Korean history, so that their children would not forget who they were.

An older friend, Yoon Won Kim, worked with H.M. Yoon Won's wife was kind to H.M., treating him like one of her own children. She let him sleep on her porch and fed him as well. He always regarded her as his mother and did everything possible to repay her kindness. One of the boys H.M. grew up with was Han Jong Won. He spoke fluent Korean as well as Spanish and was later asked by President Syngman Rhee to teach Spanish in one of Korea's universities. He came to see us in Los Angeles before leaving for Korea.

At the age of twenty, H.M. married a friend's daughter, but their life together was brief. His wife died from burns caused by an explosion while she was refilling the fuel on her alcohol stove. In 1914, a year after his wife died, H.M. came to San Francisco to start a new life. There were many Koreans in the area. They worked in the vegetable farms and fruit orchards, mostly in Fresno County. In the winter months they worked in town. He made many friends, but one was very special — Syngman Rhee, who many years later became president of South Korea.* Around 1917, H.M. went to Willows with friends to work in the rice fields. He didn't have a cent to his name, and he had to wait until the rice harvest to get paid.

Then something happened to change his luck. He heard that a banker from San Francisco was in Willows looking for a tenant farmer to raise rice on his property. The banker wanted to get in on the rice boom and high market prices. World War I was ending, but all grain products were still in great demand. H.M. was not a farmer, but he had learned from others how to grow

*See Appendix A for a discussion of Lee's relationship with Rhee. *Editor*

rice, which is much easier to raise than other crops. He was the first person to make what became known as the "10 percent deal." The landowner furnished everything to raise the crop and gave H.M. 10 percent of the rice after the harvest, delivered to the warehouse, which was considered a generous contract. Mr. A.P. Cross owned the land — 4,500 acres about five miles outside of Willows — but his son P.B. Cross took care of all the details of finding tenants.

H.M. asked for a Ford pickup truck, so he could travel back and forth for supplies, and he established three camps on the property. He asked all his friends to join him in the venture. He had the land surveyed and had contours made to hold the water at certain levels; then he started work. Luck was with him. Everything worked out nicely, he had a bumper crop, and the market price was the highest ever. Mr. Herbert Hoover sent a letter of thanks to H.M. for his generous support in growing rice for the war effort. Unfortunately we lost the letter, along with all our old pictures and household belongings, in a fire a few years later.

For the first time in his life, H.M. had more than a few dollars in his pocket. When the rice harvest ended in December, his friends were eager to return to their homes in San Francisco, Stockton, and Sacramento. They urged him to get married right away so they could witness the wedding. That's why we were married at the American Presbyterian Church in Willows on January 1, 1919.

The minister kindly offered his church free of charge, and he fired up the furnace to keep out the cold and windy weather. The congregation decorated the church with flowers. I wondered where the flowers came from, because there were none in town. We asked the Reverend David Lee of San Francisco to marry us. Mary and Dorothy Moon were my bridesmaids, and Mr. Yoon was best man. Dorothy Moon's mother made my wedding dress and veil. I was surprised and overwhelmed by everyone's kindness. We went to church in a friend's car. After the ceremony, I found a new car parked in front of the church. I asked H.M. whose car it was. He said, "It's ours!" It was a new 1919 model Chevrolet called the Baby Grand. I had a day full of delightful surprises. After the church ceremony, everybody went to the only Chinese restaurant in town, where a nice lunch was served. We received many presents from H.M.'s friends. We were sorry to see them leave, but they were eager to return to their families, so we said goodby and parted in a happy mood.

We rented the house that the Lee family had lived in. It was an old building with no bathroom or bathtub. The toilet was built onto the house, outside, after the outhouses were removed. We didn't have a hot water tank, so we had to heat the bathwater in buckets on the gas stove and we used a large tin tub for baths. There were electric lights, however. The house had four small rooms, a kitchen, and a dining area. I felt rich with so many things for the first time in my life. I had my first experience with a toothbrush and tooth paste, which took some time to get used to.

By 1919 airplanes were used for things besides war. Rice planting was made much easier by sowing the seed from the air. It was very interesting and educational to watch — so different from any other kind of farming. After the land had been properly prepared and seeded, a little water was let in from the irrigation ditch to moisten the ground and get the seeds sprouted. Then more water was let in gradually. As the rice plants grew, the level of water was increased until it reached about four feet deep after three or four months. The rice plants are quite tall, but a tough weed called "watergrass" grows faster and taller than the rice plants and must be pulled out by hand. The men stood in stagnant water up to their waists all day under the hot summer sun. This caused painful skin irritations and other medical problems. The stagnant water had a scum on top. It must have had harmful bacteria that affected the skin. Most men recovered after the harvest, but H.M. continued to suffer and was miserable with the effects for thirty years. He consulted many doctors, but not one of them knew what the problem was or what treatment to prescribe. Nothing they suggested gave him any relief. One night the itching was so bad he felt a burning sensation. He woke up to find his body covered with a rash with big bumps. It was a frightening sight. His face and body were swollen like a balloon, and his eyes were swollen tight.

We had heard about a sulphur hot springs in the mountains above Williams, a small town about fifty miles from Willows, so we decided to go there and see if H.M. could find some relief. There were very few paved roads then; the roads up the mountains were just dirt strewn with big rocks that had rolled down from the slopes. We had to stop every so often to clear them before advancing. After what seemed like many nerve-racking hours, we reached the top to find a big hotel, many small cabins for rent, a big sulphur swimming pool, and mud baths everywhere. A strong odor of sulphur filled the air. The mud baths were of different temperatures. H.M. first sat in the warm bath; then he sat in the hotter second bath for one hour. Finally, for another hour, he sat in the third bath, which was steaming. It worked like a miracle. All his rash disappeared; his skin was smooth again. Then he went for a swim in the clear sulphur pool to cool off. He felt and looked like a new man, and he was so relieved and happy. We went home feeling good, but the next morning the rash came back again. It was very frustrating. We went to the sulphur springs every weekend, and the swelling subsided somewhat, but the painful itching continued. When the rash was bad, a yellow pus came out all over his body. It was a very messy situation.

The work on the farm increased as the rice plants got taller, so we had to hire more men. At harvest time there were a hundred men working in the fields. Because 4,500 acres is a huge farm, H.M. built three camps at equal distances from one another. He hired a cook for each camp and a young man to go to town every so often to get supplies, groceries, and meat. We had made an agreement with the stores that we would pay them after the harvest in December. The name of Mr. P.B. Cross was their guarantee.

Once, when we stayed in camp for a month, I saw something very unusual and beautiful. In the early evening, just before dark, I heard a strange sucking sound out in the field. I was curious to see where it came from. As I walked along the contours built to keep the water in place, the sound became a bit louder. I approached cautiously and, at the point where the river water flows into the field, I saw four huge carp with their heads out of the water, sucking in the fresh water and evidently enjoying it very much. Their beautiful rainbow-colored bodies were shining and glistening in the light.

I hurried back to camp where the men were eating their dinner and told them about it. They thought I was joking and they laughed, but a couple of them rose, saying that this was something they had to see for themselves. One man grabbed a shovel as he left. I told them not to make any noise, and I hoped the carp would still be there. The men were just as surprised as I had been. Before I could say anything, the man with the shovel had hit one

Flooded rice fields, Willows, 1919.

of the carp on the head and stunned it for a few minutes. The other carp swam away in fright. The men had a hard time pulling the fish out of the water. They pushed the shovel handle through the gills and each man shouldered part of the handle. The men stood about five feet ten or eleven inches tall, but the carp's tail was dragging on the ground. Everybody in camp was surprised at the huge size and beautiful colors of the fish. I wished at the time that we had a good camera to take a picture of it, but no one could afford to have that luxury then. I was sorry to see such a beautiful thing killed, but the men sure enjoyed eating it. As long as we were in camp, I went to see the carp early every morning and evening. Each time, it was a thrill to see more of them.

The varieties of rice raised in Willows were Edith, Early Wataribune, and Blue Rose. When the rice was mature enough, the water was drained off slowly. The big fish left the field, but the little ones floundered around and were eaten by ducks and geese. By late November, the rhythmic marching song of the wild geese flying by reminded us that winter was not far off. The wild ducks stopped by for food and rest before continuing on their annual flights to their winter quarters. Hundreds of them flew in close formation, looking like a mass of dark clouds, circling the field and covering it like a blanket. They were so hungry they could devour everything in one night if left alone. Everyone with a gun came out to shoot and scare them away, but to no avail. There were so many, it was impossible to prevent some from landing.

We tried airplanes at first to get rid of the birds, but that proved to be too dangerous for the fliers. We put many noise-making machines all over the field, set to go off every few minutes, which helped some. Or someone would point a gun upwards, without aiming at anything, and would pull the trigger. A bunch of ducks would drop down on the ground. The ducks were beautiful things. The geese were larger. Both were good to eat, and everybody had plenty. Since our farm was owned by a banker in San Francisco, he brought his friends and the members of gun clubs to hunt every weekend. They always returned home with sacks full of ducks and geese.

Living in the country gives one the privilege of discovering that humans are not the only ones to have feelings of love and caring. Ducks and geese mate for life. If one is sick or injured, the other will bring it food and will try to protect it. I have seen many that were shot and unable to leave with their group. Their mates stayed with them until the wounded ones died; then they flew away to rejoin their group. Witnessing such devotion makes one feel humble.

Even after sharing our 1920 rice crop with all our unexpected "guests," we had a bumper crop. The market prices were still high and everyone made a good profit. But in the postwar recession, the demand for grain dropped; that meant disaster for rice farmers. A year after we sold our share of rice in the warehouse, the price dropped so low that rice farming was no longer profitable. Everybody started moving to other places. Father heard that some friends were farming in Toppenish, Washington, and he decided to move, but things did not work out there, either. My sister Florence was born in Toppenish, Washington, on August 28, 1922. Father wrote again later, saying he wanted to move to Tremonton, Utah, where friends who were growing sugar beets needed help. To enable my Paik family to move, H.M. made out a check for $3,500 and took it to Father personally.

Around this time, our old friend Syngman Rhee came to Willows to see how all the Koreans were getting along and to thank them for supporting him through the years. He had attended Princeton University and had received his Ph.D. in 1910. While there, he became acquainted with Professor Woodrow Wilson, who later became president of the United States. They became good friends. Later, he also met General MacArthur in Washington, D.C., who told him that he would do all he could to see that Korea would gain its independence. While Rhee was studying, his expenses were partly met by donations from Koreans all over the United States, but mostly from California. In later years, we paid our share every year to support his political activities, because we felt he deserved it. After he became famous, he made several visits to California to see how the Koreans were progressing and to thank them for their support.

During his visit, he stayed with us in our old house in Willows for one week. We apologized for our poor surroundings, with no bathroom, no telephone, and so forth. He laughed, saying that it was good to recall the old days when he himself had worked in the fruit orchards. On his second visit, a year later, he looked tired and worn out. He said that this would be his last trip. His secretary was busy all night, typing the notes taken during the day. Many years later, after he became president of South Korea, he and his wife made a farewell trip to Los Angeles, where we saw them again for the last time.

H.M. paid the bills we owed to all the stores that had been patiently waiting for our harvest. His condition was not getting any better, so we decided to go to San Francisco. We stayed there a month while he went to the Stanford University Medical Center. The doctors there tried every kind of test they could think of, but they could not find what was wrong with him or a remedy to stop the itching. It was a wasted and expensive trip. I had an operation at the St. Francis Hospital. Then we went back to Willows and made plans to move to Los Angeles. H.M. said he would go first and find out what we could do there to earn a living. Meanwhile, I packed all our belongings and piled them on our neighbor's porch. After we found a place in Los Angeles, she was to send them to us.

Three weeks later, H.M. came back and said some friends in Los Angeles had told him about two Korean men who were selling a fruit stand in Anaheim because their business wasn't going well. H.M. had made a down payment on the fruit stand, with the rest to be paid in monthly installments. So, in 1921, we left Willows with only our bedding and a few cooking utensils in our car. We stopped in Los Angeles to visit friends. There were no Korean churches then, but we heard that services were being held at Philip Ahn's house. I was glad to see Philip again and asked if he remembered me. It had been fifteen years since we had seen each other in Riverside. We talked about the childish pranks we had played on the old Chinese peddler, and how we had stolen the mulberries.

Los Angeles then was not the huge metropolis it is today; I remember there were not many automobiles. We went on to Anaheim, where H.M. had rented a house on Oak Street, next door to an old friend. The house had five rooms, a bathroom with a real bathtub and toilet, and a gas stove in the kitchen with a hot water tank on the back porch. We had a real house at last, with a big backyard and a fig tree. It was the first time we ever had everything just like the white people did. It really felt good.

The first thing we did was to send a telegram to our friend in Willows, asking her to send our belongings to us. She sent a telegram back, saying, "Very sorry. Had a fire in our house. Everything burned up. Nothing left." We didn't have enough money to replace anything. Luckily we had our mattress and blankets. We slept on the floor, and we used lettuce crates with boards on top for a table, and we sat on boxes. We had just enough money to buy some groceries and start our business. It took two years to pay for the fruit stand. Then we saved enough to buy one piece of furniture at a time — a bed first of all, then a table and chairs, and so on.

Our stand was inside the Safeway store on Main Street, in the center of town. The stand was in the middle of the store, the first thing one saw as one entered. It was about twenty feet by twenty feet, with shelves all the way around. We were the only good fruit and vegetable stand in town, and we had a very good business from the start. H.M. trimmed all the vegetables, washing and scrubbing them in the back room, where there was a big sink and a long drain board. Then he brought them out front to me on a long platform on wheels. I stacked them on the stand, polished all the apples, and tried to make everything attractive. All the fruit stands at that time just used old newspapers to wrap their vegetables and paper bags for their fruits. I was the first one to put purple crepe paper under the apples, which made them look better when I stacked them. In two months everyone was copying my style.

All the stores opened for business at 7 A.M., closing at 6 P.M. on weekdays and at 9 P.M. on Saturdays. We had to get up at 4 A.M., eat breakfast, and have everything ready for business by 7 A.M. There were many Japanese-owned farms outside of town. All of our suppliers were Japanese, but H.M. spoke enough Japanese to talk about prices and so forth. They would bring truckloads of products to the stand at 4 A.M. every morning. There weren't any other Koreans in Anaheim, and although we had friendly business relations with the Japanese farmers, we did not see them socially. One Japanese man brought us bunch vegetables every morning — beets, carrots, turnips, radishes, and so on. The first time he came, when we asked what his price was, he quoted a price below the market price for that day. So H.M. told him what the price should be. He was surprised and very thankful that he was paid more than he had asked for. From then on, he always stopped at our place first to learn the price for the day. He kept us supplied with as much produce as we needed. Usually we would tell him what to bring the next time, but if there was a change in plans — for instance, if we unexpectedly sold out of something — H.M. would drive out to his farm to put in the order. He had to go out there because the farmer did not have a telephone. Our business improved so much that we hired a delivery boy and a girl to help wait on customers. They were Caucasian high school stu-

Mr. and Mrs. H. M. Lee with their first son, Henry,
in Anaheim, 1926.

dents who came in looking for jobs. The weekly sulphur baths
in Williams had improved H.M.'s condition. He was almost well
and feeling fine. Sometimes H.M. would go to the lemon-packing
house and get cull lemons that weren't good enough for shipping.

We would wash them off in a big tub of soapy water, rinse and dry them, and then sell them to other stores.

We met Mr. Walter Knott when he first came to us with his blackberries. We bought most of his load. In those days he had a small farm in Buena Park. As business improved, he increased his acreage and planted raspberries and boysenberries as well, which became very popular later. His wife had a small roadside stand where she sold her berry jams and jellies. Later on she also sold pies, and still later, fried chicken and biscuits. That was the start of their million-dollar business. All their children and relatives pitched in to create a huge success.

The residents of Anaheim were mostly German Americans, and they did not think much of Orientals. When I first moved there, I was surprised to see the "For Whites Only" signs everywhere in town. One afternoon as I was preparing to close up, a young man came in, obviously very drunk. He slapped me hard on the back and said, "Hi Mary!" in a loud voice. I was so surprised and annoyed that I turned around and hit him as hard as I could on his back and said, "Hi Charlie!" He replied angrily, "My name's not Charlie!" Then he staggered over to the lunch counter in the middle of the market, saying what he thought of the "so and sos."

Two days later, he came in, apologized, and said, "Something bothers me. Why did you call me Charlie?" I replied, "Why did you call me Mary?" He said, "I thought all you Jap women were Mary." That really got to me. "How stupid can you be?" I asked. "Do you mean to tell me that all the women in Japan have the same name? Even animals have a different grunt for each other and birds have different chirps and songs. Why should humans who can talk have the same names? The reason I called you Charlie is because people like you always call all Oriental men by that name. Isn't that true?" He nodded yes. "Also, you call all black men 'boy' —young and old. White people always say 'Hey boy!'" He had to admit that was also true, and that he hadn't thought about it and had just gone along with whatever others were doing. He was nice enough to admit he was wrong and stupid. We became good friends after that. Every time he came in, he wanted to know more about Oriental people and Asian countries.

One beautiful Sunday afternoon all the flowers in the park were in bloom, so H.M. and I went for a walk. As we passed a group of people, I said hello to a lady who was a good customer of ours. She turned and pretended not to know me. I didn't care; it had happened so often I didn't give it a thought. The following day she rushed into the store, obviously very angry, and said, "How dare you speak to me in public! You humiliated me in front of my friends. Don't you dare do that again!" I didn't say anything in reply; just turned around and went on with my work. I thought she would never come in again, but she did. But I never spoke to her after that.

Anaheim had a large, beautiful city park. The man in charge of it lived in a house on the corner. His wife came to our stand one hot afternoon and mentioned how nice it was to have a swimming pool to cool off. I said, "Yes, I wish I could go there." She said, "Why not? Everyone is welcome." I said, "What about that sign above the door?" She said, "What sign?" Then a friend of ours came in, and she turned away. The next day she said, "How come I never saw that sign before?" I said, "Because you don't have to be careful like I do. People like me have to look before going any- where." Not being allowed to enter the public restrooms was the greatest hardship. But most people became friendly after they got to know us better, perhaps because we spoke good English.

After we got settled in Anaheim, I wrote to Mrs. Stewart, who used to come to our Korean church in Riverside quite often, and who had given me my first doll. Before we left Riverside, she asked me always to write to her and let her know where we were. In my letter, I told her about my family. The last time I had seen her I was ten years old. She lived in Upland, not too far from Anaheim. I was so surprised to see her walking into the Safeway market one day. She had aged somewhat, but I recognized her right away. She was such a nice person and a true friend. She asked why I didn't have children. I told her about my ailment, and that all the doctors I had seen told me I could never have children. She said a very good friend of hers, a Dr. Farrow, was a well-known lady doctor who specialized in female disorders and might be able to help me. She wrote a letter of introduction for me to take to her. Some customers came in then. There was no time for visiting, so we said goodby and parted.

Soon after that I took a bus to Pomona and another bus to Dr. Farrow's house on top of a hill. When I told her what the other doctors had diagnosed, she shook her head and said, "Men don't know about women's bodies." After an examination, she told me the situation didn't look hopeless, and that she might be able to help me. She was already over eighty years old but was still strong and vigorous, a very nice person. Although she had retired, she took care of friends and neighbors in her home office. I went to her four times, each time a week apart, and soon I became pregnant. I told her that my first-born would be named after her. I gave birth to Henry Farrow Lee in Anaheim on September 24, 1925.

In 1926, we decided to go to Utah to visit my parents. The Pasadena Rose Parade was coming up, so we planned first to go there and see it. We left home at 5 A.M. and found that everybody else had the same idea. The roads were so crowded that it was slow going. The streets along the parade route were jammed with people who were sitting along the sidewalks wrapped in blankets. They must have camped there all night; they had little alcohol stoves with coffee boiling and sandwiches. Children were sleeping, wrapped in blankets. We just stood on the edge of the sidewalk, H.M. carrying Henry on his shoulders. The air was heavy with the fragrance of all the flowers on the floats, which were in the park nearby. Although it is a very tiring ordeal to stand and wait for so long, the Rose Parade must be seen to be really appreciated. The beauty of all the flowers, their brilliant colors and refreshing fragrance, cannot be experienced through television. People who can afford to reserve a seat in the bleachers are lucky, although they also get tired waiting in the cold air and sometimes in the rain. But everyone forgets all the discomfort when the floats start coming by. I am glad we were able to see it once.

We bought a secondhand Buick coupe and headed for Tremonton, Utah. The weather was nice and we arrived there in a few days. It shocked us to see how much my parents had aged. They looked so weary and beaten down; it was evident that they were

The Paik and Lee families in Tremonton, Utah, 1926. Left to right, front row, sitting: Ralph, Young, and Arthur; middle row: Eddie, Florence, Charlotte, and Kuang Sun with Henry in her arms; back row: Stanford, Mrs. Paik, Mr. Paik, H. M. Lee, Meung Sun, and Ernest.

just hanging on through sheer will power. The family lived in a typical old broken-down farmhouse. They had several horses and a few pigs and chickens. The sugar beet market price was so low, they were just barely making a living. It was a pitiful situation. The boys had all grown up. Charlotte was eleven, and Florence was seven, but we had never lived together long enough for them to consider me as a sister.

In the house, a big wall blackboard had the Korean alphabet written on it. It reminded me of the time in Riverside when Meung and I were first taught to read and write in Korean. Father was still trying to do the impossible. Because of his tireless efforts, all the children could speak our language just enough to get by with their elders.

There was plenty of work to do during the day, but after supper

The Korean alphabet written on a blackboard made by
Paik Sin Koo, Tremonton, 1926. Left to right, front row:
Kuang Sun, Charlotte, and Florence; back row: Young,
Ralph, and Eddie.

Charlotte Paik with the stone mill made by her father in
1914 when the family was living in Idria, Tremonton, 1926.

we talked all night, telling them the news of their friends in California. Father thought that raising chickens and selling the eggs might help, so we promised to help him. H.M. bought a second-hand Ford for them, to make their life a bit easier. But life for my parents was just as hopeless as ever. After a long visit, we drove back to Anaheim wondering what we should do next. The first thing we did was to send Father a check for $2,000, so he could start raising his chickens.

A year later, Meung came to Anaheim. He said the sugar beet farming was not going very well, so he had decided to come to Los Angeles to look for a job. He stayed with us for several months while he went around trying to find some way to make a living. He had married a Korean girl named Rose Park, whose family lived in Idaho, and they were living with our parents. After several months he found a job as a salesman for the Jan-U-Wine chop suey factory, which was owned and operated by a Korean family in Los Angeles. They canned different kinds of Chinese food, mainly chow mein with crisp fried noodles. They raised their own bean sprouts in the factory and sold them fresh and canned. Meung's job was to go to all the restaurants and show the cooks how the food should be served. Jan-U-Wine was the first canned Chinese food business in Los Angeles. It became quite successful. The products were very popular, and the business grew to be a million-dollar venture. After Meung got started, he rented a house near the factory and brought his family to Los Angeles.

Ernest came after Meung had left, and he stayed with us for a while. H.M. rented a small place in Long Beach and showed him what he had to do to sell produce. He caught on very fast and earned enough to get a pickup truck, which he fixed up for a fruit and vegetable peddling business. He drove around to the homes in Whittier and sold enough to move to something better. He eventually found a good job in a large food-chain store as manager of their fruit and vegetable section. By that time the real estate restrictions against Orientals had relaxed a bit and he was allowed to buy a house close to the railroad tracks. The freight train used to come to the sausage plant close by, and there was an ice cream factory across the street. It was the sort of location most buyers would not want. Ernest had lived in Whittier long enough for most residents to know and like him, so he was allowed to buy the house. When he married a Korean girl named Rose Choy, whose family lived in Wyoming, they moved into that house.

My second son, Allan Paik Lee, was born in Anaheim on January 16, 1929.

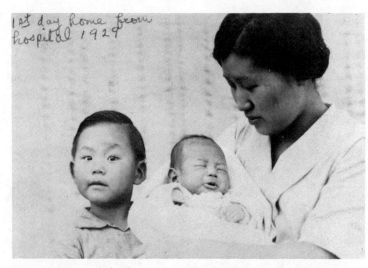

Henry and Allan Lee and their mother, Anaheim, 1929.

H.M. and I were very lucky to have had eleven years of good business in Anaheim. Then the great depression in the early 1930s wiped out most of our savings, and H.M.'s old health problems started up again. Twelve years of hard work in the damp store-room, with his hands in water all day, caused the rash to reappear on his hands and face. The doctor said he should find work out-doors in the sunshine; besides, his appearance made it bad for him to handle fresh produce.

Business was so good that several people were eager to buy us out, but we refused until we were forced to sell. A Japanese man who had been watching our business for some time made a very good cash offer, so we finally sold out to him. We certainly hated to give up such a good business, but in a way we were relieved. Both of us were very tired, and the loss of our savings had made us feel pretty low.

had told H.M. when we left Willows that I never wanted to farm again, but, because of his skin condition, we had to go back to that way of life. A Mr. Bauer came to our house one day and said he was looking for someone to farm his land in El Modeno, a short distance away. Someone must have told him that we had sold our fruit stand and were looking for another business. H.M. went to see the place and came back with good news. He said the farm was forty acres on a hillside, had a big two-story house on top of the hill, a barn, and a caretaker, who lived in a shack below the house, who looked after the property when the owner was away.

Mr. Bauer said he had business up north and wanted to move his family there. At that time there was a law that Asians could not rent or lease land unless they were citizens, but some land-owners just made oral agreements, if both parties consented. We used Stanford's name later to rent the farm when he came to Los Angeles, because he was an American citizen. Mr. Bauer said we could live in his house rent-free. It sounded too good to be true.

The original owner must have been a very wealthy man. Every-thing in the house was completely modern. The rooms were all spacious. The house had a big kitchen with tile all over, two gas stoves, and two big refrigerators. The huge living room had wide windows and a big stone fireplace on one side. There were two bedrooms with two bathrooms and two shower stalls on the first floor, as well as a music room. The dining room had wide windows so one could see all the flowers outside. The area around the house was planted with all sorts of ornamental trees and flowers, just like a miniature park. The second floor had three large bedrooms with two bathrooms and two shower stalls. We looked around in amazement, feeling like Alice in Wonderland. We couldn't believe that we were being allowed to live in such a house.

Mr. Bauer seemed very friendly and anxious for us to settle in,

Henry Lee and his parents in front of the Bauer house, El Modeno, 1934.

but one look at his wife told us that she was very unhappy about the situation. As her husband was talking to H.M., she took me aside and said that she hoped we would not ruin her home, that she had never wanted "dirty Japs" to live there. She was furious, but I guess her husband was the boss in the family. She said she would be back in three months to check up on us. I just nodded and said, "Don't worry. We won't ruin anything." They had two sons and one daughter who all seemed to be six feet tall. They ranged from about twenty to thirty years of age.

There were orange trees planted below the house. We walked to the adjoining hills where we were to farm. There was a huge space dug up on top, evidently for a swimming pool. The arable land was on a gentle slope; it looked good to us. An old barn with a work horse was nearby, along with all the equipment we needed to start working.

After we moved into the house and looked around, I was surprised to see how dirty everything was. No effort had been made to keep it clean. Mrs. Bauer was either lazy or didn't know anything about housework. I told H.M. that I was going to show her how her house should be cleaned. It was a shame, such a beautiful home being neglected for so long. Anyway, we were living there rent-free, so I decided my cleaning would be the rent. I worked all day in the field and almost all night scrubbing the filth that had built up. After all the soot was removed from the stones on the fireplace, we were surprised to see the beautiful colors of the various stones. By the third month, all the rooms were sparkling.

When the Bauer family came back three months later, Mrs. Bauer rushed into the house, fearing the worst. She looked around quickly into every room and didn't say a word. Finally she pointed to the fireplace and asked why we had painted it. I said, "It's not painted. I just scrubbed the dirt and soot off, and the natural colors came out." Then she wanted to know why her dark blue curtains had been removed. I had sewn light, flowered curtains which made the living room brighter. I said her curtains were in the closet, and that I would hang them up when we left. The whole house looked different and bright, so clean and shiny. She was speechless, but her husband was kind enough to say that he appreciated all the work I must have done. He told me he didn't know his house was so beautiful.

They stayed on the second floor for several days. Of course we had to invite them to eat with us. I wondered if Mrs. Bauer would object to eating at the same table with us, but I guess she was so hungry that she didn't care any more. It so happened that I was cooking a beef tongue the day they returned; the odor of it wafted up to the second floor. She came down and asked what smelled so good. I thought it best not to say what it was, so I answered that it was a pot roast. The whole family came downstairs. It was funny: I had the feeling they were very hungry and could hardly wait until dinner time. I was nervous and embarrassed because I didn't have anything to offer them—no sodas or ice cream. We never could afford such luxury items. They sat silently, waiting for dinner.

As soon as I announced dinner was ready, they rushed into the dining room like children. I didn't know whether they would eat rice or not, but that was all we had, so I made a big pot of it. I served *kimchee*—a Korean relish made of Chinese cabbage—long white radishes with hot pepper seasoning, marinated vegetables from our garden, fried chicken, and beef tongue sliced very thin. They must not have eaten all day, because they just wolfed everything down without asking what they were eating. They seemed to enjoy it very much. Then they went upstairs.

I was wondering what to feed them for breakfast. We had no ham, bacon, or sausages—just eggs from our chickens. Then I remembered the two large yellowtail fish H.M. had caught the day before when he had gone ocean fishing. I told him I was going to fry them. He said, "Not for breakfast!" I said, "They are five grown people who appear to be starving. We have to serve plenty of food to satisfy them." So, in the morning I made lots of muffins, fried the two fish, fried the eggs, and made coffee. It was an odd combination, and we watched in wonder as they wolfed everything down. All the food disappeared in half an hour. We were so surprised. We were glad to see them leave the next day. They came back several times and became quite friendly—except for Mrs. Bauer, who didn't want to admit we were civilized people.

H.M. was a natural farmer. He raised good crops, but nature was on a rampage that year. The hot Santa Ana wind from the desert blew for several days. All the string beans disappeared overnight, leaving only the bare stalks. The neighboring orange, lemon, and avocado farmers woke up to find all their fruit scattered on the ground. It was a bad year for farmers. The next year's crop was also good, but an unexpected early frost froze everything solid, so all farmers suffered alike again. Such is the life of farmers — a big gamble.

Although we lost money at the Bauer's place, we had the pleasure and wonderful experience of living in a beautiful home "just like the white people," as our friends used to say. I am grateful for the happy memories I have of that period.

After two years at Mr. Bauer's house, we moved down the hill and across the highway to Mr. Nuckoll's orange grove. I bought 100 chicks every spring, built a shed for them, and let them run around the orange grove. We ate the eggs and the chickens. We lived in a tall two-story house, just a plain farmhouse again, and farmed in various places, barely making a living. We had come back down to our poverty-stricken existence. While we lived at Mr. Nuckoll's place, we farmed in Santa Fe Springs, La Habra, Norwalk, and other places between Los Angeles and Whittier. H.M. looked for pieces of land lying idle and asked the owners if he could farm them. We had to make private oral agreements because Orientals were not allowed to lease land. For a small plot of ten acres, however, the authorities did not ask any questions. All of our landlords were Caucasian. We rotated crops from year to year, depending on the market prices and the soil. We grew zucchini, string beans, tomatoes, cabbage, onions, and cucumbers. We always lived off of what we grew and bought only rice and soy sauce. One year, we had eighty-five acres of tomatoes in Brea on top of a high hill. The owner was a German who grew black-eyed peas on a nearby hill. He kept pigs, which was rather unusual. One year, when he couldn't sell his black-eyed peas, he fed them to the pigs. Those peas are as hard as marbles, and I wondered how the pigs could eat them.

Around that time, my brothers started coming out to California to find a better way of life. Stanford, Ralph, Young, and Arthur

The Norwalk kindergarten class, 1934. Allan Lee is in the
front row, third from right.

stayed with us in the two-story farmhouse and helped us out on
the farm once in a while. Then they went to Los Angeles to find
what they could do there. Stanford started a small fruit stand in
Los Angeles. Later he worked at Lockheed Aircraft Company for
many years. Ralph went back to Utah, but he returned later and
reported that Father could not stay there any longer, that we had
to do something. We were broke. We had only thirty-five dollars on hand and nothing in the bank. We gave Ralph one of our
trucks and told him to bring the family out.

We got a loan from the bank, rented a house on Lambert Road
in Whittier, and bought enough groceries and supplies to help
my parents, brothers, and sisters to start housekeeping. When the
family arrived in Whittier, we were glad to see them again, but
they were in a pitiful condition. My parents had nothing to show
for all the sacrifices they had made through the years. They were
old before their time, in poor health, and very tired. We felt sad
to see them that way. The little house we rented was too small
for all of them. My brothers made temporary quarters for themselves elsewhere. Charlotte and Florence were in high school, so
no wonder they looked at me as a stranger. I gave them money
to get permanents for their hair. I remembered my experience in
high school when the other students laughed at my appearance.
Charlotte learned to play the accordian and formed a small band
that played at school functions and private parties.

While they were living in Whittier, Father heard that his old
friend Dr. Moffett, the missionary, had retired from his duties in

Korea and was living nearby. He went to see him, and they spent all day talking about their experiences. Father learned more about our family in Korea. He came home feeling very happy to have seen an old friend at last.

We were living in Anaheim when the lady who took care of my husband in Mexico came to live near us. Her husband had died and left her with seven children. Several years later she remarried, and her new husband brought the family to a farm in Villa Park, near El Modeno. H.M. was very happy to see her again. It gave him the opportunity to try and repay her kindness to him in Mexico. He regarded her as his mother. Her husband had a small farm, but he wasn't doing very well. Every Saturday night, after closing our stand, we took several boxes of vegetables and fruits to her. When we left Anaheim and started farming, they leased a farm close by.

H.M. went ocean fishing as often as possible, not only to fish but to refresh himself with the ocean air and to wash his face in the ocean water. His rash was not bad, and there was very little swelling, but the itching drove him crazy. He couldn't sleep at night and he always felt somewhat relieved after exposure to the ocean air. He was an expert fisherman and always brought home one or two sacks of big fish: sea bass, barracuda, yellowtail, and albacore. There was no limit to the number of fish a person could catch then.

When people boarded the fishing boat, each one put a dollar bill in the "jackpot." The person catching the largest fish won the jackpot. H.M. was always the lucky winner, so the expenses of his trips were not a problem. One time he was very lucky and caught three huge white sea bass. One was fifty pounds, one forty pounds, and one thirty pounds. He sold two of them to a Chinese restaurant on the way home and brought the fifty-pound one home. I bought a big pressure cooker and canned the albacore, which is really the "chicken of the sea," and salted all the others, which we shared with our friends.

Although farming was not very profitable, we had plenty to eat. I canned everything at night during the summer months, and the supply lasted us all through the winter. We shared everything with H.M.'s "mother" and her family and other friends.

The Lee family's produce stand, in front of Mrs. McGee's house on Leffingwell Road, Whittier, manned by Allan Lee, 1940.

We moved once more, this time to Mrs. McGee's house at 4844 Leffingwell Road, Whittier. We set up a roadside stand in front of the house, and we farmed in back on Cole's Ranch. Allan took care of customers at the roadside stand. He was only ten years old then. Mrs. McGee owned the orange grove behind the house. We raised tomatoes, string beans, zucchini, and other vegetables. There was a shady spot with a small stream of water flowing through the property. Watercress was plentiful on top of the water. The old trees were the perfect place for the tree mushrooms to spring out after a heavy fog or rain. These mushrooms look like an open fan. Some grow as large as a man's palm, and they are very delicious cooked in any way. I used to can as many quarts as possible during the fall and winter. We always had good crops, but the weather and market prices did not cooperate very often.

My youngest son, Anthony Paik Lee, was born in Whittier on June 18, 1940.

When we lived on Leffingwell Road, the Nixon family lived nearby on Whittier Boulevard. They had a gas station and a grocery store, where we bought our groceries. We were separated by a lemon grove and a lemon-packing house. Mrs. Hannah Nixon worked hard waiting on customers, baking pies, and so forth. Although she was always busy, she was never too busy to be friendly to everyone. We became good friends. I used to stop by every evening to buy something for supper. Richard Nixon's wife, Pat, taught typing and shorthand at Whittier High School at that time. Richard Nixon opened his first law offices in Whittier and La Habra. I used to see him often on the streets. His brothers, Donald and Edward, were always in their store, so we knew them well also. Edward Nixon and my son Allan belonged to the same Boy Scout troop.

In 1940 we were farming in South Whittier, in an area known as the "Blue Hills." We had fifty acres, and we raised zucchini, string beans, and tomatoes, rotating crops every season. Our neighbors were Japanese farmers who grew flowers. Some specialized in chrysanthemums, owned their land, and built nice homes. The chrysanthemum growers had Japanese women working in the fields. Each plant had only one huge flower on it, as big as a cabbage, and the women worked on their hands and knees all day taking care of those single blossoms. Every morning they shook the dew from the flowers so there wouldn't be any spots. Sometimes forty acres of chrysanthemums would be covered with cheesecloth to protect them from the cold. Each flower was worth five dollars, a fortune in those days. One Japanese farmer had several hundred acres of tomatoes nearby. He hired Mexican workers, with Japanese bosses to oversee them. He was taken away after Pearl Harbor because he was the leader of a patriotic Japanese association.

When the tragedy of Pearl Harbor struck, all the Japanese were forced to leave their homes and property and were taken to concentration camps. Our neighbors asked if we would look after their farms; they told us to take anything we wanted from their homes. They were our friends, so we couldn't do that, but we said we would look after their things as much as possible.

One friend asked us to live on his property, rent-free, to keep out strangers who might be coming around to take whatever they could. We told all of them that we would do our best. It was not a through road, so not too many people came by. After the Japanese left, however, many white people came in trucks, intending to take away all kinds of belongings. But when they saw us watching, they left. Many prominent Japanese were taken away quickly. We heard that many Japanese homes were looted, especially in the cities, but no one protested such actions. Another Japanese neighbor asked us to watch his land and live in his house when he was taken away. I said, "I won't live in your house, but I'll live in one of the shacks you built for your workers." So, we moved again, from one chicken shack into another. That address was 12933 S. Saint Gertrude's Road, Whittier.

The day of Pearl Harbor, we had left home very early and had worked all day in the field. We had no way of knowing what had occurred. After taking the workers home, around 7 P.M., I stopped by the Nixon's grocery store to buy something. I left my one-year-old son, Tony, in the truck, thinking I'd be back in two minutes. I was surprised to see the room full of people who stared at me with hateful expressions. One man said, "There's one of them damned Japs now. What's she doing here?" Mrs. Hannah Nixon came over to me and said to her friends, "Shame on you, all of you. You have known Mrs. Lee for years. You know she's not Japanese, and even if she were, she is not to blame for what happened at Pearl Harbor! This is the time to remember your religion and practice it." What a wonderful, courageous woman to take such an unpopular stand for me, an Oriental, upon whom every white person was looking with hatred. Later, whenever I heard President Nixon refer to his mother as an angel, my thoughts went back to that sad day in her grocery store.

I left the store and came out to my truck, just in time to see three teen-aged boys with their fists upraised, ready to strike my one-year-old son, who was standing on the front seat. I shouted at them, "Does it take three of you to beat up a one-year-old baby?" My second son, Allan, was also intimidated: he was slapped and cursed by customers at our roadside stand. I don't understand how women with young children at home could hit a child for something that had happened somewhere else. They just assumed that all Orientals were Japanese; they didn't even bother to find out before committing violence. Even after all the Japanese were taken away to concentration camps, other Orientals were subjected to all kinds of violence. They were afraid to go out at night; many were beaten even during the day. Their cars were wrecked. The tires were slashed, the radios and batteries removed. Some friends driving on the highways were stopped and their cars were overturned. It was a bad time for all of us.

Once when I went to the J. C. Penney's store in Whittier, the clerk was rude. She wrapped my purchase and threw it down on the counter so hard that it bounced off to the floor. I asked how much it cost, counted the exact amount, and threw it on the counter, where it scattered all over the floor. As I was leaving, the manager, seeing that something was wrong, asked what had happened. He wanted to know which clerk had treated me that way. He said he was going to fire her. I said it didn't matter; everybody was acting the same way. He said, "It won't happen again here, as long as I am the manager of this store." It was comforting to know that someone was sensible enough not to join the frenzy of others.

Since most of the vegetable farmers had been Japanese, the wholesale business in Los Angeles was deserted. That meant good prices for the remaining farmers, us included. We had several years of good crops and high market prices, which made up for all those years of nothing in the past. Very few men were available for farm work after Pearl Harbor, so we hired Mexican women and teen-aged girls, about fifty to sixty of them during the planting season and the same number during the months of picking and packing vegetables. Planting took about two weeks, but picking took much longer, about three months. The first crop did not take as long to pick and it produced better vegetables. The second crop was usually not that good for the stores. Four men, two of them Korean friends, worked in the packing shed. All vegetables had to be graded according to size: number ones brought the top price, and number twos brought less.

On our farm, we had a very efficient and experienced team of four persons, each of whom had special duties. Henry did all the heavy field work, plowing with the tractor, disking, and loading the truck. Once Allan asked why Henry got to "ride around in the truck," so we let him try plowing. He discovered that it was much harder than he had thought: each furrow of earth had to be flopped over at just the right distance. Allan did the irrigating, however, which was also a difficult job, going up and down the hillside in our old Dodge pickup, watching the water in the furrows. The irrigation pipes would turn on like a faucet and would scatter the water into the furrows. It was important to make sure not too much water ran out, and Allan became very good at it. H.M. supervised the packing in the shed and managed all the business of the farm. I was the forelady in the fields, leading and showing the women how to do everything.

I went out into the field with the Mexican women every morning at seven o'clock. At that time of the morning, the vegetables were wet with dew and the tiny barbs on the squash leaves stung like nettles. We all wore overalls or pants, except for the old ladies, who still wore dresses, and each of us wore white gloves and carried a basket. The dew sprinkled off the plants as we worked. By 9 A.M., we were wet to our hips and were stinging from the leaves. I went in front to set an example, because zucchini has to be cut just so, diagonally with a short-bladed knife. The squash could not be too big or too small for the market. H.M. would lecture the women before we went out into the field. At the time, other farmers were paying twenty cents an hour. H.M. told them, "I'll pay you twenty-five cents an hour. But that doesn't mean to work fast. Work slow and even, and do it right. When you cut the zucchini, leave an inch — not too close, not too far. And don't cut the ones that are too small." We worked until six every evening, with a one-hour lunch break. The workers ate breakfast and dinner at home and brought their own lunches to the fields. We supplied five-gallon bottles of water, set here and there in the fields, and we built outhouses for their use. There were times when I cried from exhaustion while I was working, with the sweat running down my back and stomach. It would be 8 or 9 P.M. by the time I got back from taking the workers home. The family would be waiting for me so they could eat, and then after supper I had to wash the children's clothes and dry them in the oven so they could wear them to school the next day.

We had a contract with Safeway and guaranteed an "honest pack," which meant that the vegetables on top of the pack would be the same size as the layers below. (Some farmers put the big deformed ones underneath the good ones.) H.M. kept the oversized squash in a separate box in the packing shed and gave them to the workers. We had our own trademark — Lee's Farm — and Safeway ordered 5,000 lugs from us every season.*

Once a man came out from Safeway with a rush order for an exclusive club. They needed 2,000 lugs of zucchini. It was already afternoon, but I said to the women, "Maybe we can do it." I told them we might have to work late, but we'd pay them extra. We stayed in the field until dark and filled the order.

At the end of each day, the men helped load the truck to take the produce to Los Angeles that evening. We also had to pick up the workers at 6 A.M. every morning and take them home at the end of the day. H.M. went to La Habra, and I went to Carmelita or Norwalk to fetch them. The workers lived in camps, in buildings like chicken shacks. Every morning they waited out in front for farmers to take them to the fields. They learned who were the good bosses. They liked H.M. because he spoke Spanish and he treated them like friends.

After supper, H.M. took the load to Los Angeles and came back home in time for a brief rest before breakfast at 5 A.M. He never had much time for sleep or rest. Saturday was the only day off, but there were so many other things to do. He had to take care of the horse, give it a rubdown, clean the barn, and do other chores. I had to do the weekly laundry, housework, and shopping. We were always busy. It's hard enough for a healthy person, but H.M. was still suffering with his terrible itching. He had to wear a corset-like brace to hold him up. It was hard and stiff like a cast, also like a saddle on a horse. He had to endure all that torment while working all day. He forced himself to keep up, said he must keep going while market prices were high. But the pressure was wearing him down; he was reduced to skin and bones. He just gritted his teeth and kept moving through sheer will power. Of course, I was the only one who knew what torture he was going through, so I couldn't blame him for "blowing up" sometimes when someone

---

*Mary Paik Lee's recollection differs from that of her son, Allan Lee. (See Appendix B.)

did something wrong. He never mentioned his illness to friends; very few persons knew about it.

H.M.'s knowledge of Spanish was a great advantage in our relations with the workers. They appreciated being spoken to in correct Spanish — always addressed as Señora and Señor So-and-So, never as "Hey you!" One day the women were singing "La Paloma" and couldn't remember all the words. H.M. happened to be walking by, so he sang all the verses for them. They were so surprised and happy. That song was popular in Mexico when he was living there. At the end of every picking season we had a big party in the packing shed for all the workers. H.M. gave Señora Josefa one hundred dollars and told her to gather the women to make tamales for all the workers, and to buy beer, soda, watermelons, and other food. Someone brought a guitar to the party, and everyone sang all the old songs they could remember. H.M. told jokes that Spanish people appreciate. Everyone had a happy time. During the war, farmworkers were scarce, but whenever we sent word that we needed them, they all came back to us.

When our Japanese neighbors came back from the concentration camps, we moved to an old Japanese schoolhouse nearby, owned by a Mr. Behenke. He put in a sink, a sideboard, a cold water pipe, and a stove. We bought butane gas for the stove. We had a big tank outside and heated our bath water in a bucket on the stove. At least there was a bathtub and a toilet. The schoolhouse had one long hall in the middle, several small rooms on each side, and a large assembly room in the back, which served as our combination kitchen, dining area, and living room.

When Henry turned eighteen, he had to report to the draft board. When they learned that he was helping his father farm fifty acres of vegetables, they deferred him for two years to help feed the people at home. When Henry joined the army two years later, we tried to continue farming, but found it very difficult. When Allan also left for military duty, it was impossible to farm anymore. In a way we were relieved, because H.M. was at the end of his endurance, though he never complained, never mentioned his suffering to anyone.

From time to time we gave Father money to help the Paik family along. My brothers were working, but they were just getting started, so they couldn't help much. Five of them were drafted into the armed services as they came of age. Stanford served with the army in Europe. When he returned, he went back to work inspecting aircraft at Lockheed, but he had lost his seniority and had to work his way back up to his old job. Ralph was a war photographer. He accompanied the planes on their bombing missions and was quite lucky to return home uninjured. Arthur worked in communications in the army. He went ahead of the troops, helping to lay telephone lines and set up radio stations. He was shot in the back of the head, and the doctors had to insert a metal plate to cover the crack in his skull. The plate caused him much pain for the rest of his life. Both cold and heat gave him terrible headaches, so he was never able to hold regular employment. He always did odd jobs, like painting. Young was a chauffeur for an army colonel in New Guinea. When the war ended, he went to Australia, married, and brought his wife to Whittier. Edward served in the air force during the war. Soon after he came home, he married a Korean girl who lived in Berkeley.

Father passed away in Ernest's house in Whittier on July 20, 1947, at the age of seventy-four, from a massive cerebral hemorrhage. All seven brothers were pallbearers at his funeral.

When we quit farming in 1950, I went to Whittier, the "City of Brotherly Love," to try to rent a house. When I knocked on doors, every person took one look at me and shut the door without a word; so we were forced to move to Los Angeles.

All during our farming years, we donated what we could to help build and maintain our Korean Presbyterian Church on Jefferson Boulevard in Los Angeles. We paid our tithe of three hundred dollars yearly as well as special donations for the Thanksgiving dinners, Christmas fund, and Mother's Day celebrations. The largest share went to the maintenance fund to keep the church going. Since Sunday was the busiest day on the farm, we could not attend services. Nevertheless, we supported the church for many years.

In addition, H.M.'s half-brother in Korea kept writing, begging for help to support his family; so we had to help him, also. We carried the load of three families for many years: the Paik family, H.M.'s family in Seoul, and our own family here. I don't know how we ever managed, but we did, despite everything.

H.M. found a house in Los Angeles at 3916 La Salle Avenue. I went to see it, and we agreed to buy it for $9,000. Henry helped us with some money from his army pay. We sold all our farm equipment—two trucks, one tractor, a disk, and an old Dodge pickup—and moved. Everywhere we have moved, we have found old friends nearby. All our friends were in the apartment business, so we too looked around and made a down payment on a twelve-unit, unfurnished, one-bedroom apartment building on Broadway Place, near the old Jan-U-Wine chop suey factory, where Meung was working at that time. We hired painters for the outside, but H.M. painted the interior and I did all the cleaning. He did the maintenance work as much as possible. Believe me, it was harder than farm work. I thought it was better to work with the clean earth than to clean up other people's filth and mess. After all the work was done, the building looked nice and clean. Pretty soon a Japanese man came around and wanted to know what price we wanted for the building. After much talking and haggling, he bought it at a price which netted us a good profit.

The first apartment building purchased by Mr. and Mrs.
H. M. Lee, Broadway Place, Los Angeles, 1950.

While we were living on La Salle Avenue, President Syngman
Rhee and his wife made their farewell visit to the United States
and came to Los Angeles. Mr. and Mrs. Leo Song gave a wonderful party for them in their beautiful patio at 1064 Gramercy
Place, Los Angeles. It was the perfect place for a fabulous party. I
bought fifty pounds of black-eyed peas and spent three days hard
at work making *muk* for the occasion. Mr. Song had ordered many
special Chinese dishes for the party, but President Rhee looked
very old and tired and apologized for not being able to sample
all the dishes set before him. Knowing that he liked *muk*, I asked
Mrs. Song to offer some to him. When President Rhee saw the
muk, he turned to his wife and said, "This is just the thing I need,"
and ate two helpings. That was my reward. Although the guests
were by "invitation only," the party was so crowded everyone had
to stand. Only President Rhee, his wife, and a few close friends
of theirs sat at a table. The crowd included several busloads of
Korean navy cadets who were in San Diego on their U.S. training
trip. That occasion was our last meeting with, and final farewell
to, an old friend.

An unexpected thing happened around then. I read about the

discovery of penicillin in England by Dr. Alexander Fleming and told H.M. about it. He decided to get some penicillin shots. After two injections at fifteen dollars each, his itching disappeared! After thirty years of constant torment, he found relief at last. What a pity to have suffered so long!

As we looked around at our friends in Los Angeles, we could see the progress our people had made since 1906. The only work available for men at that time had been farm work, eight to ten hours a day at ten to fifteen cents an hour, depending on the good nature and kindness of the employer. It was several years before women were allowed to do housework in American homes. Although not being able to speak English was a big problem, after long hours of hard labor, no one had the time or energy to study English.

As their children grew up and helped them with their language problems, Orientals were able to try something else. Some families started small grocery stores, tobacco shops, chop suey joints, dry-cleaning and pressing shops, or laundries. Those enterprises were the first step up toward a better way of life. Fruit and vegetable stands became very popular with Americans, which helped in many ways to break down the barriers between people.

Our black friends, who had lived here longer, were in the same situation as Orientals. They spoke English, but that did not help them in their struggle for a better life. My black girl friend cried as she related all the hardships of her people. "Why did God make me black to be hated and ignored by white people?" she asked. She told me I was lucky not to be black. I replied that her color did not seem to be the problem, that we were all in the same situation. The Mexican people were here first, but they were in the same hopeless state. Due to our mutual problems, all minorities felt a sympathetic bond with one another. We patronized one another's stores, to help out. The first generation laid the foundation for the future by teaching their children to be honest — never to steal or do anything that might cause ill feeling towards our people. We felt that was the only way we could prove to Americans that we are also human beings.

Our daily relations with Americans were improving, but once in a while something happened to remind us of the past. When my oldest son Henry was in the fifth grade, he came home one afternoon in high spirits because his class had had a spelling match, the guys against the girls, and he had won. The teacher had told them that the real match would be the next day, and there would be a prize for the winner. I felt like saying something, but decided to wait and see. He returned home the next day, feeling very angry and disgusted with school. He said that though he had won the match, "old lady Stone" had given the prize to the girl. I told him what my father had told me a long time ago, when the same thing had happened to me. "It doesn't matter who got the prize as long as you know the correct answer. The person who won so easily, without knowing the correct answer, has not learned anything. Just be sure that you know it and don't forget it. The knowledge you have in your brain can never be taken away by anyone."

A few days later, a young lady about twenty years old came to our roadside stand on Leffingwell Road. She said she was Henry's teacher. I asked, "Are you 'old lady Stone'?" "That's what the children call me," she replied. "I wanted to explain why I didn't give Henry the prize the other day. The girl's mother is the president of the PTA. I knew she would have me fired if I gave Henry the prize. I am very sorry and want to apologize. I am trying to earn enough money to go to college and get my teacher's certificate. It's very difficult to find a job these days. That's why I was forced to give the prize to the girl." I was so surprised by her unexpected thoughtfulness and courage in speaking to me like that. It reminded me of what my father told us long ago — that there are good people everywhere, but we just had not met them yet. Times were getting better.

Once an American lady friend asked me if I was going to vote that day. I said I was too busy and couldn't get away. She started to give me a lecture about my civic duty. I looked at her in wonder. She considered herself well educated and thought she knew everything. Yet she didn't know that the reason I didn't vote was that Orientals were not allowed to be citizens, so we didn't have the right to vote. She became very angry and said, "That's not so! Everyone in America has equal rights." But she came back a few days later and said a lawyer friend had told her that I was right. We remained good friends, anyway.

In the 1950s, most of the "For Whites Only" signs on public restrooms, swimming pools, and so forth, were removed. But although there were no signs on barber shops, theaters, and churches, Orientals were told at the door that they were not welcome. In northern California, some gas stations and towns had signs on the highway stating: "Japs are not wanted here."

Young Korean students who were just starting their careers with high hopes found themselves caught in the fury of this anti-Oriental sentiment. We had a young friend who had graduated from medical college with honors and was serving his internship at the Stanford University Hospital. One evening a man from a prominent family was badly injured in an automobile accident, lost a lot of blood, and needed an immediate blood transfusion. No one present would volunteer his blood, so our friend offered his to save the man's life. The family refused it, saying they didn't want "dirty Jap blood" put into the man's body. So the man died. The incident broke the spirit and ambition of our friend. He was too young and naive to realize what our world was like. Years later, our black friends laughed when the doctors told them that their blood was acceptable for the blood bank.

As the Japanese families were being taken to concentration camps, their sons of military age volunteered or were drafted for army duty. They proved their courage and loyalty to America by joining the famous Japanese battalion that was sent to Europe. The battalion won more medals than any other unit of its size in the army. Many men were killed. One captain in that battalion later became Senator Daniel Inuoye from Hawaii. He was wounded and had one arm in a sling when he landed in San Francisco after the war. He thought he should get a haircut and make himself presentable before joining his family in Hawaii. He was wearing his captain's uniform as he entered the barber shop. The barber took one look at him and said, "I don't serve Japs in my shop." His uniform didn't mean a thing to the barber.

In Los Angeles in 1950 we found many minority women working in sewing factories making garments of every sort for fifty

Tony Lee and his parents, Los Angeles, 1950.

cents an hour, eight hours a day. After several years, the wage went up to one dollar an hour. The sewing rooms were dirty and very dusty, with lint and dust filling the air like fog. The rooms had no air conditioning and no windows. The dust settling on the heads of the women made their hair look gray by the end of the day. The loud power-driven sewing machines working at full speed all at once made a thundering noise that deafened the ear. It was a frightful thing to listen to for eight hours every weekday. I tried it once for several months; the experience made me admire all those women who endured it for years in order to send their children to colleges and universities. I have seen those children return home as doctors, lawyers, and engineers, thus rewarding their parents for their sacrifices. Those pioneers took the first step toward raising the standard of living for the second and third generations of Orientals here.

There is a good example among Koreans which makes me feel proud of what people can accomplish despite hardship. Mr. and Mrs. Lee (no relation to us) had a son named Sammy. The first time I saw him, he was only eleven months old. I watched his progress all the way through the University of Southern California School of Medicine, where he became a doctor, specializing in ear, nose, and throat ailments. He was always playing in the swimming pools and became interested in high diving. The coach at USC took an interest in him and helped him to develop into an expert high-platform diver. Sammy Lee won the Olympic Gold Medal for high-platform diving in 1948 and successfully defended his title in 1952. In 1953 he became the first non-Caucasian to win the James E. Sullivan Memorial Trophy. His parents helped with all his expenses by working in their chop suey restaurant for many years.

Orientals were not the only ones who suffered from discrimination. A neighbor told me her family had to move to Los Angeles because her son was not accepted in most universities back East because he was Jewish. There was discrimination of every kind in those days, and it has not disappeared completely. As recently as 1982 a Chinese man was killed by two white men. They had been laid off their jobs at an automobile plant because of all the Japanese

Mr. and Mrs. H. M. Lee in front of their house, La Salle
Avenue, Los Angeles, 1960.

cars coming into America. Without knowing or even thinking
that there are many Orientals who are not Japanese, they vented
their rage on the first Oriental man they saw. He was savagely
beaten with a baseball bat. The local police were reluctant to do

anything about it until the Chinese community rose up in sorrow and anger and complained to the federal government. The two men were convicted, but their sentences were light, considering the crime they had committed.*

*Mrs. Lee is referring to the Vincent Chin case, in which a Chinese American was clubbed to death by two unemployed white autoworkers in Detroit. One of them was acquitted and the other, though convicted and sentenced to twenty-five years in prison, never served time, because his conviction was overturned on a technicality. *Editor.*

While Henry was in the army, he served as an interpreter for Koreans who were being ordered out of Japan. After several months in Japan's severe cold and snow, he became very ill and was sent to Fitzsimmons Army Hospital in Denver, Colorado. He had pleurisy in both lungs and had caught tuberculosis. He had to stay in bed for several years. During his illness, he sent for correspondence courses from Georgetown University in Washington, D.C. He did all the required writing and reading, so his time in the hospital was not wasted. Since he majored in foreign trade and service, he also learned to speak Japanese.

Henry was very fortunate to be finishing his education at a time when restrictions against Orientals were beginning to be lifted. While he was attending Georgetown, he was elected student body president in 1954, the first minority person to hold that post. Some of his American friends also asked him to join their fraternity and prepared a party for the event, but on the evening of the party, someone looked up the charter for the fraternity and found that nonwhites were not allowed as members. His friends were embarrassed and apologized to him. When Henry told us about this incident, what mattered to us was the fact that the members had wanted him to join them. His name was included in the 1954 *Who's Who among University Students in the U.S.*

We sent Henry one hundred dollars every month to help with his expenses at Georgetown University, but that was not enough, so he did odd jobs during vacation. One time, while we were living on La Salle Avenue, he brought twenty Korean Assembly members from Seoul to Los Angeles. The U.S. government paid him to conduct tours to America to show them places of interest. Some friends and I prepared a Korean dinner for them, thinking they might be tired of strange American food. They certainly enjoyed everything. We talked all night, exchanging ideas.

In 1959 Henry married Ellen Kim in Washington, D.C. The trip there was my first airplane flight. I felt airsick and nervous, but H.M. felt fine. The captain said there would be a two-hour delay for refueling in Memphis, Tennessee, which would give the passengers a chance to leave the plane and refresh themselves. A black couple sitting in front of us were the only people who did not get off the plane, and I wondered why they stayed. Then, as I walked around the airport building looking for the restrooms, I saw something that sent a chill down my spine, like a ghost from the past. Several young men were glaring at us, and on the wall above them, in large print, was the familiar old sign "For Whites Only." The young men seemed to be daring me to go in. It had been some years since those signs had disappeared in California, and I had forgotten all about them. It came as a shock to see one again in 1959 in Memphis. Seeing that sign brought back all the unpleasant memories of the past. Now I understood why the black couple had stayed on the plane. Black people were obviously still suffering from such restrictions.

This unpleasant experience was forgotten in Washington, D.C., where we met friends and witnessed a beautiful wedding ceremony. We were happy to have a wonderful daughter-in-law join our family. After a short visit, we returned home and made plans for a party to introduce Ellen to all our relatives and friends. We invited about two hundred and fifty guests to our party, which was held in one of the best Chinese restaurants in town. It was a happy meeting of relatives and friends. There were many presents for the newlyweds. Afterwards they returned to Washington to continue their education.

After Henry received his M.A. at Georgetown University, he taught at the Wharton School of Commerce and Finance for four years while working for his Ph.D. at the University of Pennsylvania. When he became Dr. Henry Lee, the Federal Reserve Bank asked him to work for them — probably the first time they ever allowed an Oriental in their agency. They sent him to South America, where his knowledge of Spanish was useful. He went to many Third World countries, reporting to the Federal Reserve about what was needed most and how the U.S. could best help

Mr. and Mrs. H. M. Lee with Henry Lee's family, Los Angeles, 1969. Left to right: Henry with Michael on his lap, Mrs. Lee, Mr. Lee, Ellen with Stephen on her lap, and Allan.

them. He made many trips to the small Asian countries, explaining how to get American foreign aid and how to repay it with products manufactured in their own countries. This helped to start some of the "cottage industries" that have helped small countries to be self-sufficient. Henry told us one time that a friend, Mr. Sal Sun Kim, asked him to consult the U.S. government about starting a modern textile industry in Korea. The U.S. government agreed to give some American textile manufacturers new machinery if they would send their old equipment to Korea. After a slow start, the textile industry in Korea became a huge success, contributing greatly to that country's recovery after the war. Henry traveled all over to find enough cotton to send to Korea; he even went to India. He was very pleased to see the success of that venture. Today, many stuffed animals in American stores have "Made in Korea" labels. Also, all sorts of wearing apparel from Korea is sold in the United States. What a difference the years of progress have made!

Henry said that, wherever he went, he met officials who had been classmates of his at Georgetown or Pennsylvania, which helped to better his relations and made his work more enjoyable because he could avoid some of the diplomatic ceremonies. The people in Asian countries appreciated the fact that an Oriental person was sent to represent the U.S. in such important work. The Fox Movietone Company took pictures of Henry's first arrival in an Asian country. The people were so surprised and happy to see him. It caused a wave of friendship among Orientals that made for better understanding in that part of the world. Henry worked in the State Department during the Vietnam War, making many trips back and forth. Then he was asked to work for the Treasury Department. He and Ellen had three children — Michael on July 8, 1965; Stephen on November 21, 1966; and Laura on November 28, 1970.

Henry's success reflects the sort of attitude change we had been hoping for since 1906, a change that took nearly one hundred years to bring about. In 1942, after all the excitement and confusion of Pearl Harbor had faded somewhat, most of the American firms suddenly made it known that they would hire Orientals who were qualified to work in their establishments. We regarded that as a miracle from Heaven, because it happened at a time when everything seemed hopeless for all of us. We gave thanks to God for bringing about this sudden change. It brought new hope to everyone that we might have a better future. I am always happy to see Orientals able to work almost everywhere now. America is the only place in the world where people of all races can live in peace and harmony with one another. It is the responsibility of all persons to obey the laws of the country and do their part to maintain this harmony. As my mother always said: "God is surely leading us in the right direction."

Allan has also had success in his career. When he went to the University of California at Los Angeles, his father was so proud of him he bought him a new Ford to drive to school and back. Allan was just getting started in college when he was drafted and sent to Europe for several years. He returned from the war in good health, with no injuries, and went back to UCLA. He graduated cum laude, receiving a B.S. in Business Administration in Production Management. He is a licensed real estate broker and building

contractor and has built three high-rise office buildings in northern California. Now he is a managing general partner in a real
estate investment and development company. He was married in
1966 and divorced in 1977. He has two daughters — Sarah, born
in 1972, and Katie, born in 1974.

My youngest son, Tony, has had a difficult life. Although I was
very ill at the time he was born, I noticed something wrong with
his eyes and asked the doctor about it. The doctor refused to
discuss it, saying, "All you Japs have small eyes. What are you worried about?" He was impatient with me for bringing it up several
times. Because he insisted there was nothing wrong with Tony's
eyes, and because Tony never complained of any pain, I put the
whole thing out of my mind for several years. Then, in 1946, while
we were living in Norwalk, Tony started school. When he came
home from his first day at school, he brought me a piece of paper
with writing that he said he had copied from the blackboard. The
writing was upside down. That's when I realized he had something seriously wrong with his eyes. I took him to Dr. Mills in Los
Angeles, who said he had drooping eyelids. Evidently he was born
without muscles in his eyelids. Dr. Mills said it would take several
operations to correct the problem. He was eight years old at the
time of his first operation in August 1948. The second and third
operations were each five years apart, in July 1953 and July 1958.
The doctors gave the muscles time to heal before operating again.
The skin above and below the eyes had to be peeled back in order
to transplant muscles to his eyelids. It was a very slow and painful
ordeal that lasted for years, but he never cried or complained. At
the hospital, all the other children cried and screamed when their
stitches were removed, but Tony always suffered in silence. Dr.
Mills was so pleased by how good he was, he always gave him a
quarter when he saw him. He also had plastic surgery years later
to remove the scars on his face. But that was not the end of his
suffering.

In 1948 a severe polio epidemic had struck Norwalk, and schools
were closed for several months. We felt relieved that Tony was
not sick, but years later, after we moved to La Salle Avenue, we

noticed that he walked with his shoulders bent slightly forward. I used to tell him to straighten up. One day, when he removed his T shirt, I saw that one side of his back curved in slightly in a manner that alarmed me. I took him to Children's Orthopedic Hospital in Los Angeles. Dr. Norquist, a specialist in spinal cases, asked if Tony had ever been exposed to polio. I told him about the epidemic in Norwalk. He shook his head and said he had most of those children there now. Although Tony had not been sick at the time, the doctor said the polio virus could enter the body and break out later wherever there was a weak spot. He later told me that Tony had three weak spots in his spine that needed to be strengthened. In the beginning, Tony was placed for six weeks in a turn-buckle cast, a real torture instrument, to straighten the curve in his spine. Every hour, the nurse would turn the screw to hasten the process. Then, in May 1954, the doctor made the first spinal fusion. Tony was then fourteen years old. I asked where he would get the bones for the "welding." He said there is plenty on the spine. He cut off a bit to wedge into the weak spots. The second fusion was in June 1954, and the third, in March 1955. While Tony was in the hospital, his whole body was bound in the old-style plaster cast from head to toe, like a mummy. He could not move even an inch and had to be fed by a nurse. The pain was so great, he could not eat; he just asked for candy bars and juice. A short time later, Dr. Norquist gave him a different kind of cast made of light plastic, with air holes to relieve the heat and itching inside.

In June, they began to shorten Tony's cast bit by bit, trimming away the top and bottom. By September, it had been reduced to corset size. We were allowed to take him home to recuperate, but he had to remain in bed. A friend let us borrow a hospital bed. We rented a pulley to attach to a rod above. Even with a short cast, Tony was too heavy for me to turn over in bed. Being at home and able to move his body a bit was a big relief. He felt like eating again, and he began to improve day by day. The cast was finally sawed off in November 1955. His body was a mass of terrible-looking sores. Just imagine how much torture that must have been. He had been reduced to skin and bones, and he was a pitiful sight. An American boy who lived across the street came to see him every day, which made him laugh again.

Although the ordeal had lasted two years, the intense pain was so agonizing it seemed like ten. After two years of "hell" and inactivity, all Tony's muscles were soft and flabby. His legs could not function. We started exercising slowly, bit by bit. Every half hour I held him up as he tried to move his legs. The effort was like a baby's first attempt at walking. We walked around in the house for several weeks; then, gradually, we went outside. After two months, we were walking around the block. The school sent a home teacher to help him keep up with his classmates, but pain prevented him from concentrating on anything. So she mostly just read to him. Later, when he felt able and strong enough, he went back to the Manual Arts High School, where he graduated. There was no government assistance then — no one to help us with all the bills that kept coming in every month — but we managed to pay for everything.

Once he was able to take care of himself, Tony got a job as a janitor at Macy's in downtown San Francisco. Because of his illness, he has never had the opportunities other people have had. I admire his strong, patient spirit; his ability to endure misfortune without blaming anyone; and the way he tries to be optimistic about life.

Someone wanted to buy our apartment building on Broadway and made us a good offer, so H.M. sold it and bought the St. James apartment building at 848 W. 23rd Street in Los Angeles. It was an old three-story building with an elevator and twenty-seven furnished studio units, each of which we rented for fifty-four dollars per month, including utilities. We sold our house on La Salle Avenue and moved into a one-bedroom apartment in the St. James building. Tony also had a studio apartment there. We worked hard to clean up the place, did a lot of painting inside and cleaning up outside. Tony helped with the maintenance work, dusting the stairways, keeping the halls clean and vacuuming the hall rugs. By this time H.M.'s health was getting poorer. He couldn't keep up with all the work that had to be done. His eyesight was failing; he had cataracts in both eyes and was unable to repair pipes and electric wiring. He had one eye operation, and then another several months later. Although the operations improved his eyesight somewhat, the rest of his body was failing rapidly. He was seventy years old. The years of hard labor and suffering were taking their toll. It was time for him to retire. The real estate boom was still on, so we decided to take advantage of it and sell again.

There was a Jewish man who kept coming around looking into our building, asking questions, commenting on the cleanliness of our yard, garbage cans, and so forth. We asked him why he was hanging around so much. He said he would like to buy some income property. He was looking for a building like ours and asked what our price would be. I said that we had such a good business that my husband did not want to sell. Then I asked, "What is your offer?" He mentioned a price. I laughed and said, "You're crazy. We're not going to give it away." H.M. was in the hospital then, recuperating from his second eye operation. When I told him the offer, he said, "We might be able to make a good profit on this deal." After he came home, he and the Jewish man haggled about the price and finally came to an agreement. It was an unexpectedly good deal; we got more than we had hoped for. We made an inventory of everything in each apartment. When we came to our apartment, I told the new owner that the bookcase was my personal property, that I was going to take it when we moved. He agreed, but on moving day he refused to let me take it, which made me really angry. The bookcase was one that Henry had made when he was in the fifth grade.

Our next move was to 1416½ W. 25th Street. The building was owned by an old friend of ours. For the first time in our lives we were able to take it easy with no more work to do. It was good to be able to relax and have a little fun. We went to Redondo Beach with friends to catch clams and abalone at low tide. The men dived for abalone, which we cooked on the beach for lunch. There were no restrictions or limits then on any kind of fishing. We went to Pismo Beach one time to dig for clams at 2 A.M., when the tide was at its lowest. We built a fire and cooked them for our lunches. Pismo Beach is noted for its clear white sand and a special kind of large clams. When they became known to the public, restrictions were imposed. The beach was fenced in, and guards made sure all regulations were enforced. Each person going in was given a pitchfork and a five-inch measuring stick. Only five abalones were allowed each person, and the abalones had to be at least five inches in width.

H.M. went ocean fishing from Newport Beach. He boarded the large boats there and came back with big barracuda, white sea bass, and large albacore. He went to Catalina Island for clams and lobsters. Near the pier at Newport Beach there was a place where one could get one's fish smoked. It was the custom to give the owner half the catch in return for his smoking it. Those were the "good old days." It was the happiest, most carefree time we ever had. The memory of it will always be with me. In the evenings the men played cards — mostly poker, with bets of pennies, nickels, and dimes. I made doughnuts and coffee. The women brought their knitting and crocheting, or just visited until midnight. Sometimes I went to a nearby restaurant and bought chow mein for everyone. The hard times were over, and we could relax a bit.

At a certain time during the summer, a wondrous event of nature takes place along the southern California coast. Small, slender fish called "grunion" come up on the beaches with the high tide at night to lay their eggs in the warm sand. The male grunions follow to fertilize the eggs. The females are pushed up on the beaches by the strong waves and immediately wiggle their bodies to make a shallow depression in the sand. They lay their eggs and wait for the next wave to carry them back to sea. [Then the males surge in.] The beaches are covered with a blanket of sparkling, shimmering silver — a marvelous spectacle one is privileged to witness. People go out with buckets and scoop up the fish. The grunion are helpless while on the beach and fall victim to human beings. They resemble smelt but are smaller and very slender.

In 1960 H.M. and I became American citizens. I asked to have my name changed from Kuang Sun Paik to Mary Paik Lee. We never received any Social Security money, because farmers were not included in that program. Years later, after we had quit farming, an amendment to Social Security gave farmers some compensation. But we were grateful to have the benefits of Medicare.

Then we moved again, to 3611 Chesapeake Avenue, Apartment 4, our last address in Los Angeles. We were now able to retire from work, but old age and physical ailments became problems. H.M. was now seventy-three years old, in poor health, and barely hanging on. The hard labor, lack of proper rest, and mental anguish over the years, trying to help three families and friends, had made him a physical wreck. He was too generous for his own good; he could not refuse to help anyone who asked for aid.

His half-brother in Seoul, Korea, was always asking for more money. We helped whenever possible. During the Korean War, a bomb fell on his half-brother's house, killing his two sons, one daughter, and several relatives who happened to be in the house. The half-brother, his wife, and another daughter were not at home that day. After the tragedy, he wrote asking for help, so H.M. returned to Korea for the first time since his departure in 1905. He

Fiftieth wedding anniversary of Mr. and Mrs. H. M. Lee,
Los Angeles, 1969.

found them huddled in temporary quarters. He bought them a
two-story house, furniture, clothes for everyone, and enough food
to last them for some time — all for $4,000 in American money,
which was a fortune in Korean money. In his frail state of health,
H.M. couldn't take proper care of himself. He had several diarrhea attacks and was forced to return to Los Angeles feeling very
weak, barely able to walk. After his return, he was sick in bed for
a month.

A year later, his half-brother wrote again, saying his only surviving daughter needed an operation to save her life. So H.M.
sent them five hundred dollars. He told them he was not able to
help them anymore; that was the limit of his generosity. Sometime
later, his half-brother sent an invitation to his grandson's wedding. H.M. dreaded the thought of going to Korea again, but after
thinking it over, he said that this trip would be his final farewell to
his own family. He took along $1,000 to give to his grandnephew
as a wedding present. He brought back pictures of the family and
the wedding reception. He was so weak and ill when he came back
that he could hardly stand up. He went straight to bed and took
several weeks to recover.

The last big event in our lives was the celebration of our fiftieth wedding anniversary. All our relatives and old friends helped
make it a memorable occasion. The thought of it always brings
back happy memories. Cherished memories are like the jewels that
wealthy people keep in safe-deposit boxes in the bank—to take
out and enjoy on occasion. Whenever I feel low, I think back to
all the happy times we had with family and old friends who have
remained dear to us through the years. Whenever we meet, we
pick up where we left off the last time. The feeling between us remains the same. I'm very fortunate to have so many loving friends
everywhere.

While we were living on Chesapeake Avenue, Stanford did a
wonderful thing. He rented a two-bedroom apartment near us
and brought Mother to live with him. He bought all the furniture
and took care of her. He made her breakfast every morning before leaving for work. I went over every day to clean her house,
bathe her, cook her lunch, and prepare something for supper. I
was glad to see her relaxing with no work to do, just reading her
Bible and listening to music or watching television. Stanford kept
the refrigerator full of food that Mother liked. Sometime later, she
developed kidney trouble and couldn't urinate. We had to put her
in a nursing home nearby where a nurse could use a catheter on
her. I went to the nursing home at eight every morning and stayed
with her all day until eight at night. Mother could not speak or
understand English. She felt scared when I left, but the manager
told me no one was allowed to stay overnight. Her doctor said
her condition was hopeless: it was too late to do anything, and the
end was near. She suffered for three months. She had difficulty
swallowing even water, which had to be squirted into her throat
with a syringe. She refused food because she couldn't swallow it.
But she never complained or asked for anything.

Daniel, a Baptist minister, and his wife Margaret (my niece)
came to see her a few days before she died and gave her Holy
Communion, which made her feel happy and relieved. I had no
idea she wanted it, and I shall be forever grateful for Daniel's and
Margaret's thoughtful gesture. She was happy to go after that, and
she passed away on March 12, 1969, at eighty-nine years of age.

All the Paik siblings after their mother's funeral, Los Angeles, 1969. Left to right, front row: Florence, Charlotte, and Kuang Sun; back row: Eddie, Young, Ralph, Arthur, Stanford, Ernest, and Meung Sun.

I had a feeling Mother was going to die that night, and I asked the manager if she could be moved to another room where I could be with her. But she refused to let me stay. It made me so angry and frustrated. What if Mother had asked for me, and I was not there to comfort her at the end? It seems cruel to treat a dying person that way and leave a family with regrets. I hope that nursing homes in the future will allow dying persons the comfort of having someone stay with them until the end. Mother was buried in the Rosedale Cemetery in Los Angeles.

During the three months that I was at the nursing home with my mother, my ailing husband at home was in and out of bed. I cooked enough food for him at night so he could warm it over and help himself during the day. He never complained about the inconvenience. He was such a patient and understanding man. He told me not to worry about him.

During this period, my brother Young and his wife moved to

San Francisco where Young became a bus driver on Market Street for several years. One day his wife received a letter from Australia saying that her mother had passed away. She went back to Australia to claim her inheritance and discovered that she was not allowed to take money out of the country. She had to choose between a life of luxury in Australia and a poor life here, so she chose to stay in Australia. It turned out to be a wise decision, because Young was dying of malaria. I wrote to him once in a while from Los Angeles, and he always sent me a hundred or so dollars for Mother when he answered. He wanted me to get her everything she needed. His back hurt him so much he had stopped driving the bus and had started driving a taxi. He suffered for many years until death released him from pain and sorrow on February 26, 1974. He died alone in his apartment and was buried near our parents in the Rosedale Cemetery. I think of him often and wish I could have helped him, but I could never get away from my other duties.

Our last car was an old Ford Thunderbird. I urged H.M. to sell it while he was able to do so. He was very reluctant, saying that meant the end of everything for him. He felt sad the day it was sold. From then on, it was the beginning of the end for him. He had difficulty walking; his legs were so weak he just barely shuffled along; his hearing was impaired; his eyesight was poor. To make matters worse, an aneurysm of the aorta caused him much pain. The doctor said the aneurysm was as large as a small orange; that it could burst at any moment. He recommended an immediate operation, but H.M. refused, saying that it was too late for anything. He became unconscious twice. I called the paramedics. They came, gave him oxygen, and took him to Daniel Freeman Hospital in Inglewood. When he came to, he refused to stay in the hospital. He said he wanted to die at home. "If this happens again," he said, "don't to do anything. Just let me go." He was living in a dream world, with all kinds of hallucinations; he thought snakes were coming down from the ceiling to attack him several times a day. And he was incontinent. I had to put diapers on him. He wanted his back massaged several times a day to relieve itching and he was constantly in and out of a coma.

In his brief moments of consciousness, H.M. did something surprising and unexpected. He thanked me several times for taking such good care of him and said he appreciated all my efforts to help him. He thanked me for working with him throughout our life together to accomplish all the things we were able to do, and he said he couldn't have done it without my cooperation. I was so surprised that he was able to think of such things in his confused state of mind. He kept repeating his love for me, and he said his farewell before sinking into the last coma. He died with a big smile on his face on June 29, 1975, aged eighty-three years. His burial plot is Pineview lot 420, Inglewood Park Cemetery. He left me a priceless legacy, more valuable than material things. He gave me a feeling of great solace that makes life worth living and that enables me to carry on alone. H.M. was a man of generous nature, always willing to help friends and families in need. Having grown up an orphan, he could never refuse aid when approached. Some people took advantage of this. Our early life here was sometimes rough and grim, but we had our lighter moments and our happy times with friends. We made our own amusements in spite of all the restrictions imposed on us.

I will never forget our considerate old friend James Kim. He drove us to H.M.'s doctor's appointments and came over every afternoon to talk to H.M., keeping him company while I shopped and did other errands. He and his wife Sarah were true friends.

Not long before H.M. died, Henry was appointed assistant director of the Asian Development Bank in Manila. He was told to be ready to leave for the Philippines in August. My daughter-in-law Ellen telephoned to tell us the good news. It made my husband feel good to hear about it; he said he would like to see Manila, but he knew that was impossible. When H.M. died, Henry, his daughter Laura, Allan, and Tony came to the funeral. Before Henry and Laura went back to Washington, Henry asked me to come to Manila with his family for a change of scenery and a rest. The flight left from Los Angeles, so we agreed to meet at Allan's house in Moraga later in August and then travel to Los Angeles together. Henry brought his family, and we all had a nice visit with Allan, his wife, and two daughters. In Los Angeles we boarded a plane to Hawaii. Henry had to see the state finance officer there; so we took a bus around Honolulu, and the children swam. The next day we went to Tokyo, where Henry also visited the finance minister. We stayed a week and took bus rides to see the countryside, although a terrible typhoon was blowing. Our last stop was in Korea. Henry was always busy with his work while we toured Seoul. All the cities are beginning to look alike; the world has certainly improved everywhere. We were entertained at dinner parties in the hotel and received gifts from the government. But we were beginning to feel sick with diarrhea, and I was glad to reach Manila at last.

The house assigned to Henry in Manila was wonderful. I had never lived in such a house. Although it was 100 degrees outside, it stayed cool inside. The Asian Development Bank office, where Henry worked, was constructed by the U.S.; all the American aid for East Asia is distributed from there. The large, beautiful building looks like a museum, with many Oriental art objects on display. The American Embassy is nearby, and there are schools for American children, and a bus that goes around to pick them up. After we unpacked and settled down to regular living, the children started going to school on the bus. Henry was very busy with his work at the bank and the embassy, often going by plane to visit all the little islands around there. Whenever there was time, Ellen and I went sightseeing. It was really luxury living for us. But I had not been feeling well when I started the trip and, as time went by, I felt myself getting worse. So I decided to go back to the U.S. after Christmas. I didn't tell Ellen the real reason for my leaving; I just said Allan wanted me back in San Francisco to keep the apartment he had found for me. I left Manila on January 1, 1976.

Soon after I arrived in San Francisco I became violently ill and had to call Allan to get an ambulance for me. I was freezing cold one minute and burning hot the next; I thought I had malaria. It took the hospital two weeks to find out that I had bacterial endocarditis from a germ I might have picked up in Manila. I had to have a painful penicillin treatment to clean out my veins and was in the hospital for two months. I was glad I had come back in time

H. M. Lee with his half-brother and nephew in Seoul, Korea, 1972.

for Medicare to help me, but I still had to pay $1,500 of the bills myself. It took a long time to get my strength back, and I had to plan what to do with the rest of my life. I had always wanted to learn oil painting, so even though it seemed a little late to start learning at the age of seventy-six, I asked around and found a senior citizens' center close to my apartment. About 250 seniors went to the center, which is located in the basement of the old First Presbyterian Church on the corner of Van Ness and Sacramento Streets. The oil painting classes met once a week, and the volunteer teacher was excellent. I was happy to find such a perfect place, and I was beginning to feel better and stronger.

Then, on September 11, 1976, Allan came to see me in San Francisco. I could see by his expression that something was wrong. He said he had news from the Philippines that Henry's airplane had crashed into a mountainside during a rainstorm. The news felt like a hard blow on my head. I couldn't cry or say anything. Everything in my body stopped working. After a while I asked who had been with him and where it had happened. Allan said that eleven men were with Henry, all coworkers from the bank and the embassy. To make our agony worse, we had to wait eleven days for the army to find the wrecked plane. Thinking the men might have survived the crash and were suffering was torture for all the families, and we consoled ourselves with the thought that sudden death was more merciful. Services were held at the Presbyterian church in Washington, D.C., on October 2, 1976, attended by representatives from the State Department, Treasury Department, Board of Governors of the Federal Reserve System, Asian Development Bank, and so forth. President Ford sent a personal letter of condolence to Ellen. Henry was buried with full honors in the military cemetery in Winchester, Virginia. Two close friends of his who also died in the crash were buried nearby. Henry's oldest son, Mike, was then eleven years old, Stephen was ten, and Laura was six. They don't remember their father well, but he loved them very much. It is a pity things happened the way they did. Ellen still lives in the same house. She has a master's degree in social work and an office where she counsels people.

After Henry died, I walked around like a zombie for two years. I couldn't remember my name, address, or phone number and had to carry a card with that information. I thought I was crazy and I felt frozen inside. Two years later I was in the hospital for an operation, and the thought of Henry made me start crying. I could not stop crying all night. It seemed to loosen up my nerves and release the tension in my body. Afterwards I felt better, and I resumed my normal life. I went to a Korean senior center for a visit, and as soon as they found out I could speak English, they wanted me to interpret for them. My job helped me to forget the past and to think of present problems. I greeted new arrivals from Korea at the airport, told them about services available to Koreans in America, helped them when they needed to see a doctor, and so forth. Ever since 1950, the new Korean arrivals have been from educated, high-class backgrounds. Life in America has changed so much that they don't understand the hardship we old-timers had to go through in this country. I told them: "You have arrived in Heaven compared with the place we came to in 1906."

My brother Arthur died in December 1976 at the age of sixty-six. He was buried next to our parents in the Rosedale Cemetery. When we were children, he had been the one who brought laughter into our home. He was full of pep, whereas all the other boys were quiet and did not play inside the house. He never married. Unfortunately, his injury from the war made him a physical wreck for the rest of his life. Although we missed him after he died, we were relieved his suffering was finally over.

Charlotte went to Hawaii and married a Korean man there. She had one son and adopted a little Korean girl. A few years later, her husband was killed in an automobile accident. She worked in a bakery decorating cakes for many years, and she passed away in March of 1977. She is buried in Hawaii. We heard from friends that her daughter is married and her son is working.

As Meung grew older, he had health problems that made him uncomfortable. After a long illness, he passed away in a hospital on August 2, 1982. He also is buried in the Rosedale Cemetery. I felt a great loss and sorrow when he died, as though a part of me was being buried with him in his grave. That happened only a few years ago, but my thoughts of him will last forever. Meung's five daughters and one son are all married now and have nice families of their own. They are all well educated and work in responsible positions in various business places in Los Angeles.

After Ernest's children were grown, his wife Rose became ill

Mrs. Lee, her sons, Tony and Allan, and two of her grand-
daughters, Sarah and Katie, Santa Cruz, 1987.

and eventually passed away in Whittier. Ernest himself died in
June 1988. His older daughter was a public school nurse in Whittier for many years; she now works with surgeons in the operating
room. His younger daughter is married to a schoolteacher and has
a son and a daughter. His son is married and lives and works near
Whittier.

After Mother's funeral, Stanford moved to Lancaster, where he
worked at Lockheed until he reached retirement age. He never
married. He is relaxing in his old age, riding his motorcycle and
enjoying his retirement.

Ralph and his wife Esther have two sons and three daughters.
One son is a dentist and the other is a veterinarian who runs his
own animal hospital in San Diego. One daughter is a successful
artist and another is a lawyer. The third generation of Orientals
are fortunate to be born into a different world, where everything
is possible if they work hard enough.

Edward worked for the Lytton Company and was sent all over
the country to introduce the microwave oven to dealers. He was
very successful and received an award for being the top salesman

one year. His wife taught grammar school for many years until she retired. They bought a beautiful house on a hill with a wonderful view, and they have two daughters and three grandchildren.

Florence struggled to further her education after high school. Although she had to work hard, it was not as difficult a life as in the old days. She married a Korean student named George Paik (no relation). They have two sons and live in Pasadena.

After ten years of interpreting, I told everyone that I needed to resign because of old age. I was eighty-five years old at the time. Now I am free of cares and worry and am just trying to relax and enjoy what little time is left. I attend a church regularly where most of the members are black, because it is there I feel most comfortable.

I n thinking back to my parents, the Bible describes their way of life: "Now faith is the assurance of things hoped for, the conviction of things not seen" (Hebrews 11:1). I am glad they lived long enough to see the promise of a better way of life for their children and grandchildren. I am the only one left who remembers them as they were in 1905 when we left Korea. They were a handsome couple. Father had thick, curly black hair and looked strong and healthy. He had a dignified personality that commanded respect from everyone. Mother had long, thick black hair that touched the ground, a fair complexion, and a slender figure. I was proud of them.

Mother was a gentle person. She never indulged in gossip, never had harsh words for anyone. She knew a lot but never bragged about it. Father was full of vitality then. He had all kinds of ambitious plans for our future and was always telling us funny stories and jokes. He was also a very practical person, always looking for ways to improve our situation no matter how hopeless the conditions. I remember one time when he chopped a tree in the yard — he piled all the kindling in one place and all the long logs in another. When anyone else does a job like that, there is a mess for weeks — but he was such a neat man. He had the knack of using whatever was available for doing and making things. I have noticed that all my brothers have inherited that ability. He was an expert tailor in Korea and made all of our clothes in the early years. After working all day in the fields, he spent much time in the evenings teaching us the Korean alphabet, telling us about Korean history, describing his boyhood days fishing for trout in the stream that ran through Grandfather's property — trying to give us an idea of who we were. I appreciated my parents more as I grew older and realized how much effort and love they had showered on us. He was the only father among all our friends who even tried to teach his children to read a Korean newspaper. I may not have under-

Mr. and Mrs. Paik Sin Koo, Tremonton, 1926.

stood everything, but I could get a general idea, and I can still read and write some Korean.

My parents came to America with high hopes for a better way of life. Mother said they had expected life to be difficult — not knowing the language, without money — but they had put their faith in God and were determined to survive whatever hardships

Mary Kuang Sun Paik Lee, San Francisco, 1987.

came their way. That faith was their only comfort and refuge throughout their lives. Mother managed to make a tasty meal with whatever she could find growing in the empty lots and open fields. Her homemade bread was just as good as and even better than that sold in stores. The year we lived in Colusa in 1911 was the only time we really went hungry. Years of backbreaking work without enough food and relaxation took its toll on my parents, but they just hung on through sheer will power. Their wretched physical condition was painful to see.

The fourth generation of young Koreans growing up in comfortable homes with every advantage open to them will find it difficult to realize the sacrifices made by the first generation. It is very gratifying to me to see the progress our family has made from poverty to where we are today. It is nothing spectacular, but a good firm foundation has been laid on which our future generations will find it easier to build their dreams.

On the first day of March 1919, thirty-three brave Korean patriots signed their names on the Korean Declaration of Independence, knowing full well they would be killed by the Japanese soldiers. Every year, on the first day of March, we remember their courage and their sacrifices as well as Korea's independence.

APPENDIX A ❀ THE HISTORIOGRAPHER'S ROLE

The changes an editor makes in other people's writing are seldom neutral. I believe that choosing what to say, as well as how to say it, always involves a point of view. Because this book has been shaped by the values I hold as a scholar, I will discuss in some detail both my editorial approach and my research methodology.

My decision to edit Mary Paik Lee's autobiography, rather than simply to publish her original draft, was prompted by her story's intrinsic merit and its unique historical value. Her autobiography deserves to be made as meaningful as possible to students and scholars as well as to the general reading public. My share in this scholarly edition has been to augment Mrs. Lee's text with a comprehensive explication, to verify her factual statements, and to edit for increased readability her lively and perceptive prose.

Augmenting the Text

In addition to placing Mrs. Lee's account in its historical context with an Introduction and Appendixes, I solicited further autobiographical information. I wanted her memoir to be as full as possible because we know so little about the experiences of the early Asian immigrants. I asked her to write down whatever else she could remember. I also interviewed her for ten hours. Jenni Currie, my editorial assistant, listened to these taped conversations and transcribed the portions that contained information not found in the original text, but we discovered that about 90 percent of what Mrs. Lee wrote at my request and what she told me in person duplicated (sometimes verbatim) the material she had already prepared. Thus, in the end, only some details about her husband's childhood and youth, the careers of her three sons, and her siblings' mature years were added to the narrative at appropriate places.

There were a number of topics she either did not wish to discuss or simply did not know anything about. On the personal level, she declined to elaborate on her operations, her son Allan's marriage, and her relationships with her two younger sisters. To some questions, she had no answers. For example, for some of the individuals mentioned in her story, she could not provide first names or further details.

I queried Mrs. Lee about the interaction between early Japanese and Korean immigrants. Given the strong anti-Japanese feelings harbored by many Koreans, I wanted to know how Korean and Japanese immigrants in California had related to each other. She said that during her childhood, she had no contact with any Japanese because Koreans "always avoided them." I asked how that was possible, since both groups usually lived near the areas inhabited by the earlier-arriving Chinese.

"Didn't Koreans ever just run into Japanese?"

"No. Whenever we saw them coming, we'd cross the street or start walking the other way."

"How could you tell who was Japanese?"

"Somehow we could."

"How?"

"I don't know . . . maybe by the way they walked."

If Mrs. Lee's recollections are accurate, then it seems that avoidance — at least on the part of the Koreans — characterized the relationship between the two groups. But that does not mean Korean immigrants had no *feelings* toward their Japanese peers: a number of incidents Mrs. Lee recounted reveal that whenever she was mistaken for a Japanese, she became extremely angry. On the other hand, after her marriage, when she and her husband sold produce and farmed, the couple did interact with Japanese immigrants through business dealings and as neighbors, and the relationships sounded cordial enough.

I also asked about her family's social background. I wanted to know whether her paternal family was of *yangban* ("two classes," i.e., military and civil officials who comprised the traditional Korean elite) or *chungin* ("middle people," i.e., petty officials and practitioners of certain professions) status. She did not know, as her parents never mentioned such words (possibly because, as Christians, they had discarded some of the Confucian values upon which such class distinctions were based). Given the occupations of her paternal grandfather, uncle, and father, the family could have been either *yangban* or *chungin*. Her maternal grandfather, on the other hand, being a farmer, was almost certainly *sangmin* ("common people"). I asked about her family's class background partly because we have only skimpy information about what kinds of people emigrated, and also because I wanted to know if such ascribed status mattered in America. Apparently it did not—at least not in Mrs. Lee's own life.

It is significant that she knew neither the names of her maternal grandparents nor the social origins of her paternal ones but was familiar with the names of several American missionaries in Korea. I think we can argue that for those Koreans who converted to Christianity, a new reference group took the place of the old ones. Some students of European immigration have noted that their subjects often did not represent a cross section of the population in their homelands. This certainly has also been true of Korean immigrants, a disproportionately large percentage of whom were Christians. Mrs. Lee's father repeatedly counseled his daughter to treat others with Christian charity, but the child Kuang Sun Paik had an irrepressible urge to challenge injustice: it was difficult for her to accept attitudes and behavior that discriminated against her. Thus, I suspect her desire to write and publish her autobiography is a retrospective attempt to come to terms with the tensions of being a Christian *and* an Asian immigrant in America.

That her story is an act of reconciliation rather than a full disclosure is corroborated by my not-entirely-successful efforts to elicit more information from her. As I interviewed her, I came to realize that the story told here is what Mary Paik Lee wants to pass down to posterity. It is a self-conscious testament, complete unto itself. For that reason, although she has many living relatives, I made no attempt to interview them, for this is an autobiography and not a biography. I did, however, talk to Allan Lee to get more information on the irrigation method the Lees used to cultivate a hillside plot in southern California, because Mrs. Lee herself could not give me any details, as she did not supervise Allan's work. But it should be noted that having such information fulfills not Mrs. Lee's needs but mine, as historiographer, to understand better the *technical* bases of Asian American success in California agriculture. I have summarized what Allan Lee told me in Appendix B. I also searched through extant documentary records to reconstruct the story of Korean rice cultivation — in which both her father and her husband participated — in the Sacramento Valley. That information is found in Appendix C.

Historical Verification

Although I worked primarily from a written manuscript rather than from transcripts of taped interviews, the problems I encountered in editing Mary Paik Lee's autobiography are similar to those confronted by the oral historian. Oral history's recorded conversations indeed breathe life into times past, but they present some challenges for the researcher. Not only is human memory fallible, but personal recollections are often colored by what motivates the speakers to tell their stories to the world and by their perception of who their audience might be. Thus, personal recollections, whether oral or written, must be checked by the historian against available corroborative evidence.

By trying to "locate" Mrs. Lee's account in its proper historical context, and by discussing the research that went into validating it, I have sought to turn one woman's memoir into a credible and representative historical record. Had another scholar worked on Mrs. Lee's manuscript, this probably would have been a different book. Three other writers have referred to the Paik Sin Koo family, but none of them, to my knowledge, has checked the oral history against documentary evidence.[1] Also, although several oral history compilations of Asian immigrants are now available, only one, so far, has been annotated.[2] I believe that the documentary research I did to check the historical accuracy of Mrs. Lee's story is the first attempt of this nature in Asian American Studies.

In order to illustrate the limitations and challenges of contemporary Asian American historiography, I shall go into considerable detail on what kinds of sources I consulted, where and how I found them, what information was in them, what I failed to find, and my reasons for accepting or rejecting particular statements.

My efforts were selective rather than exhaustive. I chose to concentrate mainly on the early years of the author's life — to the mid-1920s — because those years are of the greatest historical interest. Also, a practical consideration guided my choice — namely, there are far fewer public records of the activities of Asian immigrants from the mid-1920s through the early 1950s than for the years before 1920. This is so because Asian immigrants, categorized as "aliens ineligible to citizenship," were wary of running afoul of the law. Discriminatory measures such as the 1913 and 1920 Alien Land Acts of California and their 1923 and 1927 amendments, which codified anti-Asian sentiment and subjected Asian-born farmers to heavy penalties (including forfeiture of their holdings) in cases of violation, meant that both the Asian tenant farmers and their white landlords resorted to unwritten agreements, as Mrs. Lee has revealed.

For purposes of illustration, I shall focus on five of the areas in which I sought corroborative evidence: the relationship of the Paik family to American missionaries in Korea; H. M. Lee's early years; the Paik family's emigration; Mary Paik Lee's own childhood and young adulthood; and the Lee family's acquaintance with well-known public figures in the United States.

Quoted material in this Appendix is from Mrs. Lee's original manuscript and not from the edited version found in this book.

The Paik Family and American Missionaries in Korea

Mrs. Lee does not name her grandparents in her text, but I ascertained their names during our interviews. Her paternal grandfather was Paik Goon Un; her paternal grandmother was Sin Bok Duk; and her uncle was Paik Sin Chil. (She did not know the names of her maternal grandparents.) I tried to find corroborative evidence for the following claims: the family had converted to Christianity before her birth; Dr. Moffett (mispelled "Moffitt") had baptized her brother Paik Meung Sun, born 1897, and herself, born 1900; her uncle was a minister and the principal of a boys' high school in Pyongyang; her father Paik Sin Koo had also studied for the ministry; her grandmother established the first girls' school in Pyongyang; and her father visited Dr. Moffett after the missionary had retired.

From the available English-language works on Protestant missions in Korea, I gathered the following information about the introduction of Christianity to the city of Pyongyang, where the Paik family lived.[3] Henry G. Appenzeller, a Methodist, was the first American missionary to visit Pyongyang, in April 1887. Over the next six years, he and Horace G. Underwood; the latter's wife, Lillias Horton Underwood, M.D.; William Scranton, M.D.; Samuel A. Moffett; Homer B. Hulbert; James Scarth Gale; Hugh Brown, M.D.; Cadwallader C. Vinton, M.D.; and Graham Lee also visited the city—some of them more than once—but none of them settled there until Moffett did so in 1893. During those visits, the longest of which lasted two weeks, the missionaries preached, passed out literature (mostly translations of the Scriptures into Chinese, which educated Koreans could read), and made contact with a handful of Koreans who had already converted to Christianity.

Graham Lee joined Moffett in Pyongyang in 1894, and they set up a Presbyterian Mission. But in August of that year, they had to evacuate the city when one of the major battles of the Sino-Japanese War (1894–95) was fought there. The two missionaries returned, however, in October. In the midst of all the troubles, a young man, Kim Chong Sup, convinced Moffett that he knew the Scriptures well enough to be baptized. Kim became the first Korean Presbyterian elder, evangelist, and candidate for the ministry in Pyongyang. Six others were baptized that same year. The first woman to be converted was Yi Sie Sin Haing. She later served for twenty-five years as president of the Women's Missionary Society. In 1895 J. Hunter Wells, M.D., arrived to begin medical work. Annie Baird and Margaret Best opened a Sunday School for women in 1897. The mission also purchased a building for "women's work" that year. At that time, the Presbyterians were holding five Sunday School sessions in the morning and one church service in the afternoon.

In June 1900 the cornerstone was laid for Central Church, which became the most important Presbyterian house of worship in northern Korea. By 1903 the attendance at prayer meetings at Central Church averaged 1,000 to 1,200 persons. Kil Sun Chu, the second Korean (after Kim Chong Sup) to become an assistant pastor, was installed as the pastor of Central Church in 1907 — the first Korean to serve as full pastor in a Presbyterian church in his country.

Mrs. Lee's natal family, the Paiks, must have been converted some time between 1893, when Moffett settled in Pyongyang, and 1897, when her older brother, Meung Sun, was born. I did not find their names, however, in any of the available English-language sources, but that is not surprising, given the large number of converts in Pyongyang. Also, there is no reason to doubt Mrs. Lee's claim that she and her brother were baptized by Moffett, as he baptized many children as well as adults.

As for the religious education and calling of Mrs. Lee's uncle, Paik Sin Chil, and her father, Paik Sin Koo, they could very well have been among the students the missionaries taught in their first theology classes, which began in 1903 with six students in attendance. Three years later, the enrollment had gone up to fifty. I did not find the two Paik brothers listed in the sources I consulted, but that does not mean they were not there. It is more likely, however, that they were not studying for the ministry in the strict sense of the word. Rather, chances are they attended some of the Bible institutes the missionaries held, each of which lasted several weeks and attracted hundreds — and later, thousands — of men and women every year. These institutes trained individuals to serve as pastors' assistants, Sunday School teachers, and Bible women. Mrs. Lee indicates that her father was never ordained, so technically it is incorrect to call him the Reverend Paik Sin Koo, but out of deference to her desire to honor his memory, in editing her text I did not remove the title she confers on him in the Dedication.

The missionaries established schools almost as soon as they arrived. By 1898 there were two schools for boys and two for girls in Pyongyang and a dozen in the countryside. The combined enrollment in the primary and intermediate schools was 650 in 1904, and 4,000 ten years later. It is not clear to what institution Mrs. Lee is referring when she writes: "My uncle was the principal of the Pyong Yang high school." (I asked her if she knew the name of his school; she did not.) He could have been the "Mr. Pak" referred to in the official history of the Presbyterian Mission in Korea: "For several months during the early part of 1898, the Rev. W. M. Baird conducted classes 'for the larger boys and young men' with the help of a Korean teacher, Mr. Pak."[4] (Korean surnames were then often being inconsistently transliterated into English.) Given the relatively large number of educational institutions founded by the missionaries in Pyongyang, it would have been difficult to locate Paik Sin Chil in the rolls, even had I gone to Korea or searched through the Presbyterian archives in Philadelphia.

To try to find her grandmother, I looked through Yung-Chung Kim's English translation of the history of Korean women — the only detailed source available to me — but I failed in my efforts.[5] (Mrs. Lee did not know the name of her grandmother's school for girls, either.) There is no reason, however, to doubt her assertion: we have quite a few accounts of how some Korean women, after their conversion to Christianity, became strong, independent, and totally dedicated to the education of other women as well as of their own children,[6] so the career of Mrs. Lee's grandmother, Sin Bok Duk, is not only plausible but is very likely true.

Finally, Mrs. Lee writes that her father visited Moffett after the latter retired. This is quite credible, since Moffett retired in 1934 and died in 1939 in Monrovia, California, a town about twelve miles north of Whittier. Mrs. Lee's father came back to California from Utah in 1932 and settled in a house that his daughter had rented for the family in Whittier. Since Moffett did not retire until 1934, it must have been more than two years after Paik Sin Koo's return to California that he saw his missionary friend.[7]

Hung Man Lee's Early Years

Because I cannot read Korean, I had no way of verifying what Mrs. Lee has written about her husband's grandfather, Lee Kwong Kun, and his father, Lee Juhn Kew. But I was able to check three points: that her husband's father had assisted missionary James Scarth Gale in publishing a newspaper; that her husband, Hung Man Lee, had played with Gale's son; and that H.M. had gone to Mexico as a stowaway in 1905.

A detailed biography of Gale is found in Rutt's edition of Gale's *History of the Korean People*.[8] A Canadian of Scottish ancestry, Gale was sent to Korea by the Toronto Young Men's Christian Association, arriving at the end of 1888. At first he tried to set up a station in Haeju, the capital of Hwanghae province, about one hundred miles northwest of Seoul, but this effort failed because no one would sell him a house. During his first trip in the country, however, he met two Koreans who would prove indispensable to him: So Kyong-jo, who was the younger brother of So Sang-yun (a Korean baptized by missionary John Ross in Manchuria); and Yi Chang-jik, who became his first language teacher. After spending the summer of 1889 in Seoul, Gale moved to Pusan, but he was persuaded by another missionary, John Heron, who visited him and pitied the poor conditions under which he lived, to return to Seoul the following year.

In Seoul, he joined Horace H. Underwood and Homer B. Hulbert in founding the Korean Tract Society. In 1900, he was appointed to the Permanent Executive Bible Committee of Korea — thereafter devoting more and more of his time to translating the Bible and classics of English literature into Korean and compiling a Korean-English dictionary. In 1891, he left the auspices of the

Toronto YMCA and became a member of the American Presbyterian Mission. From 1892 to 1895, he served in Wonsan, on the northeast coast of Korea. He then went to Yokohama, Japan, to supervise the printing of his dictionary and remained there until 1897, when he went to the United States on furlough. He returned to Korea in 1898 and served again briefly in Wonsan, but he left the following year when the different denominations divided up the country into service regions. (The area where Wonsan is located was turned over to the Canadian Presbyterian Mission.) Gale then worked in Seoul from 1899 until his retirement in 1927. Thus, Gale resided in Seoul during 1889–92 and 1899–1927.

In 1892, Gale married Harriett Gibson Heron, the widow of John Heron, who had drowned. His wife had two daughters by her first marriage; she died of ill health in 1908. They had no children. Gale married Ada Louise Sale in 1910, by whom he had two sons — one of whom died in infancy — and a daughter.

Mrs. Lee claims that her father-in-law Lee Juhn Kew (whose family name could also have been transliterated as Yi, Yee, or Li) "worked for Dr. Gale, helping to publish a Christian newspaper." Gale indeed edited a biweekly Korean-language newspaper, *The Christian News* (*Kurisudo sinmun*), in 1901, and again from 1905 to 1910. The name of this publication changed several times: it became *The Church Herald* (*Yesugyo sinbo*) in 1907 and *The Christian News* (*Yesugyo hoebo*) in 1910. In the latter year, a Korean, Han Sokchin, took over the editorship.[9] Gale's detailed biography does not mention Lee Juhn Kew's name, but the latter could very well have served on the newspaper's publication staff.

The statement that Hung Man Lee played with Gale's son, however, cannot be true. H.M. was born in 1892 and he left Korea in 1905. While the missionary was indeed in Seoul from the time H.M. was seven years old until H.M. left for Mexico, Gale had no children by his first marriage, and his first son, George, by his second marriage was not born until 1911, *after* H.M.'s departure. Thus, there was no "son" in the Gale household during the period when H.M. might have played with one. It is possible — but not very likely — that he could have played with one of Gale's stepdaughters; that is why I did not delete the two sentences in Mrs.

Lee's original manuscript which say: "Hung Man Lee played with Dr. Gale's son. They became good friends and learned English from him." Instead, I rewrote the sentences to read: "H.M. played with Dr. Gale's children, with whom he became good friends and from whom he learned English." (Note that the "they" in Mrs. Lee's second sentence is ambiguous: the other party referred to could have been Gale himself. When I queried her about this, she said her husband probably meant the son.) As for Gale's step-daughters, one was seven years and the other five years older than H.M.[10] Thus the likelihood they "played" with him is not very great, although they might have taught him a little English.

H.M. ran away from home and traveled to Mexico as a stowaway in 1905. The only English-language source with information on the Koreans who went to Mexico is the English version of War-ren Y. [Won Yong] Kim's history.[11] According to Kim, who based his account on the extant records of various Korean associations as well as on his personal knowledge, 1,033 Koreans (802 men, 207 women, and 24 children) were illegally recruited for Mexico by a Mr. Myers, with the assistance of "Genichi Taisho, a Japanese operating a private development company in Korea, and his asso-ciate, Jun-Hyek Yi."[12] The agents had no trouble finding people because they offered each one a bonus of 150 *won* (Korean cur-rency unit) above and beyond what recruitees to Hawaii received. Recruitment for Mexico lasted from October 1904 to January 1905. Myers tried to ship his human cargo out of Pusan, where the Korean government had no emigration office, but failed in his efforts. Ultimately he had to take them to Inchon, where a French official (for unknown reasons) helped to prevail upon the government to let Myers's charges leave the country "without an investigation."[13]

The group left Inchon in March 1905. Two children died en route, and the 1,031 who landed in Vera Cruz, Mexico, on May 15 were allowed to rest three days before being taken to Merida City on the Yucatán peninsula. The Mexico Development Company divided the laborers into small groups and sent them to work in henequen plantations. This was the one and only shipment of Korean workers to Mexico, because a traveling Korean ginseng merchant, upon witnessing the extreme maltreatment accorded his compatriots, reported their plight to the "Kong-Lip Association" (transliterated in a more standard way as *Kongnip Hyop hoe* — an organization founded by Ahn Chang-ho in 1905) in San Francisco. The association then sent the information to newspapers in Korea; the resultant adverse publicity caused such a public outcry that the Korean government banned further emigration not only to Mexico but also to Hawaii.[14]

We shall never know if Hung Man Lee was counted among the 1,031 arrivals, or whether, as a stowaway, he was not enumerated, but there is no doubt that the only way he could have reached Mexico was to have been on that ship. There is also no way to find out if he indeed attended high school in Mexico City and if he worked as an interpreter and sanitary inspector.

Mrs. Lee's account differs in two minor ways from Warren Y.[Won Yong] Kim's. She writes that "[t]he Chamber of Commerce and Agriculture of Yucatán, Mexico, sent a ship to recruit people to work in their hemp plantations." Kim, on the other hand, says that the Mexico Development Company was in charge. Having no other sources on this topic, I did not change Mrs. Lee's statement. It could very well have been that Myers was the Korea-based agent of the Chamber of Commerce and Agriculture of Yucatán, while the Mexico Development Company was the agent responsible for distributing the workers after they landed. I also did not change "hemp" to "henequen" in Mrs. Lee's account, because "hemp" can be a generic term for fiber used in making rope. Botanically, the two plants are not the same: henequen (also spelled "henequin") is the fiber of *Agave fourcroydes*, which grows in Yucatán, while hemp is the fiber of *Cannabis sativa*, a native of Asia now cultivated in many parts of the world.

Passage to Hawaii and California

Mrs. Lee not only gives the names of the ships that took her family to Hawaii and California but also specific dates for their journey, although it is not clear whether the dates she gives are of departure or of arrival. She has written, "we went to Hawaii on the S. S.

Siberia, on May 6, 1905." Without going to Hawaii, I could not look through Hawaiian newspapers for 1905, but I discovered that San Francisco newspapers carried news of ships docking at other ports. The *San Francisco Examiner* of May 9, 1905, noted on page 15, under "Island Ports," that the steamer *Siberia* had arrived in Honolulu on May 8. Thus, Mrs. Lee is off by two days, so I have revised her sentence to read, "arriving on May 8, 1905."

As for the Paik family's journey to California, Mrs. Lee has written, "our passage to America on board the S. S. *China*. We landed in San Francisco on December 3, 1906." On page 15, under "Shipping News," the *San Francisco Examiner* of December 3, 1906, announced that the steamer *China* was "due at this port" from Hong Kong that day. A day later, the same newspaper, on page 14, elaborated that the ship had stopped in Honolulu on November 26 and had "brought 160 tons of freight for local people and land [*sic*] 8 cabin and 290 steerage passengers for Honolulu." On the same day, the steamer departed at 5 P.M. for San Francisco "with a fair crowd of passengers." The following page carried the additional information that the *China*, part of the Pacific Mail Steamship Company fleet, had taken "27 days, 7 hours, 21 minutes" to sail from Hong Kong to Honolulu, via Yokohama, and had taken "6 days, 9 hours, 2 minutes" to get from Honolulu to San Francisco. Thus, the Paik family's trip, even in steerage, could not have been too strenuous during the shorter second leg of the ship's journey.

When I told Mrs. Lee I had found references to the ships in which her family had sailed, she remembered that her safe deposit box contained the passport issued to her father by the Korean government. I photographed this document, which is printed in three languages: Chinese characters (then in use in Korea), English, and French (see p. 7). The Chinese section of the document contains more information than the English or French sections. The Chinese section lists all four members of the family, but names only her father, brother, and herself. (Her mother is merely recorded as "wife.") The English section names only her father. The family's destination is given as "Hawaii, America" in the Chinese section, but as "American" [*sic*] in the English section. The Chinese section indicates that her father was a native of the city of Pyongyang in the province of Pyongan.

Mrs. Lee has said that her family departed from Inchon, twenty-five miles west of Seoul, but the passport records that they began their journey from Chinampo, a port about thirty miles southwest of Pyongyang. In the English and French sections, however, it is shown that Seoul is the place where the document was issued. Thus, the family could have walked from Pyongyang to Chinampo, taken a coastal vessel from there to Inchon, and then transferred to a larger steamship. The date of issuance was the tenth day of the fourth lunar month in the ninth year of Kwangmu. The Chinese section has spaces for the name of the guarantor and for the luggage and money carried, but nothing is written under these headings. The ages of the family members are also given in the Chinese section: Paik Sin Koo was 32; his wife, 23; Meung Sun, 9; and Kuang Sun, 5.

Kuang Sun Paik in California

To locate Mrs. Lee (née Kuang Sun Paik) in the public records of California, I searched through the manuscript schedules of the 1910 U.S. Census of Population, extant records of school districts, vital statistics records, and lease and mortgage documents in the offices of various county recorders. (The manuscript schedules for censuses after 1910 have not yet been made public.) Mrs. Lee has said that her family arrived in Riverside in December 1906 and lived there for "four or five years" before moving to the town of Claremont. She also has stated that her brother Arthur was born in Claremont on December 2, 1910. Thus, the family must have left Riverside for Claremont some time before Arthur's birth. That means that they could have been either in Riverside County or in San Jose Township — the subdivision of Los Angeles County where Claremont was situated — from the latter part of April through early June, when the 1910 census was taken. I did not find the Paik family in either place in the manuscript schedules. Neither did I find her playmate Philip Ahn.[15] Martha Kim, who Mrs. Lee had said lived in Claremont, was also not in the manuscript schedules.

My failure to locate these Koreans does not mean they were not around, because the census grossly undercounted the group. The published census lists only 462 Koreans in the entire continental United States in 1910, but immigration records indicate that over 1,000 had migrated from Hawaii to the Pacific Coast between 1905 and 1910, and that approximately 300 had left the mainland for Korea during the same five-year period, leaving a net influx of about 700.[16] Adding this number to the approximately 200 Koreans who had entered the United States directly from Korea, census takers should have counted at least 900. Thus, the enumerators apparently found only about half of the Koreans who were in the country. Living in shacks out in the citrus groves, the Paik family could easily have been among those whom census takers missed.

There *were* Koreans in the census schedules I looked through, however. The most interesting thing about them is that the census takers did not know what "race or color" they belonged to. The census takers had initially written "Jap," but someone had crossed this out and written "Asia – Korean." We do not know whether this change was a result of Korean protest. Information under "Name" and "Birthplace" confirms the Korean origins of such individuals.

I also tried to locate the Mrs. Stewart who gave Mrs. Lee the first and only doll she ever owned. Mrs. Lee did not know her first name. I wondered whether this could be the same woman whom Bong-Youn Choy, relying on Warren Y.[Won Yong] Kim's Korean-language account, had identified as Mary E. Steward (spelled with a "d"), "a native of Missouri and a Christian" who "owned an orange orchard in Upland" and employed Korean workers, who camped on her property. Apparently, this woman had protected her Korean laborers against "white farmers and workers" who "attacked them with stones and rocks."[17] The town of Upland is located in Upland Township at the western edge of San Bernardino County. I searched through the manuscript schedules of this township three times but did not find any Mrs. Steward or Stewart. There was a Mrs. Stewart (whose first name was illegible) – a woman married to a George D. B. Stewart, the minister of the Presbyterian church in Indio, Riverside County –

who might have been Mrs. Lee's childhood benefactress, but she was not living in Upland, at least not during the time when the census was taken, so it is doubtful she was the one.

More useful than the manuscript schedules of the census were school records. Mrs. Lee does not always give the dates of her attendance at various schools, but she does list the dates and places of birth of her younger siblings. From these, I was able to pin down where she went to school during what years: Riverside (Riverside County), 1907–10; Claremont (Los Angeles County), 1910–11; Colusa (Colusa County), 1911–12; Roberts Island (San Joaquin County), 1912 to February 1914; Idria (San Benito County), 1914–16; Hollister (San Benito County), 1916–17; and Willows (Glenn County), 1917–18. A photograph in Mrs. Lee's possession shows that she was in the first grade in Riverside in 1907; San Benito County records indicate that she graduated from the eighth grade in 1916. Thus, it apparently took her nine years to complete eight grades. Somewhere along the way, she lost a year of schooling – a fact she does not mention in her memoirs. But given her family's migratory existence, this is not surprising.

I did not search for her in the school records of Riverside County, because I consider the photograph of her first grade class as sufficient "proof" of her presence there (see p. 17). Neither did I look for the records of Los Angeles County (for Claremont), for two reasons. First, Mrs. Lee does not remember the name of the school she attended; without this information, given the fact that Claremont had more than one elementary school, it is virtually impossible to locate her records. Second, from past research experience with such local records, I know that populous counties like Los Angeles usually dispose of the records they are not required by law to keep, so even if Mrs. Lee had remembered the name of her school, it is highly unlikely that its records would still be available. Less populous counties, on the other hand, often have very old records still in storage. Therefore, I contacted the offices of the County Superintendent of Schools or the Office of Education in Colusa, San Joaquin, San Benito, and Glenn Counties and sought their help. I found nothing for Colusa or San Joaquin Counties. Colusa County has records only from 1924 onward (Mrs. Lee went to school there in 1911–12), while people working in the Office of Education in San Joaquin County do not know where the 1912–13 records for Roberts Island are, or if they still exist. But my efforts bore fruit in San Benito and Glenn Counties.

I found four documents at the Office of Education in Hollister, county seat of San Benito County, on which the names Meung Paik, Kuang Paik, and Taw Paik (Daw Sun Paik, Mrs. Lee's younger brother, whom she named "Ernest") appear. In those days, seventh and eighth graders had to take a statewide examination every June. Each school district was required to send in a report on who had passed. All the reports for each year were bound into a volume entitled "Reports. Promotions. Graduations." The performance of Mrs. Lee and her brothers was recorded in the reports sent in by the teachers at the New Idria School District. These documents, however, contradict the statement of Mrs. Lee's teacher, who apparently had told her that she and Meung were the only students to have graduated from that school (up to that point). This is not what the records show. The 1914 report lists three graduates: Meung Paik, aged 16, Tillie Ashurst, aged 14, and Tony Gonzales, aged 16. The 1915 report shows one graduate, Rita Larios, aged 15, but it also includes a seventh grader, Kuang Paik who had passed the state examination and was to be promoted to the eighth grade. The 1916 report lists Kuang Paik, aged 15, as the sole graduate that year, while the report for 1917 shows four seventh graders — one of whom was eleven-year-old Taw Paik — who had passed the state exams, but no graduates. Thus, other students besides Mrs. Lee and her brother finished eighth grade at the New Idria school.

The Paik family was in Idria because her father worked at the quicksilver mine there. The 1918 report of the California State Mining Bureau indicates that during that year, the mines owned by the New Idria Quicksilver Mining Company, the largest in the United States, produced 10,715 flasks of mercury — one-third of the entire U.S. output.[18] Another source says that the company employed over four hundred workers, most of them Chilenos and Mexicans.[19] Since the mine closed down in 1974 and I could not

determine whether its records have been preserved, I was not able
to look for Paik Sin Koo's name in the company's salary rolls.

I also found the transcript for the year Mrs. Lee attended
San Benito High School in Hollister (see p. 49). This document,
together with the ones from the New Idria School District, alerted
me to another problem: Mrs. Lee has written that her sister "Charlotte was born in Idria on September 6, 1915. . . . That was the day
before I had planned to leave for Hollister. I didn't know what to
do but Mother said it was alright, that I should leave as planned."
Mrs. Lee may have made a mistake about the year Charlotte was
born, or she may have stayed two years in Hollister, or she may
have mixed her departure for Hollister with some earlier leave-
taking in 1915. Both the 1916 report from the New Idria School
District and the transcript from the high school show that she
went to the high school in 1916–17, not 1915–16. Had Charlotte
been born in 1915, she would have been a year old, and not a
day old, when Mrs. Lee left Idria. Internal evidence in Mrs. Lee's
narrative also indicates that Charlotte was born in 1915, and not
1916. Mrs. Lee has written that when she returned to Willows in
June 1917, Charlotte was two years old and Eddie three months
old; Charlotte was seventeen when Mrs. Lee's parents moved back
to California from Utah in 1932; and she was sixty-two when she
died in Hawaii in 1977. I asked Mrs. Lee about this discrepancy.
She insisted Charlotte was only a day old when she left, but she
also remembered that Charlotte was talking and walking when she
returned, so she concluded Charlotte might have been close to
two years old in June 1917.

"Were you in Hollister for one or two years?" I asked.

"Only one."

"Then how could Charlotte have been almost two years old
when you returned if she had been born the day before you left?"

"I don't know how to explain that. *You* figure it out. All I can
tell you is what I remember. I remember her birth so clearly, because I had been unaware that Mother was pregnant and I should
have noticed such things at age fifteen. . . . I felt so selfish leaving
home."

After this conversation, Mrs. Lee discovered an affidavit in her safe deposit box in which her father had listed the names and birth-dates of all his American-born children. This document indicates that Charlotte, called "Lottie," was born in 1915.

The affidavit also answers another question: on which Hawaiian plantation did Mrs. Lee's father work? She had no idea, but the affidavit gives her brother Ernest's birthplace as "Ewa Plantation." The church shown on p. 11 must have been on that plantation. Scholars doing research in Hawaii may want to look for Paik Sin Koo's name in the records of Ewa Plantation.

After her year in Hollister, Mrs. Lee attended Glenn County High School in Willows. The names, Kuang Paik, Taw Paik (Daw Sun Paik, or Ernest) and Kyoung Paik (Kyung Sun Paik, or Arthur) are shown on three documents of the Willows Unified School District. On the page showing Kuang Paik's transcript for 1917–18, it is noted: "Grades in the first 5 subjects accepted from San Benito High School," and "Married to a Korean gentleman in November 1918." She received grades above 90 in English, Latin, Spanish, history, drawing, sewing, and shorthand. She did not do as well in geometry, singing, or physical education. As for her marriage, Mrs. Lee has written that her wedding took place on January 1, 1919. I asked her why the transcript stated that her marriage was in November 1918. She insisted the latter date is wrong. So I obtained copies of her marriage license and marriage certificate from the Glenn County Clerk's office. These confirm her marriage on January 1, 1919, with Dorothy Moon of Marysville, Yuba County, as her bridesmaid; H. Yoon of Willows as the witness; and David Lee, "pastor, Korean Church" in San Francisco, officiating. Mrs. Lee's age is given as nineteen, which means she was still counting her age the East Asian way—from the date of conception rather than the date of birth.

I checked other information about her years in Willows. A Judge Finch had been kind to her, but she did not know his first name. The superior court of Glenn County told me that the judge's first name was William and that he had served as superior court judge from 1905 to 1921. Librarians at the Willows Public Library helped me look for biographical information, but the only source available is John A. Apperson, *The Glenn County Edition of the Wil-*

lows Review, 1892–1893, which includes a short biographical sketch of William Finch.[20] At that time, Finch was still a bachelor and had just been elected county superintendent of schools. Without further research, it is not possible to say whether the good judge indeed had a daughter named Margaret who befriended Mrs. Lee.

Mrs. Lee's father first farmed on Roberts Island on land leased by a Mr. Kim. I searched through "Book G of Miscellaneous [Records]" (leases) and "Book I of Miscellaneous [Records]" (chattel mortgages) in San Joaquin County and found a lease between Agnes M. Solomon and four Koreans — Rhee Soong, Park Sang Sup, Park Ki Ho, and Kim Chang Yern — signed in September 1911 for fifty-six acres. The clerk had noted that Kim Chang Yern was also known as C. Y. Kim. A chattel mortgage document shows that C. Y. Kim mortgaged his horse and buggy for $105 in June 1913. Unfortunately, the legal description specifying the location of the land the Koreans had rented shows it was not on Roberts Island, so the Mr. Kim who sublet to Mrs. Lee's father was most likely a different man. No other Koreans signed leases in San Joaquin County until 1917.

I was more successful in finding documents in Colusa and Glenn Counties, where both Mrs. Lee's father and her husband grew rice. I found their names in the "Book of Leases" and the "Book of Personal Property Mortgages," as well as a lease signed by Philip Ahn. There is, however, no record of any transactions between P. B. Cross and Mrs. Lee's husband, as she claims. Neither did I come across any "10 percent deal" between landowners and Korean lessees. But there is no doubt P. B. Cross existed. Notes 13 through 17 of Appendix C (below) tell where the extant records can be found. Finally, Mrs. Lee names several rice cultivars: "Edith, Water Bune, and Blue Rose." A publication of the U.S. Department of Agriculture shows that "Water Bune" is in fact *wataribune*, a Japanese short-grain variety.[21]

Acquaintance with Public Figures

Mrs. Lee is proud of the fact that she and her husband knew two presidents — Syngman Rhee of Korea and Richard M. Nixon of the

United States. Part of what she says about Syngman Rhee, however, is difficult to reconcile with available information on Rhee's life. In her original text, she introduces Syngman Rhee thus:

> So a year later in 1914, he [Hung Man Lee] came to San Francisco to find a new life. There were many Koreans here, they worked in the vegetable farms and fruit orchards, mostly in Fresno County. In the winter months they worked in town. He made many friends but one was very special, he was Syngman Rhee who many years later became the President of South Korea. They worked together until Mr. Rhee earned enough to go back East to study.

At a later point, she writes that "after earning enough money picking fruit in Fresno County, he [Syngman Rhee] went back East to study, attended Princeton University and graduated with honors." She also claims that "while Dr. Rhee was studying, his expenses were partly donated by Koreans all over the United States but mostly from California. We paid our share every year because we felt he deserved it."

Two things seem wrong with these assertions. It is unlikely Rhee ever picked fruit in California; and even if he did, the timing given by Mrs. Lee is wrong. There are two available biographies in English of Rhee: *Korea's Syngman Rhee: An Unauthorized Portrait* by Richard C. Allen, and *Syngman Rhee: The Man Behind the Myth* by Robert T. Oliver. Of the two, Oliver's gives more details about Rhee's whereabouts at different points in time. The two authors agree that Rhee left Korea on November 4, 1904. According to Oliver, Rhee stopped overnight in Honolulu, where he met with a number of Koreans as well as the superintendent of the Methodist Mission, John Wadman, before sailing on to California. While in California between December 6 and 26, 1904, Rhee visited San Francisco, San Raphael, and Los Angeles, from whence he boarded a train to Washington, D.C. He entered George Washington University at the beginning of the spring semester in February 1905. Between then and June 1910, when Rhee received his Ph.D., he was on the East Coast continuously, except for a brief visit to California during the Christmas recess in 1907.

It is *possible* that Rhee might have spent one or more of his summers picking fruit in California, but it is highly unlikely. In any case, neither of his biographers mentions this fact. Instead, according to Oliver, Rhee earned part of his way in college and graduate school by making speeches about Korea. Oliver's account has Rhee spending the summers of 1905, 1906, and 1908 in Ocean City, New Jersey, as the guest of a rich, elderly Methodist lady. He was in New York City during the summer of 1907, and he studied at Harvard through the summer of 1909. After receiving his doctorate, Rhee sailed from New York on September 3, 1910, to return to Korea via Europe and Russia on the trans-Siberian railway. He worked for the YMCA in Seoul for seventeen months before going to Minnesota to attend an international conference of Methodists. He then traveled in the United States for six months until he was invited by Park Yong-man to serve as the principal of a Korean school in Hawaii. Hawaii remained his base until he went to Washington, D.C., in the spring of 1919 to lobby for Korean independence.[22]

It is clear that at no time between December 1904 and April 1919 did Rhee visit California for any extended period. Mrs. Lee, on the other hand, has him working with her husband *after* the latter arrived in 1914, when, in fact, Rhee was already in Hawaii. By 1914 Rhee had long since finished his education and had become a recognized leader in the Korean immigrant community. When I suggested to Mrs. Lee that what she had written could not be true, she replied that it was what her husband had told her.

According to Mrs. Lee, Rhee visited them twice — in 1920 and "a year later" — while they were living in Willows. This assertion, unlike the one above, is based on her personal knowledge, but it is also problematic in terms of timing, at least with respect to the first visit. According to Rhee's biographers, he left the United States in November 1919, with an assistant named Ben Limb, traveling by train from the East Coast across the continent to California and by ship to Hawaii. There, Rhee and Limb smuggled themselves onto a ship that was sailing directly to Shanghai, in order to elude the Japanese police in Japan. They hid in the hold of the vessel till it was well out to sea. Upon his arrival in Shanghai, Rhee became "chief of executive" of the provisional government. He remained in China until May 28, 1921, when he sailed via Manila back to Hawaii, arriving on June 29. He stayed in Hawaii for two months, then went to Washington, D.C.[23]

If this chronology is correct, then Rhee *could* have visited the Lees en route to Shanghai in November 1919 (not 1920), and again on his way to Washington, D.C., in late August 1921. Though Rhee's biographers do not mention any such stops, he might have made them as part of his efforts to keep his supporters loyal and forthcoming with donations. Mrs. Lee puts it this way:

[Rhee] made several visits to California to see how the Koreans were progressing and to thank them for their support. In 1920 he stayed with us in our old house in Willows for one week. We apologized for our poor surroundings, no bathroom, no telephone, etc. He laughed, saying that it's good to remember the old days when he was working in the fruit orchards with H.M.

The above passage suggests that the myth about working in the fruit orchards might have been created and perpetuated by Rhee himself, rather than by Mrs. Lee's husband. Rhee was very clever at garnering financial support, and his efforts to show he was "one of them" might have been a means he used to maintain a bond of sympathy between himself and his followers. As Mrs. Lee recalls in an earlier passage: "We paid our share every year *because we felt he deserved it*" (italics added). Why did she (and many other Korean immigrants) think he deserved it? Because he was one of them, because he was the first Korean to obtain a Ph.D. (a great honor, in their eyes), and because he was their leader in the fight to regain Korean independence. In light of these findings, I rewrote Mrs. Lee's sentences to remove the dubious phrases, but I did not delete the references to Rhee.

Mrs. Lee's final assertion about Rhee concerns the latter's visit to Los Angeles in the 1950s. In this instance, written records validate most of what she has said. The *New York Times* Index reveals that Rhee and his entourage began their official trip when they left Seoul on July 26, 1954. After stops at various places on the

East Coast, Rhee and his party flew to Los Angeles on August 6. An article on the front page of the *Los Angeles Times* of August 6, 1954, quotes Rhee as saying that this was his "first visit to Los Angeles since 1904." At 7:30 P.M., the Rhees went to "the home of Leo S. Song, 1064 S. Gramercy Place, where about 100 guests attended an official reception given by the Dong Ji Hoi [*Tongji-hoe*], Korean patriotic society." Thus, though Mrs. Lee does not state the date for this event, she gives the correct address. Her statement, however, that Rhee was "over ninety years old" at the time is incorrect. Born in 1875, Rhee was seventy-nine years old in 1954.

And who was Rhee's host, Leo Song? According to Bong-Youn Choy (*Koreans in America*, 1979), "Song was a constant supporter of Syngman Rhee from his student days. He joined Rhee's political organization, *Tongji-hoe*." Song apparently had made his fortune as a wholesaler. After working for the Kim Brothers Company in Reedley in the early 1920s, he and a partner "formed the K. & S. Company, which became one of the most successful wholesaling operations in Los Angeles's Korean community. Most of the Orientals who had retail vegetable stores became customers of the K. & S. Co. Its total assets were estimated at about three hundred thousand dollars at the end of 1945."[24] No wonder Leo Song had a home fit for entertaining South Korea's president! One other Korean enterprise Mrs. Lee mentions is the Jan-U-Wine (misspelled "Janvine") Food Corporation, where her brother Meung worked. Established by Peter Hyun, it began as the Oriental Food Product Corporation in 1926 in Los Angeles, canning bean sprouts, mushrooms, chop suey, chow mein, and soya sauce. It adopted the name Jan-U-Wine a few years later.[25]

Syngman Rhee was not the only president the Lees knew. While farming in southern California, they became acquainted with the family of Richard M. Nixon. In *Richard Nixon: The Shaping of His Character*, Fawn M. Brodie states that the Nixon family store was situated at the corner of Whittier Boulevard and Leffingwell Road.[26] Mrs. Lee and her family lived in a house they rented from one Mrs. McGee at 4844 Leffingwell Road, Whittier, in the late 1930s and early 1940s. The Nixon family was, indeed, down the road. Mrs. Lee wrote that Nixon first practiced law in La Habra; this is not entirely accurate. Nixon worked for the law firm of Wingert and Bewley (later Wingert, Bewley, and Nixon) in Whittier, but he later opened a part-time office in La Habra.[27] So I added the words "Whittier and" to Mrs. Lee's sentence, "He opened his first law office in [Whittier and] La Habra, used to see him often on the streets." Mrs. Lee also notes that Pat Nixon "was the business course teacher in Whittier High School then." This is correct: Pat Nixon taught typing and shorthand.[28] The Nixon parents, Frank and Hannah, had five children, all boys, two of whom died. The youngest, Edward, was born in 1930. Mrs. Lee recalls he was in the same Boy Scout troop as her middle son, Allan. Since Allan was born in 1929, he and Donald were about the same age.

Mrs. Lee also refers to two other public figures: Sammy Lee and Walter Knott. Sammy Lee was the Korean American diving champion, who, according to the *Guinness Book of Olympic Facts and Feats* by Stan Greenberg, won the bronze medal for springboard diving and the gold medal for highboard diving in 1948 in London, and the gold medal for highboard diving in 1952 in Helsinki.[29] Mrs. Lee correctly cites these medals, but she errs in the locations of the 1948 and 1952 Olympics. I simply deleted her references to the locations. I also deleted her claim that Richard Nixon had facilitated Sammy Lee's purchase of a home in a white neighborhood in Washington, D.C., simply because there was no way to prove or disprove that fact without contacting the principals involved.

Mrs. Lee met Walter Knott "when he first came to us with his blackberries. . . . He had a small farm in Buena Park. As business improved, he increased his acreage and planted other varieties as well, raspberries, boysonberries [sic], which became very popular later." At that time, Mrs. Lee and her husband had a produce stand inside the Safeway supermarket in Anaheim. A label on a bottle of preserves on a supermarket shelf gave me the current location of the corporate headquarters of Knott's Berry Farms: Placentia, California, just outside of the city of Anaheim. I called the company and was told that the original ten-acre farm owned by Mr. Knott in Buena Park to the west of Anaheim still stands, but no one today, of course, would know whether he had indeed sold his berries to a Korean produce stand inside the Safeway store back in the 1930s.

From the above discussion, we can see that, though Mrs. Lee made some factual errors, on the whole her recollections have been substantiated by both public records and secondary sources. The edited version of her memoirs, therefore, is a historical document that can be quoted with confidence.

Editorial Decisions

Mrs. Lee conveys her ideas in a vigorous and lively manner. My purpose in editing her prose was to increase its readability through carefully considered stylistic changes. To make sure my renderings did not alter Mrs. Lee's tone, I edited the text five times, comparing each version with the original to preserve her distinctive voice.

Many of Mrs. Lee's sentences had no subject, especially in the first or third person singular. Jenni Currie, my editorial assistant, added "I," "he," "she," "it," and sometimes "we," and "they," wherever needed and made other grammatical corrections. For smoothness, I combined short, choppy sentences into longer ones. When words or phrases were repeated in close proximity, I substituted synonyms or alternative ways of saying the same things.

To impose some organization on the narrative and to straighten out chronology, I moved sentences and paragraphs around. Like her sentences, Mrs. Lee's paragraphs were often short and incomplete, so I restructured these to increase their thematic coherence. I also divided the original run-on text into chapters with titles. The final product can be likened to a necklace, for which Mrs. Lee provided the original beads, which I sometimes polished or reshaped before stringing them together into a finished product.

Besides making stylistic changes, I also edited Mrs. Lee's text substantively. I thought it crucial that her attitude towards the various people with whom she has come in contact be captured as accurately as possible. She often dealt with prejudice and discrimination in a spirited way, so her behavior could be interpreted as evidence of "minority" consciousness. There is no question that she protested against certain kinds of mistreatment; I took great care, however, not to inject more militance into her tale than she herself had expressed. Nonetheless, one reader of the manuscript suggested that Mrs. Lee might have recalled some incidents through a "retrospective" ideology, reflecting later civil-rights attitudes that subsequently colored her recollections. He based his judgment on his knowledge of race relations in California where, according to him, Asians were "fleeing from [their] black neighbors in L.A. [in the early 1950s]." To him it seemed improbable that Mrs. Lee could have identified with members of other minority groups as much as she did.

The question raised by this scholar is an important one, but it can be answered only by careful research into the spatial distribution of various ethnic groups in specific localities at particular points in time. Furthermore, objective studies of large, structural patterns serve a different purpose from that served by expressions of subjective consciousness. An account such as Mrs. Lee's is valuable precisely because it allows historians to paint a more nuanced picture — one based on qualitative as well as quantitative data — than we could otherwise provide. Mrs. Lee did not participate in the civil rights movement of the 1960s and 1970s, nor does her language appear to reflect the rhetoric of the movement's newspaper or television coverage. Without persuasive contrary evidence, there is no reason *not* to accept her recollections at their face value.

Paradoxically, I wrestled with an opposite problem with respect to Mrs. Lee's perspective on life and people. In the midst of recounting tales of discrimination, she made a number of what might be called ingratiating statements, expressing appreciation for the small kindnesses shown her. My editorial assistant asked, "How can she be grateful to people who were simply treating her like a human being?" and suggested that we remove what, in "modern" eyes, seems out of place. Though I did take out a few redundant utterances, I kept enough to show Mrs. Lee's *contradictory* postures, for I believe this very ambivalence to be the hallmark of the Asian American experience.

Like the rest of us, Mary Paik Lee is a product of her times: during much of her life, Asian Americans were *not* treated like human beings. Nonetheless, just as Filipino immigrant writer Carlos Bulosan (*America Is in the Heart*) never lost his vision of what the United States *could* be, so too, Mary Paik Lee has kept her faith. Without such vision and such faith, Asian pioneers would have found it much more difficult to survive in a white world that did not welcome them. Letting her tell her story as she sees fit is the best way to respect her integrity—and to pay tribute to the courage, strength, and graciousness that such remarkable women have possessed.

For that reason, I have retained the word *Oriental,* a term Mrs. Lee has used all her life and with which she feels comfortable, even though an increasing number of younger Asian Americans now prefer *Asian* or *Asian American.* In their view, *Oriental,* which means "eastern," has Europe as its point of reference and smacks of the legacy of Western imperialism in Asia.

Some things I did remove, however. I checked as many of the assertions she had made about events outside of her family as available resources allowed. Wherever she erred, if the details were not essential, I deleted the phrases or sentences. For example, she had written, "The treaty [between Korea and the United States signed in 1882] was ratified by Chester A. Arthur, the 21st President of the United States." Treaties are not ratified by the president, but by Congress, but since the point is irrelevant to her story, nothing is lost by removing the sentence. I also discarded several incidents she had heard at second hand because, since she did not know even the approximate year of their occurrence, they could not be verified through corroborating sources. She had recounted such events to illustrate discrimination faced by nonwhites, but wherever the connection between the example and the point she wished to make seemed tangential, I removed the details.

Where small changes would right mistakes in statements I deemed significant enough to keep, I made them. (I added nothing to her text, however, that had not come from Mrs. Lee in one form or another.) For example, she had written: "The first American Presbyterian missionaries from America settled in Pyong Yong. They were Drs. Moffitt and Underwood." In actual fact, Moffett and Underwood were among the first, but were not the first, American missionaries in Korea. Furthermore, Moffett's name is misspelled; Pyongyang is not transliterated in standard form; and, while Underwood visited that ancient city many times, he never resided there. I revised the sentences to read: "*Two of* the first American Presbyterian missionaries to come to *Korea* were Dr. *Moffett* and Dr. Underwood; *Moffett* eventually settled in *Pyongyang*." In another place, she had said: "Dr. Gale and Dr. Appenzeller were the first American Presbyterian ministers to settle in Seoul." Here, too, while James Scarth Gale and Henry G. Appenzeller were two of the first, they were not the first American missionaries in Seoul; moreover, Gale was a Presbyterian, while Appenzeller, born into a Dutch Reformed Church family, later became a Methodist and served under that denomination's auspices in Korea. The sentence, corrected, now reads: "Dr. Gale and Dr. Appenzeller were *two of* the first American *Protestant* missionaries to settle in Seoul." I rewrote, rather than deleted, these statements because the fact that Mrs. Lee's family knew these pioneer missionaries is of some historical significance and has a direct bearing on her own life.

In transliterating Korean and Chinese words, since I anticipate that scholars will be only a small fraction of those who will read this book, I chose not to use apostrophes and diacritical marks. Readers will notice that there is no uniformity in the transliteration of proper nouns. For those sections that refer to people in Korea, the names of individuals are given in the East Asian order: family name first, followed by given name. Exceptions are Philip Jaisohn and Syngman Rhee, who Anglicized their names in an unconventional manner. For the sections set in the United States, the American convention of given names followed by the family name is adopted. There is as yet no agreement on whether the two characters in the given names of Koreans should be hyphenated. A few individuals, such as Yi Sung-man (Syngman Rhee), have always spelled their given name as a single word, placing it first; Mrs. Lee, her siblings, and some of her compatriots have transliterated their given names as two separate words, capitalizing each one; still other Koreans (and I) have preferred to hyphenate the given names, lower-casing the second word. In the bibliographic essay, I have reproduced the Korean authors' names as published in English sources, but it should be noted that some of them did not transliterate their names consistently in their various works.

The photographs come from the family albums of Mrs. Lee and Allan Lee. I obtained most of the documents from California county offices. I designed the two maps, which Adrienne Morgan, a professional cartographer, rendered into publishable form.

The choice of the title for the book is mine. Mrs. Lee had called her typewritten manuscript "One Korean Family in America." For the book she suggested *Life Is Bittersweet*, but when I requested additional possibilities she asked me to contribute the title. I chose *Quiet Odyssey* not only to reflect the fact that her family had moved around a great deal but also to suggest that, though their contributions to America, like those of other Asian immigrants, have generally not been appreciated, there has nevertheless been a heroic touch to their arduous journey.

NOTES

1. Sonia Shinn Sunoo, "Interview with Mary Kuang-sun Paik Lee," in *Korean Kaleidoscope*, edited by Sonia Shinn Sunoo (Davis, CA: Korean Oral History Project, Sierra Mission Area, United Presbyterian Church, U.S.A., 1982), pp. 89–110; Eun Sik Yang, "Korean Women of America: From Subordination to Partnership, 1903–1930," *Amerasia Journal* 11, no. 2 (1984):1–28; and Brenda Paik Sunoo, "Journey to Kumgang-san: A *Samsei* Perspective," *Amerasia Journal* 14, no. 1 (1988):69–78. A somewhat different version of Yang's article appeared as "Korean Women in America, 1903–1930," in *Korean Women in Transition: At Home and Abroad*, edited by Eui-Young Yu and Earl H. Phillips (Los Angeles: Center for Korean-American and Korean Studies, California State University, Los Angeles, 1987), pp. 167–82.

2. Kazuo Ito, *Issei: A History of Japanese Immigrants in North America*, trans. Shinichiro Nakamura and Jean S. Gerard (Seattle: Executive Committee for Publication of *Issei*, 1973), the most substantial anthology of Asian American oral histories, weaves transcripts of the oral histories into a narrative divided into twenty-one parts, comprising a total of eighty-nine chapters. The Issei Oral History Project based in Sacramento has produced *Issei Christians: Selected Interviews from the Issei Oral History Project* (Sacramento: Issei Oral History Project, 1977); and Eileen Sunada Sarasohn, *The Issei: Portrait of a Pioneer: An Oral History* (Palo Alto, CA: Pacific Books, 1983). The first is a collection of individual life histories, while the second – its title is misleading – is a collective portrait that combines the experiences of many individuals in each thematic chapter. The compilers of the above works do not seem to have checked their informants' accounts against other evidence. Sue Kunitomi Embrey et al., *Manzanar Martyr: An Interview with Harry Y. Ueno* (Fullerton, CA: California State University, Fullerton, Oral History Program, 1986), on the other hand, contains three introductions and detailed notes that reveal clearly how the taped interview was transcribed, edited, and substantiated, according to the standards of professional historians. Akemi Kikumura, *Through Harsh Winters: The Life of a Japanese Immigrant Woman* (Novato, CA: Chandler and Sharp, 1981) contains a valuable methodological essay, an epilogue, and appendixes that show how the author's mother's life history was prepared, following the methods used by anthropologists.

3. L. George Paik, *The History of Protestant Mission in Korea (1882–1910)* (Pyongyang: Union Christian College Press, 1919); Harry A. Rhodes, ed., *History of the Korea Mission, Presbyterian Church, U.S.A.*, vol. 1, 1884–1934 (Seoul: Chosen Mission Presbyterian Church, U.S.A., 1934), and vol. 2, 1935–1959 (New York: Commission on Ecumenical Mission and Relations, The United Presbyterian Church in the U.S.A., 1965); Charles A. Sauer, ed., *Within the Gate* (Seoul: The Korea Methodist News Service, 1934); Allen D. Clark, *History of the Korean Church* (Seoul: Korean Christian Literature Society, 1961); Everett N. Hunt, Jr., *Protestant Pioneers in Korea* (Maryknoll, NY: Orbis Books, 1980); and Martha Huntley, *Caring, Growing, Changing: A History of the Protestant Mission in Korea* (New York: Friendship Press, 1984).

4. Rhodes, *Korea Mission*, vol. 1, p. 164.

5. Yung-chung Kim, ed. and trans., *Women of Korea: A History from Ancient Times to 1945* (Seoul: Ewha Woman's University Press, 1982).

6. Induk Pahk, *September Monkey* (New York: Harper and Brothers,

1951); Louise Yim, *My Forty Year Fight for Korea* (New York: A. A. Wyn, Inc., 1951); and Helen Kim, *Grace Sufficient* (Nashville, TN: The Upper Room, 1964).

7. Rhodes, *Korea Mission*, vol. 2, pp. 420, 447.

8. Richard Rutt, ed., *James Scarth Gale and His History of the Korean People* (Seoul: Royal Asiatic Society, Korea Branch, 1972), pp. 1–88.

9. Ibid., p. 46.

10. Ibid., pp. 47–48.

11. Warren Y. [Won Yong] Kim, *Koreans in America* (Seoul: Po Chin Chai, 1971).

12. Ibid., p. 14.

13. Ibid., p. 15.

14. Wayne K. Patterson, *The Korean Frontier in America: Immigration to Hawaii, 1896–1910* (Honolulu: University of Hawaii Press, 1988), pp. 128, 146–47.

15. Bong-Youn Choy, *Koreans in America* (Chicago: Nelson-Hall, Inc., 1979), p. 82, states that Philip Ahn's father, Ahn Chang-ho, returned to Korea in 1907 but when he came back to California in 1911, "he found that his wife had been working as a housemaid in order to support herself and their two children (the first son is Philip Ahn, who became the first Oriental actor in Hollywood.)" Choy offers no clue, however, as to where Mrs. Ahn and her children were in 1910, when the census was taken.

16. Hyung June Moon, "The Korean Immigrants in America: The Quest for Identity in the Formative Years" (Ph.D. diss., University of Nevada, Reno, 1977), pp. 92–93.

17. Choy, *Koreans*, p. 109.

18. California State Mining Bureau, *California Mineral Production for 1918* (Sacramento: State Printing Office, 1918), pp. 64–65, 67–69.

19. J. M. Guinn, *History and Biographical Record of Monterey and San Benito Counties and History of the State of California* (Los Angeles: Historic Record Co., 1910), p. 329; and San Benito County Board of Education, *San Benito County Long Ago and Today* (Hollister: Office of the San Benito County Superintendent of Schools, 1980), pp. 38–40.

20. John A. Apperson, *The Glenn County Edition of the Willows Review, 1892–1893* (Willows, CA: n.p., 1893), p. 6.

21. U.S. Department of Agriculture, *How to Grow Rice in the Sacramento Valley*, Farmers' Bulletin No. 1240 (Washington, D.C.: Government Printing Office, 1924), p. 12.

22. Robert T. Oliver, *Syngman Rhee: The Man Behind the Myth* (New York: Dodd Mead and Co., 1954), pp. 76–114.

23. Ibid., pp. 148–52.

24. Choy, *Koreans*, p. 131.

25. Ibid., p. 132.

26. Fawn M. Brodie, *Richard Nixon: The Shaping of His Character* (New York: W. W. Norton & Co., 1981), p. 81.

27. Ibid., p. 154.

28. Richard M. Nixon, *The Memoirs of Richard Nixon* (New York: Grosset & Dunlap, 1978), p. 24.

29. Stan Greenberg, *The Guinness Book of Olympic Facts and Feats* (London: Guinness Superlatives, Ltd., 1983), pp. 57–58, 164.

For about eight decades, between 1860 and 1940, agriculture provided a living for a large number of Asian immigrants and their families in the western United States. Much has been written about Japanese immigrant farmers, but little is known of other Asian American cultivators. My recent book, *This Bittersweet Soil: The Chinese in California Agriculture, 1860–1910*, paints a broad picture of the Chinese involvement in developing California agriculture. But neither the existing literature on the Japanese nor my own work provides much detail on the actual operation of the farms and on their division of labor. In an interview with me on March 30, 1987, Allan P. Lee offered some glimpses of how his family carried out the hard work of farming, adding important information that his mother did not know. The following report is based on that interview.

From the late 1930s to 1950, Hung Man Lee and Mary Paik Lee farmed in various localities in southern California with the help of their two older sons, Henry and Allan. During this period, H.M. was sick a great deal — he broke out in an allergic rash every time the fields were plowed — but he directed the family's farming operations and figured out how best to cultivate a 60-acre tract on a steep hillside in Whittier, where the Lees grew zucchini, string beans, and garlic. Zucchini and garlic were planted on the slopes, while string beans were grown in the flat areas.

The annual planting cycle began in early winter. The earth was irrigated in preparation for plowing. The flat areas on the farm were disked with a tractor, driven by Henry, the eldest son, a hefty youngster who began to take charge of all the heavy equipment during his early teens. Then chicken manure purchased from the Downey Fertilizer Company was spread evenly over the ground and mixed with the soil by another round of disking. But the tractor could not be used on the slopes, so H.M. made a special plow with a furrowing blade to till the hillside. He surveyed and marked the contours of the land with lime, and he hired a Mexican to walk a horse that pulled the implement along these lines. The man put the reins of the horse around his neck as he plowed. After the earth was turned, the hired hand and the horse pulled a leveler (made from a piece of 1 x 12 plank with "feet" at both ends) over the ground to create narrow terraces with furrows measuring twelve inches deep and three inches across the top.

After plowing, the ground was irrigated again. Then, like other farmers, the family waited for the rains. Planting began in early February. Mary and a number of Mexican women put the zucchini seeds into the ground by hand. They covered each seed with a cellophane dome that had a hole punched at the top. Known as "hot caps," these covers protected the seedlings until they were about six inches high. So far as Allan Lee can remember, their family was the only one in the area that used such "hot caps." Perhaps because they did so, their crops ripened earlier than those of neighboring farmers, so they usually made a good profit on their first pickings.

The zucchini harvest began in April and lasted until July. String beans came after that and were picked throughout the summer. Then the garlic was gathered. Mary again served as crew boss, leading teams of Mexican women — the only farm workers available for hire in the area during World War II — into the fields at the crack of dawn when the dew was still heavy on the plants. Harvesting zucchini requires skill because the stems of the squash must be cut at a certain angle. It is also an unpleasant task because the stalks and leaves of the plant are covered with a fuzz that pricks like thousands of fine splinters. The women all wore heavy rubber gloves as well as overalls, and they covered their heads with bandanas. Nevertheless, every morning their clothing got completely wet up to the waist. Mary had to lead the women into the fields and participate in the harvesting herself, because, had she not done so, the pickers would have been reluctant to wade into the prickly rows. A woman named Josefa was Mary's chief assistant. Since H.M. spoke fluent Spanish, the Lees communicated readily enough with their workers.

Even as the harvest proceeded, the plants had to be irrigated. Allan was responsible for this task from the time he was ten years old. His father designed and built the ingenious irrigation system that was installed on the hillside. He made holes three feet apart with a welding torch in two-inch pipes, which he laid in the furrows. Water was pumped up the hill to a holding tank that fed the pipes. Allan whittled hundreds of redwood pegs of various shapes — some completely round, others with slits in them — that were plugged into the holes in the pipes. The shape of the pegs controlled the amount of water that came out of each hole. Since the pegs could be pushed in or pulled out at will, this created a "flexible" system that allowed the amount of water flowing into different furrows to vary. Given the curvature of the land and the fact that water pressure changes with elevation, water flowed out of the holes in different sections of the tract at different speeds, so, using the pegs to control the volume of effluence allowed Allan to wet the hillside evenly. He could also control the speed of the flow or vary the amount needed by different plants at successive stages of their growth cycle. To conserve water and minimize the cost of irrigation, Allan always did his work at night to reduce evaporation. To allow the harvest to proceed without a break, he irrigated alternate rows, so that the dry rows could be picked.

The Lees packed their zucchini in flats. The boys tried to persuade their father to use a brand name, but H.M. felt it was not necessary to do so.[1] They simply placed a piece of green paper on top of each flat, and that became their "trademark." The family guaranteed the quality of their produce, so their crops were always in demand. Allan recalls that, in the 1940s, they received eight dollars for each flat of zucchinis. At first, they sold their crop to brokers who came out to their farm and also directly to Safeway, but later on, because they wanted to choose the retailers themselves, they trucked the flats to the wholesale produce market in Los Angeles. Henry and Allan delivered two truckloads of zucchinis, with each truck containing several hundred flats, every night at the height of the harvest.

When Henry joined the army in 1948 and Allan in 1950, the Lees had to quit farming. Tony, the youngest boy, who is eleven years Allan's junior, could not help, partly because of his youth and partly because he had polio and other medical problems. The key role that Mary played as forewoman was not uncommon: Allan remembers that all the wives among their immediate neighbors worked in the fields. Mrs. Hamano, an *Issei* (Japanese immigrant) woman, whose family owned a flower farm, supervised the cuttings. Mrs. Mimaki, a *Nisei* (American-born, second-generation Japanese) woman, whose family grew chrysanthemums, nursed those flowers like babies. A third neighbor, a Mexican woman named Mrs. Hernandez, also toiled in the fields. Thus, regardless of their ethnic background, women in farming families did a large share of the fieldwork in addition to keeping house and raising children. Without their contribution, their immigrant husbands would have had a far more difficult time surviving.

NOTE

1. Allan Lee's recollection differs from his mother's. See p. 98.

APPENDIX C

KOREAN RICE

GROWERS IN THE

SACRAMENTO VALLEY

After decades of experimentation, rice was finally cultivated successfully on a commercial scale in California. Americans had tried to grow the crop in California since the 1880s. Because of the sizeable Chinese population in the state, growers first planted long-grain varieties, which they knew the Chinese preferred. Due to the cool and foggy nights in the Central Valley, however, the heads of the long-grain rice plants never ripened properly. The hardier short-grain varieties were not introduced until the first decade of the twentieth century. The first successful short-grain crop was raised in 1911 on a tract belonging to an agricultural experiment station. I. Ikuta, a Japanese immigrant, W. W. Mackie of the U.S. Bureau of Soils, and C. E. Chambliss of the Office of Cereal Investigations of the Bureau of Plant Industry, performed many experiments in scientific agronomy before they accomplished this feat. From 1913 onward, for almost a decade, rice acreage increased by leaps and bounds. Landowners eagerly sought Asian tenants, thinking they would be expert rice growers, even though the methods used in the upper Sacramento Valley bore little resemblance to the patterns of cultivation found in Asia.

Immigrants from China, Japan, Korea, and India all participated in the California rice boom. Korean immigrants, such as Mary Paik Lee's family, flocked to Colusa, Glenn, Butte, Yuba, and Sutter Counties from the mid-1910s to the early-1920s to grow rice on leased land. In this Appendix, I have reconstructed the history of Korean rice cultivation from extant records in these five counties.

The first two documents recording contracts between Korean tenants and white landowners were signed in 1913. In August, S. O. Kim and K. S. Lee of Colusa County borrowed $1,000 from the Moulton Irrigated Lands Company, a California corporation, at 7 percent interest, using their entire crop on a 70-acre tract of the Crocker Ranch as collateral.[1] The following month, K. H. Kim, K. H. Pyun, and S. L. Kim, also of Colusa County, and the same Moulton Irrigated Lands Company signed a chattel mortgage in which the Koreans pledged their crop of rice and beans for a loan of $1,500 at the same interest rate.[2] These documents show that Koreans joined the "rice rush" from the very beginning.

Kim Chong-lim, who eventually became known as the Korean Rice King, shows up in the official records of Colusa County in 1914, when he and Joseph Marr borrowed $800 at 8 percent interest from A. J. Woody, a rancher in Colusa County, mortgaging four horses and one rice stretcher as surety.[3] Kim was farming 150 acres in Colony No. 1 on the Boggs Tract at that time. Two months after his first loan, he borrowed an additional $1,281 from the Rumely Products Company, using a rice separator, a crankshaft band-cutter and self-feeder, and a tally box attachment to guarantee repayment.[4] Since he could not have used the horses or the equipment as collateral had he not owned them, these records indicate that Kim had already made quite an investment in both draft animals and machinery by then. The following year, he leased the Poirier Ranch, situated on the east bank of the Sacramento River, six miles north of the town of Colusa. He had also acquired a wagon and two rice binders.[5] By 1916, he had added a wind stacker and a bagger to his possessions.[6] The J. I. Case Threshing Machine Company lent him and his partner, Y. S. Park, $1,250 at 8 percent interest the year after that, while he was leasing 160 acres from the Rice Land and Products Company at $14 per acre.[7]

His peak years were from 1918 through 1920. He branched out into hay, wheat, and barley, which he grew, in addition to rice, on thousands of acres situated in Colusa County which he leased from the Sacramento Valley Irrigation Project. He obtained three loans from P. B. Cross in the spring of 1918 — one for $30,000; a second for $2,000; and a third for $38,844 — revealing both the size of his operations and his credit worthiness.[8] In late summer, he borrowed another $7,500 from Leon Speier, a broker from neighboring Glenn County, using as collateral the rice he grew on 480 acres leased jointly with D. H. Kim and Kwang H. Shin.[9]

Kim also started farming with white partners in 1919 in Glenn County, where the town of Willows eventually became his headquarters. The lease he signed with Ben C. Crouch in September 1918 gives detailed information about the terms under which he operated. Together with F. M. Porter, J. R. Scheimer, and F. B. Gilliam, he leased 3,564 acres known as the Crouch Butte City Ranch at $14 per acre for the land and $10 per acre for water for three years. He made a down payment of $5,000 in cash towards rent, the remainder of which was to be paid in installments. The landlord wanted him to plant 2,800 ("or at least 2,500") acres of the tract to rice, because he had already paid the Western Canal Company for enough water to irrigate 2,800 acres at $30 per acre. If Kim planted less than the desired 2,800 acres to rice, the water rent for the nonrice acreage would be only $6 per acre, since other crops required less water. The $28,000 he owed for the water rent started accumulating an interest of 6 percent a year from the day the lease was signed. Kim was responsible for digging a canal to carry water from the main canal of the Western Canal Company to the fields, for which Crouch reimbursed him $2,000.[10] In December, the two parties modified the lease, reducing the amount to be planted to rice to 2,000 acres, but increasing the down payment to $10,000.[11] The first record showing he had moved to Willows appeared in 1923, when he leased two Moreland trucks from Edward L. Park of Los Angeles at $2,000 a month.[12]

The more modest contracts entered into by Mary Paik Lee's father, S. K. Paik, her husband, H. M. Lee, and her childhood playmate, Philip Ahn, are also in the county records. On October 9, 1917, S. K. Paik, with partner Roy Kim, borrowed $1,000 at 8 percent interest from the First National Bank of Colusa, using as collateral two-thirds of their rice crop planted on the 75 acres they leased.[13] A year later, Paik was cultivating 465 acres on four differ-ent tracts. He borrowed $3,000 at 8 percent from the same bank, using one-third of his crop as surety.[14] Glenn County records for 1921 show that H. M. Lee, together with D. K. Kang and a white partner, leased 400 acres from L. H. Twede and his son in re-turn for one-third of the harvest to the landlords.[15] I did not find any documents recording Lee's dealings with P. B. Cross, whom Mrs. Lee mentions in her autobiography, although his name defi-nitely appeared in many county documents as well as in newspaper articles.[16] Also, contrary to Mrs. Lee's recollection, the available records show that Korean tenants received far more than "10 per-cent" of the crop. Finally, in 1926, Philip Ahn, together with two Korean and three white partners, leased a tract (acreage unspeci-fied) from E. M. Gordon to grow rice, even though the boom was long over. The partners promised the landlord one-quarter of the crops. The latter reserved the right to hunt on his property.[17]

Other Korean tenant rice farmers included J. S. Im, S. W. Lee, C. S. Lee, J. Soo Lee, A. Lee, J. K. Lim, C. H. Lim, S. K. Park, Y. S. Park, D. Y. Song, Y. H. Yoon, and M. S. Whang in Colusa County; Leo K. Chang, N. Kim, S. H. Kim, and M. S. Loo in Glenn County; Soon K. Rhee, a resident of Woodland in Yolo County who farmed in Yuba County; and S. C. Park in Yuba County.[18] Their acreages ranged from under a hundred to several hundred, but none matched those of the Korean Rice King. Brief as the boom was, and regardless of the acreages they leased, rice growing gave Korean immigrants the only prosperity they knew during their pioneer period of settlement in California.

NOTES

1. Colusa County, California, "Personal Property Mortgages," Book Z, p. 106. (In this and the following notes, page numbers refer to the first page of the document, each of which runs several pages.)

2. Ibid., p. 112.

3. Colusa County, California, "Personal Property Mortgages," Book X, p. 223.

4. Ibid., p. 235.

5. Colusa County, California, "Personal Property Mortgages," Book 1, p. 94.

6. Colusa County, California, "Personal Property Mortgages," Book 2, p. 256.

7. Colusa County, California, "Personal Property Mortgages," Book 5, p. 23.

8. Ibid., pp. 112, 161, 164.

9. Ibid., p. 222.

10. Glenn County, California, "Leases," Book 2, p. 345.

11. Ibid., p. 388.

12. Glenn County, California, "Leases," Book 4, p. 6.

13. Colusa County, California, "Personal Property Mortgages," Book 3, p. 70.

14. Ibid., p. 244.

15. Ibid., p. 172.

16. *Willows Daily Journal*, November 6, 1917, p. 1, for example, took note of the "agreement between P. B. Cross and three Japanese rice men of Colusa" to plant 3,000 acres of rice near Willows and start a camp near the Green camp. The 1918 *San Francisco City Directory*, p. 484, gave the following information about Cross: "P. B. Cross, real estate and loans, 805–809 Bank of Italy Building . . . Oakland office, 314 First Savings Bank Building; residence, 423 Lagunitas Avenue, Oakland." A. P. Cross, whom Mary Paik Lee said was P. B.'s father, had his office at 550 Montgomery Street, San Francisco, but lived in Los Angeles. The 1919 *San Francisco City Directory*, p. 431, showed that P. B. Cross had moved his office to 550 Montgomery Street, San Francisco, and his residence to the Fairmont Hotel.

17. Colusa County, California, "Leases," Book 4, p. 266.

18. Colusa County, California, "Leases," Book 3, pp. 61, 64; "Personal Property Mortgages," Book T, p. 340; Book 2, p. 359; Book 3, pp. 76, 79, 148, 193, 202, 334, 376, 427; Book 4, p. 48; Book 5, p. 417; Book 6, pp. 76, 151; Book 7, pp. 86, 126, 206, 210, 250; Book 8, pp. 33, 77; and Book 11, p. 100; Glenn County, California, "Leases," Book 3, p. 162; "Crop Mortgages," Book 5, p. 121; Book 34, pp. 58, 139, 190, 193, 202; Sutter County, California, "Crop and Chattel Mortgages," Book I, p. 70; and Yuba County, California, "Chattel Mortgages," Book 10, pp. 1, 3, 52, 188.

BIBLIOGRAPHIC ESSAY

This Bibliographic Essay focuses on the topics I discussed in my Introduction: namely, foreign incursion in Korea in the late nineteenth and early twentieth centuries, and the rise of nationalism; the impact of Protestant Christianity on the status of women and on emigration; and Korean immigrant life in America — especially the conditions faced by immigrant women. The first part, on Korean history, is highly selective; with the exception of the section on women, which is fairly complete, I cite only readily accessible materials in English. The second part, on Korean American history, by contrast, lists more than 90 percent of the works available in English. It should be noted that issue numbers are given only for *Korea Journal* and *Amerasia Journal*, which do not use continuous pagination in successive issues of each volume, as most journals do. The University of Hawaii Press will be listed as such throughout, even though for a number of years it was called the University Press of Hawaii.

Part 1: Korea

Americans first read about Korea in John Ross, *History of Korea* (Paisley, Scotland: J. and R. Parlane, 1879); Ernest Oppert, *A Forbidden Land* (London: Sampson Low, Marston, Searle, and Rivington, 1880); and William Elliot Griffis, *Corea: The Hermit Nation* (New York: Charles Scribner's Sons, 1882). Though Griffis's information was secondhand, compiled from sources he had obtained in Japan, his book was very popular and was consulted by virtually every American diplomat, missionary, and merchant headed for Korea. It went through nine printings over a thirty-year period. Another nineteenth-century work of some interest is

Percival Lowell, *The Land of Morning Calm* (Boston: Tickman and Co., 1886).

Some of the earliest scholarly studies of Korea were done by pioneer American Protestant missionaries. Three such works have been reprinted (the two historical ones include revisions and annotations): Clarence Norwood Weems, ed., *Hulbert's History of Korea* (New York: Hillary House Publishers, Ltd., 1962), a work first published in Korea in 1905; James Scarth Gale, *Korean Folk Tales: Imps, Ghosts, and Fairies* (1913; repr. Tokyo: Charles E. Tuttle Co., 1963); and Richard Rutt, ed., *James Scarth Gale and His History of the Korean People* (Seoul: Royal Asiatic Society, Korea Branch, 1972), which first appeared in installments between 1924 and 1926. Other early, but less readily available, books are Isabella Bird Bishop, *Korea and Her Neighbors* (1897; repr. Seoul: Yonsei University Press, 1972); D. L. Gifford, *Everyday Life in Korea: A Collection of Studies and Stories* (New York: Fleming H. Revell Co., 1898); Homer B. Hulbert, *The Passing of Korea* (1906; repr. Seoul: Yonsei University Press, 1969); and George Heber Jones, *Korea: The Land, People and Customs* (Cincinnati: Jennings and Graham Co., 1907).

Accessible general histories of Korea include Takashi Hatada, *A History of Korea*, translated and edited by Warren W. Smith, Jr., and Benjamin H. Hazard (Santa Barbara: ABC-Clio Press, 1969); Pow Key Sohn et al., *The History of Korea* (Seoul: Korean National Commission for UNESCO, 1970); William H. Henthorn, *A History of Korea* (New York: The Free Press, 1971); and Woo-keun Han, *The History of Korea*, translated by Kyung-shik Lee, edited by Grafton K. Mintz (Honolulu: University of Hawaii Press, 1971).

On Korean cultural and social life, see Cornelius Osgood, *The Koreans and Their Culture* (New York: Ronald Press Co., 1951); Richard Rutt, *Korean Works and Days* (Tokyo: Charles E. Tuttle Co., Inc., 1964); Paul S. Crane, *Korean Patterns* (Seoul: Hollym Corp., 1967); Shin-Yong Chung, ed., *Folk Culture in Korea*, Korean Culture Series, no. 4 (Seoul: International Cultural Foundation, 1974); Eui-Young Yu and Earl H. Phillips, eds., *Religions in Korea: Beliefs and Cultural Values* (Los Angeles: Koryo Research Institute, Center for Korean and Korean-American Studies, California State

University, Los Angeles, 1982); and Roger L. Janelli and Dawnhee Yim Janelli, *Ancestor Worship and Korean Society* (Stanford: Stanford University Press, 1982).

Robert J. Moose, *Village Life in Korea* (Nashville, TN: Publishing House of the Methodist Episcopal Church, South, 1911) is the earliest study in English of Korean villages. Rural life in twentieth-century Korea is described in Chungnim Choi Han, "Social Organization of Upper Han Hamlet in Korea" (Ph.D. diss., University of Michigan, 1949); Eugene Knez, "Sam Jong Dong: A South Korean Village" (Ph.D. diss., Syracuse University, 1959); John E. Mills, ed., *Ethno-Social Reports of Four Korean Villages* (San Francisco: United States Operations Mission to Korea, 1960); Vincent S. R. Brandt, *A Korean Village between Farm and Sea* (Cambridge: Harvard University Press, 1971); Ki-hyuk Pak and Sidney D. Gamble, *The Changing Korean Village* (Seoul: Shin-hung Co., 1975); Soon-young Yoon, "Magic, Science, and Religion on Cheju Island," *Korea Journal* 16, no. 3 (1976): 4–11; Sang-bok Han, *Korean Fishermen: Ecological Adaptation in Three Communities* (Seoul: Population and Development Studies Center, Seoul National University, 1977); Young-key Kim and Dorothea Sich, "A Study of Traditional Healing Techniques and Illness Behavior in a Rural Korean Township," *Anthropological Studies* (Korea) 3 (1977): 75–108; Dorothea Sich, "A Study on the Childbearing Behavior of Rural Korean Women and Their Families," *Transactions of the Royal Asiatic Society, Korea Branch* 53 (1978): 27–55; Griffin M. Dix, "How to Do Things with Ritual: The Logic of Ancestor Worship and Other Offerings in Rural Korea," in *Studies on Korea in Transition*, ed. D. McCann et al. (Honolulu: Center for Korean Studies, University of Hawaii, 1979), pp. 57–88; Laurel Kendall, "Wood Imps, Ghosts, and Other Noxious Influences: The Ideology of Affliction in a Korean Village," *Journal of Korean Studies* 3 (1981): 113–45; Dorothea Sich, "Traditional Concepts and Customs on Pregnancy, Birth and Post-Partum Period in Rural Korea," *Social Science and Medicine* 15 (1981): 65–69; and Clark W. Sorensen, *Over the Mountains Are Mountains: Korean Peasant Households and Their Adaptations to Rapid Industrialization* (Seattle: University of Washington Press, 1988).

On the diplomatic history of Korea around the turn of the century, see George M. McCune and John A. Harrison, eds., *Korean-American Relations: Documents Pertaining to the Far Eastern Diplomacy of the United States, vol. 1. The Initial Period, 1883–1886* (Berkeley and Los Angeles: University of California Press, 1951); Spencer J. Palmer, *Korean-American Relations: Documents Pertaining to the Far Eastern Diplomacy of the United States, vol. 2. The Period of Growing Influence, 1887–1895* (Berkeley and Los Angeles: University of California Press, 1963); Hilary Conroy, *The Japanese Seizure of Korea: 1868–1910; A Study of Realism and Idealism in International Relations* (Philadelphia: University of Pennsylvania Press, 1960); Frederick Foo Chien, *The Opening of Korea: A Study of Chinese Diplomacy, 1876–1885* (Hamden, CT: Shoestring Press, 1967); C. I. Eugene Kim and Han-kyo Kim, *Korea and the Politics of Imperialism, 1876–1910* (Berkeley and Los Angeles: University of California Press, 1967); and Martina Deuchler, *Confucian Gentlemen and Barbarian Envoys: The Opening of Korea, 1876–1885* (Seattle: University of Washington Press, 1977).

The introduction of Protestant Christianity is covered in George Heber Jones, *The Korean Mission of the Methodist Episcopal Church* (New York: Methodist Board of Missions, 1910); L. George Paik, *The History of the Protestant Mission in Korea (1882–1910)* (Pyongyang: Union Christian College Press, 1919); Harry A. Rhodes, ed., *History of the Korea Mission, Presbyterian Church, U.S.A., 1884–1934*, vol. 1 (Seoul: Chosen Mission Presbyterian Church, U.S.A., 1934); C. D. Stokes, "History of the Methodist Mission in Korea, 1885–1930" (Ph.D. diss., Yale University, 1947); Allen D. Clark, *History of the Korean Church* (Seoul: Korean Christian Literature Society, 1961); Samuel Hugh Moffett, *The Christians of Korea* (New York: Friendship Press, 1962); Spencer J. Palmer, *Korea and Christianity: The Problem of Identification with Tradition* (Seoul: Hollym Corp., 1967); In Jong You, "The Impact of the American Protestant Missions on Korean Education, 1885–1932" (Ph.D. diss., University of North Carolina, Chapel Hill, 1967); Everett N. Hunt, Jr., *Protestant Pioneers in Korea* (Maryknoll, NY: Orbis Books, 1980); and Martha Huntley,

Caring, Growing, Changing: A History of the Protestant Mission in Korea (New York: Friendship Press, 1984).

Several of the pioneer missionaries have received biographical treatment: Elizabeth McCully, *A Corn of Wheat, or the Life of the Rev. W. J. McKenzie of Korea* (Toronto: Westminster Co., Ltd., 1903); William Elliot Griffis, *A Modern Pioneer in Korea: Henry G. Appenzeller* (New York: Fleming H. Revell Co., 1912); Lillias Horton Underwood, *Underwood of Korea* (New York: Fleming H. Revell Co., 1918); Fred Harvey Harrington, *God, Mammon, and the Japanese: Dr. Horace N. Allen and Korean-American Relations, 1884–1905* (Wisconsin: University of Wisconsin Press, 1944); Clarence Norwood Weems, "Profile of Homer Bazaleel Hulbert," in Richard Norwood Weems, ed., *Hulbert's History of Korea* (New York: Hillary House Pub., Ltd., 1962), pp. 23–62; Richard H. Baird, *William M. Baird of Korea* (Oakland: n. p., 1968); Richard Rutt, "A Biography of James Scarth Gale," in Richard Rutt, ed., *James Scarth Gale and His History of the Korean People* (Seoul: Royal Asiatic Society, Korea Branch, 1972), 1–88; and Allen Clark, *Avison of Korea: The Life of Oliver R. Avison, M.D.* (Seoul: Yonsei University Press, 1979).

Some of the missionaries wrote sketches of Korean life and reminiscences about their own experiences. Three of the most interesting are by women: Lillias Horton Underwood, *Fifteen Years Among the Top-Knots* (1904; repr. Seoul: Royal Asiatic Society, Korea Branch, 1977); Annie L. Baird, *Daybreak in Korea: A Tale of Transformation in the Far East* (New York: Fleming H. Revell Co., 1909); idem, *Inside Views of Mission Life* (Philadelphia: Westminster Press, 1913). Horace N. Allen, *Korea: Fact and Fancy* (Seoul: Methodist Publishing House, 1904); Horace G. Underwood, *The Call of Korea* (New York: Fleming H. Revell Co., 1908); James Scarth Gale, *Korean Sketches* (New York: Young People's Mission Movement, 1909); and idem, *Korea in Transition* (New York: Young People's Mission Movement, 1909), offer glimpses of missionary perceptions of the society they tried to change.

Eyewitness accounts of the March First Movement (or *Mansei* Uprising) are quoted in Hugh Heung-wo Cynn, *The Rebirth of Korea: The Reawakening of the People, Its Causes, and the Outlook* (New York: The Abingdon Press, 1920); and Peter Huyn, *Man Sei! The Making of a Korean American* (Honolulu: University of Hawaii Press, 1986). Frank P. Baldwin, Jr., "The March First Movement: Korean Challenge and Japanese Response" (Ph.D. diss., Columbia University, 1969) is the most detailed study; Henry Chung, *The Case of Korea* (New York: Fleming H. Revell Co., 1921) pleads his country's case in the court of world opinion; while (Bishop) Herbert Welch, "The Korean Independence Movement of 1919," *The Christian Advocate* 94 (1919): 947–49, 971–73, 1005–7, and 1038–40; and Frederick A. McKenzie, *Korea's Fight for Freedom* (New York: Fleming H. Revell Co., 1920) are the accounts of sympathetic observers. The standard histories of Korea cited above also deal briefly with this momentous event.

Eui Whan Kim, "The Korean Church Under Japanese Occupation with Special Reference to Resistance Movement Within Presbyterianism" (Ph.D. diss., Temple University, 1966); and Gil Sop Song, "American Protestant Missionary Perceptions of the Korean Independence Movement of 1919 and Its Effects Upon the Churches of Korea" (Th.D. diss., Boston University School of Theology, 1976) discuss the involvement of Korean Christians in, and the stance of American missionaries towards, the independence movement.

Nym Wales [Helen Foster Snow] and Kim San [pseud.], *Song of Ariran: A Korean Communist in the Chinese Revolution* (New York: John Day Co., 1941) is the biography of a Korean who came of age during the anti-Japanese struggle and became a revolutionary partisan among Korean expatriates in Manchuria and China. Biographies of nationalist leaders who spent long years in the United States include Channing Liem, *America's Finest Gift to Korea: The Life of Philip Jaisohn* (New York: William-Frederick Press, 1952); Robert T. Oliver, *Syngman Rhee: The Man Behind the Myth* (New York: Dodd, Mead and Co., 1954); and Richard C. Allen, *Korea's Syngman Rhee: An Unauthorized Portrait* (Rutland, VT: Charles E. Tuttle Co., 1960).

Relatively little has been published about Korean women. The most complete study available in English is Yung-Chung Kim, ed. and trans., *Women of Korea: A History from Ancient Times to 1945* (Seoul: Ewha Woman's University Press, 1982), which is an abridged version of a three-volume study prepared by the Committee for the Compilation of the History of Korean Women at Ewha Woman's University, *Hanguk Yosongsa* [The History of Korean Women] (Seoul: Ewha Woman's University Press, 1972). The best short introduction to Korean women during the Yi dynasty is "Appendix B: Women and Family in Traditional Korea," in Youngsook Kim Harvey, *Six Korean Women: The Socialization of Shamans* (St. Paul, MN: West Publishing Co., 1979), pp. 253–71. For a brief historical overview, see Hyon-ja Kim, "The Changing Role of Women in Korea," *Korea Journal* 11, no. 5 (1975): 21–24. Two feminist analyses are given in Tae-young Lee, "Elevation of Korean Women's Rights," *Korea Journal* 4, no. 2 (1964): 4–9, 43; and Hesung Chun Koh, "Yi Dynasty Women in the Public Domain: A New Perspective on Social Stratification," *Social Science Journal* (Korea) 3 (1975): 7–19. The only glimpse available of women's intellectual life during the Yi dynasty is in Dong-uk Kim, "Women's Literary Achievements," *Korea Journal* 3, no. 11 (1963): 33–36, 39. Stories about women are found in Frances Carpenter, *Tales of a Korean Grandmother* (Seoul: Royal Asiatic Society, Korea Branch, 1973); and Richard Rutt and Chong Un Kim, trans., *Virtuous Women: Three Masterpieces of Traditional Korean Fiction* (Seoul: Royal Asiatic Society, Korea Branch, 1974).

Two anthologies, Sandra Martielli, ed., *Virtues in Conflict: Tradition and the Korean Woman Today* (Seoul: Royal Asiatic Society, Korea Branch, 1977); and Laurel Kendall and Mark Peterson, eds., *Korean Women: View from the Inner Room* (New Haven: East Rock Press, 1983) contain several essays written from a feminist perspective. (Essays in these two volumes will not be cited individually here.) Kendall and Peterson note that the new feminist scholarship has focused on two groups of autonomous women: shamans, and women who dive for marine products. Shamans, especially, have fascinated contemporary scholars: Youngsook Kim Harvey, Laurel Kendall, Kwang Iel Kim, Tae Gon Kim, and Jung Young Lee have written extensively about shamans' social position and role.

Youngsook Kim Harvey has published "The Korean *Mudang* as a Household Therapist," in *Culture-Bound Syndromes: Ethnopsychiatry and Alternate Therapies*, edited by William P. Lebra (Honolulu: University of Hawaii Press, 1976), pp. 189–98; *Six Korean Women: The Socialization of Shamans* (St. Paul, MN: West Publishing Co., 1979); and "Possession Sickness and Women Shamans in Korea," in *Unspoken Worlds: Women's Religious Lives in Non-Western Cultures*, edited by N. A. Falk and R. M. Gross (New York: Harper and Row, 1980). Harvey's interpretation of how *synbyong* (possession sickness, a condition indicative of supernatural notification to assume the role of shaman) is a "pathway out of impasse" — that is, a way for individual women to break out of the behavior prescribed for females in Korean society — casts a feminist light on why certain women become shamans.

Laurel Kendall has been prolific with "Caught between Ancestors and Spirits: Field Report of a Korean *Mansin's* Healing *Kut*," *Korea Journal* 17, no. 8 (1977): 8–23; "*Mugam*: The Dance in Shaman's Clothing," *Korea Journal* 17, no. 12 (1977): 38–44; "Receiving the *Samsin* Grandmother: Conceptual Rituals in Korea," *Transactions of the Royal Asiatic Society, Korea Branch* 52 (1977): 55–70; "Giving Rise to Dancing Spirits: *Mugam* in Korean Shaman Ritual," in *Dance as Cultural Heritage*, ed. B. T. Jones, *Dance Research Annual* 14 (1984): 224–32; "Wives, Lesser Wives, and Ghosts: Supernatural Conflict in a Korean Village," *Asian Folklore Studies* (Japan) 43 (1984): 215–25; *Shamans, Housewives, and Other Restless Spirits: Women in Korean Ritual Life* (Honolulu: University of Hawaii Press, 1985); and *The Life and Hard Times of a Korean Shaman: Of Tales and the Telling of Tales* (Honolulu: University of Hawaii Press, 1988).

Kwang Iel Kim has two pieces: "Psychoanalytic Consideration of Korean Shamanism," *Neuropsychiatry* (Korea) 11 (1972): 121–29; and "Shamanist Healing Ceremonies in Korea," *Korea Journal* 13, no. 4 (1973): 41–47. Tae Gon Kim authored "A Study of Shaman's Mystic Illness during Initiation Process in Korea," *Journal of Asian Women* (Korea) 9 (1970): 91–132; "The Influence of Shamanism in the Living Pattern of People in Contemporary Korea," in *The Modern Meaning of Shamanism*, edited by T. Kim

(Iri, Republic of Korea: Folklore Research Institute, Wongwang University, 1972); "Components of Korean Shamanism," *Korea Journal* 12, no. 12 (1972): 17–25; "Korean Shamanism and Its Outlook on Future Life," *Journal of Social Sciences and Humanities* (Korea) 39 (1974): 83–104; and "Shamanism in the Seoul Area," *Korea Journal* 18, no. 6 (1978): 39–51. Jung Young Lee produced "The Seasonal Rituals of Korean Shamanism," *History of Religions* 12 (1973): 271–87; "Shamanistic Thought and Traditional Korean Homes," *Korea Journal* 15, no. 11 (1975): 43–51; and *Korean Shamanistic Rituals* (The Hague: Mouton, 1981).

Other studies on shamanism are Bou-Yang Rhi, "Psychological Aspects of Korean Shamanism," *Korea Journal* 10, no. 9 (1970): 15–21; Tong Ni Kim, "Portrait of a Shaman," in *Flowers of Fire*, edited by P. Lee (Honolulu: University of Hawaii Press, 1974), 58–90; Arthur W. Kinsler, "Korean Fertility Cult for Children in Shaman Ritual and Myth," *Korea Journal* 17, no. 2 (1977): 27–34; and Barbara Young, "Spirits and Other Signs: An Ethnography of Divination in Seoul, Republic of Korea" (Ph.D. diss., University of Washington, 1980).

Haejoang Cho, "An Ethnographic Study of a Female Diver's Village in Korea, Focused on the Sexual Division of Labor" (Ph.D. diss., University of California, Los Angeles, 1979); and idem, "Neither Dominance: A Study of a Female Diver's Village in Korea," *Korea Journal* 19, no. 6 (1979): 23–34, describe the unusual lives of women divers and their spouses, while Daniel Bouchez, "*Kisaeng*: Mediums of the Vernacular," *Korean Culture* 2 (1981): 21–27, looks at female entertainers.

Protestant missionaries published some of the earliest observations of Korean women: George Heber Jones, "The Status of Women in Korea," *Korea Repository* 3 (1896): 223–29; idem, *The Korean Woman* (Boston: Women's Foreign Missionary Society, Methodist Episcopal Church, n.d.); Mary F. Scranton, "Women's Work in Korea," *Korean Repository* 3 (1986); idem, "Mission Work among Women of City and Country," *Korea Repository* 4 (1897): 294–97; anon., "Women's Rights in Korea," *Korea Review* 6 (1906): 51–59; anon., "Girls and Women in Korea," *Korea Mission Field* 4 (1908): 82; and Kay Cooper, "The Bible Woman," *Korea Maga-*

zine 1 (1917). See also James S. Gale, *Korean Sketches* (New York: Fleming H. Revell Co., 1898), passim; and Homer B. Hulbert, *The Passing of Korea* (New York: Doubleday, Page, and Co., 1906), passim; Helen K. Kim, "Methodism and the Development of Korean Womanhood," in *Within the Gate*, edited by C. A. Sauer (Seoul: Korea Methodist News Service, 1934); and Hyo-chae Lee, "Protestant Missionary Work and Enlightenment of Korean Women," *Korea Journal* 17, no. 11 (1977): 33–50, discuss the impact of Christianity on Korean women.

Three of the most active Korean Christian women have published their autobiographies in English: Induk Pahk, *September Monkey* (New York: Harper and Brothers, 1951); Louise Yim, *My Forty-Year Fight for Korea* (New York: A. A. Wyn, Inc., 1951); and Helen Kim, *Grace Sufficient* (Nashville, TN: The Upper Room, 1964). Education played a key role in making them into public leaders. Brief studies of women's education include Kyu-hwan Lee, "A Study of Women's Education under the Japanese Occupation," *Journal* (Korean Cultural Research Institute) 3 (1962); and Hwang-kyong Ko, "Korean Women and Education," *Korea Journal* 4, no. 2 (1964): 10–13.

Bae Kyung Sook, *Women and the Law in Korea* (Seoul: Korean League of Women Voters, 1973); In-ho Lee, "Women's Liberation in Korea," *Korea Journal* 17, no. 7 (1977): 4–11; and Uhn Cho and Hagen Koo, "Economic Development and Women's Work in a Newly Industrializing Country: The Case of Korea," *Development and Change* 14 (1983): 515–21 offer modern perspectives. Korean family life is analyzed in Doo-hun Kim, "Historical Review of Korean Family System," *Korea Journal* 3, no. 10 (1963): 4–9, 32; Chae-sok Choe, "Process of Change in Korean Family Life," *Korea Journal* 3, no. 10 (1963): 10–15; Hang-nyung Lee, "Civil Law and Korean Family System," *Korea Journal* 3, no. 10 (1963): 20–21, 32; Seong-hi Yim, "Changing Patterns in Korean Family Structure," *Korea Journal* 6, no. 8 (1966): 4–9; Hae Yong Lee, "Modernization of the Family Structure in an Urban Setting—with Special Reference to Marriage Relations," in *Aspects of Social Change in Korea*, edited by E. Kim and C. Chee (Kalamazoo, MI: Korea Research and Publications, 1969), pp. 44–69;

Chang Shub Roh, "Family Life in Korea and Japan," *Silliman Journal* (Philippines) 16 (1969): 200–15; Un Sun Song, "Marriage and the Family in Korea," in *Marriage and Family in the Modern World: A Book of Readings*, edited by Ruth Shonle Cavan (New York: Thomas Y. Crowell Co., 1969), pp. 92–98; Tae-hung Ha, *Folk Customs and Family Life* (Seoul: Yonsei University Press, 1972); Hyo-chai Lee, "Changing Korean Family and the Old," *Korea Journal* 13, no. 6 (1973): 20–25; and Cha-whan Chung, "Change and Continuity in an Urbanizing Society: Family and Kinship in Urban Korea" (Ph.D. diss., University of Hawaii, 1977).

The American military occupation of Korea (1945–48), the Korean War (1950–53), and the continued presence of some 40,000 American troops in South Korea have led to thousands of marriages between American men and Korean women. The latter's entry into the United States has formed a significant segment of post–World War II Korean emigration. This topic has not been researched in depth. But, there is a vast literature on the Korean War: David Rees, *Korea: The Limited War* (Baltimore: Penguin Books, 1964); Gregory Henderson, *Korea: The Politics of the Vortex* (Berkeley and Los Angeles, University of California Press, 1981); Bruce Cumings, *The Origins of the Korean War: Liberation and the Emergence of Separate Regimes, 1945–1947* (Princeton: Princeton University Press, 1981); Burton I. Kaufman, *The Korean War: Challenges in Crisis, Credibility, and Command* (New York: Alfred A. Knopf, 1986); and Callum A. MacDonald, *Korea: The War Before Vietnam* (New York: The Free Press, 1986) are the best starting points.

Part 2: Koreans in America

Korean immigration into the United States can be divided into four periods: (1) recruited immigration (1902–05); (2) restricted immigration (1905–45); (3) the entry of dependents of U.S. citizens (1945–65); and (4) renewed immigration (1965–present). The available literature deals mainly with the first and fourth periods. Some studies deal with women and children who entered during the third period; while the handful of articles about the second period focus on picture brides.

The most detailed study of early Korean emigration is Wayne K. Patterson, *The Korean Frontier in America: Immigration to Hawaii, 1896–1910* (Honolulu: University of Hawaii Press, 1988). Korean emigration is also discussed in Yo-jun Yun, "Early History of Korean Emigration to America," pt. 1, *Korea Journal* 14, no. 6 (1974): 21–26, and pt. 2, *Korea Journal* 14, no. 7 (1974): 40–45; Wayne K. Patterson, "Sugar-Coated Diplomacy: Horace Allen and Korean Immigration to Hawaii, 1902–1906," *Diplomatic History* 3 (1979): 29–38; and Linda Pomerantz, "The Background of Korean Emigration," in *Labor Immigration Under Capitalism: Asian Workers in the United States before World War II*, edited by Lucie Cheng and Edna Bonacich (Berkeley and Los Angeles: University of California Press, 1984), pp. 277–315.

The only available general history of Korean Americans is Bong-Youn Choy, *Koreans in America* (Chicago: Nelson-Hall, 1979); while Hyung June Moon, "The Korean Immigrants in America: The Quest for Identity in the Formative Years, 1903–1918" (Ph.D. diss., University of Nevada, Reno, 1977) has details not found elsewhere. Useful overviews, especially for classroom use, are Lee Houchins and Chang-su Houchins, "The Korean Experience in America, 1903–1924," *Pacific Historical Review* 18 (1974): 548–72 (reprinted in *The Asian American: The Historical Experience*, edited by Norris Hundley, Jr. (Santa Barbara: ABC-Clio Press, 1976), pp. 129–56); H. Brett Melendy, *Asians in America: Filipinos, Koreans, and East Indians* (Boston: Twayne Publishers, 1977), pp. 111–72; Eui-Young Yu, "Koreans in America: An Emerging Ethnic Minority," *Amerasia Journal* 4, no. 1 (1977): 117–32; and idem, "Korean Communities in America: Past, Present, and Future," *Amerasia Journal* 10, no. 2 (1983): 23–52.

Articles in several anthologies (which will not be cited individually here) provide valuable insights into various aspects of immigrant life: Hyung-chan Kim, ed., *The Korean Diaspora: Historical and Sociological Studies of Korean Immigration and Assimilation in North America* (Santa Barbara: ABC-Clio Press, 1977); Byong-suh Kim and Sang Hyun Lee, eds., *The Korean Immigrant in*

America (Montclair, N.J.: Association of Korean Christian Scholars in North America, 1980); and Eui-Young Yu et al., eds., *Koreans in Los Angeles: Prospects and Promises* (Los Angeles: Koryo Research Institute, Center for Korean and Korean-American Studies, California State University, Los Angeles, 1982).

Early Korean settlers in Hawaii have been described in Samuel F. Morse, "One Night with the Koreans in Hawaii," *Korea Review* 3 (1903): 529–32; Homer B. Hulbert, "The Koreans in Hawaii," *Korea Review* 5 (1905): 411–13; George H. Jones, "The Koreans in Hawaii," *Korea Review* 6 (1906): 401–6; idem, "Koreans Abroad," *Korea Review* 6 (1906): 446–51; William Elliot Griffis, "The First Koreans in America," *Korea Review* 4 (1922): 11–15 [this is a different journal from the one published in Korea]; anon., "Korean Youth of Hawaii," *Pan-Pacific Youth* 16 (1930): 2; Tai-sung Lee, "The Story of Korean Immigration," *The Mid-Pacific Magazine* 44 (1932): 136–40; Bernice B. Kim, "The Koreans in Hawaii," *Social Science* 9 (1934): 409–13; idem, "The Koreans in Hawaii" (M.A. thesis, University of Hawaii, 1937); Alice R. Appenzeller, "A Generation of Koreans in Hawaii, " *Paradise of the Pacific* 56 (1944): 81–83; Donald Kang, "The Koreans in Hawaii," *New Pacific* 11 (1944): 4–5; J. Kyuang Dunn, "Progress of Koreans in Hawaii," *Paradise of the Pacific* 58 (1946): 90–91; Morris Pang, "A Korean Immigrant," *Social Forces in Hawaii* 13 (1949): 19–24; Andrew Lind, "Hawaii's Koreans — Some Basic Considerations," *Bohk Dohng* 1 (1956): 3–4; Roger C. Schmidt, "Hawaii's Koreans, 1960: A Preview of Census Statistics," *Bulletin of Hawaii* (Autumn 1960): 20–22; Seung-Jae Koh, "A Study of Korean Immigrants to Hawaii," *Journal of Social Sciences and Humanities* 38 (1973): 19–33; and Samuel S. O. Lee et al., eds., *75th Anniversary of Korean Immigration to Hawaii, 1903–1978* (Honolulu: 75th Anniversary of Korean Immigration to Hawaii Committee, 1978). Short pieces in Myongsup Shin and Daniel B. Lee, eds., *Korean Immigrants in Hawaii: A Symposium on Their Background History, Acculturation and Public Policy Issues* (Honolulu: Korean Immigration Welfare Association of Hawaii and Operation Manong, College of Education, University of Hawaii, 1978) examine current issues.

For regional studies of Koreans in the continental United States, see Helen Lewis Givens, *The Korean Community in Los Angeles County* (1939; repr. San Francisco: R and E Research Associates, 1974); Dale White, "Koreans in Montana," *Asia and the Asians* 17 (1945): 156; Kyung Sook Cho Gregor, "Korean Immigrants in Gresham, Oregon: Community Life and Social Adjustment" (M.A. thesis, University of Oregon, 1963); Don Chang Lee, *Acculturation of Korean Residents in Georgia* (San Francisco: R and E Research Associates, 1975); David Namkoong, "Korean Americans," in *Asian Americans and Their Communities of Cleveland*, edited by Stephen Fujita et al. (Cleveland: Cleveland State University, 1977), pp. 123–60; William Henry Hubler, *Koreans in Emlyn: A Community in Transition*, Philip Jaisohn Memorial Papers, no. 3 (Elkins Park, PA: Philip Jaisohn Memorial Foundation, 1978); Won Moo Hurh et al., *Assimilation Patterns of Immigrants in the United States: A Case Study of Korean Immigrants in the Chicago Area* (Washington, D.C.: University Press of America, 1978); Jay Kun Yoo, *The Koreans in Seattle*, Philip Jaisohn Memorial Papers, no. 4 (Elkins Park, PA: Philip Jaisohn Memorial Foundation, 1979); and Kyung Soo Choi, "The Assimilation of Korean Immigrants in the St. Louis Area" (Ph.D. diss., St. Louis University, 1982); and Sarah R. Mason, "The Koreans," in *They Chose Minnesota: A Survey of the State's Ethnic Groups*, edited by June Drenning Holmquist (St. Paul, Minn.: Minnesota Historical Society Press, 1981), pp. 572–79.

Korean immigrant communities in the early decades of their existence were torn by factional political struggles. Warren Y. [Won Yong] Kim, *Koreans in America* (Seoul: Po Chin Chai, 1971), which is an abbreviation in English of his larger work, *Chaemi Hanin Osimnyonsa [A Fifty-Year History of the Koreans in the United States]* (Reedley, CA: Charles Ho Kim, 1959), is definitive but hard to obtain. A more readily accessible source on Korean expatriate politics is Kinsley K. Lyu, "Korean Nationalist Activities in Hawaii and the Continental United States, 1900–1945," pt. 1 (1900–1919), *Amerasia Journal* 4, no. 1 (1977): 23–90; and pt. 2 (1919–1945), *Amerasia Journal* 4, no. 2 (1977): 53–100.

The only study of Korean immigration in the decade before changes in U.S. immigration legislation made it possible for some

30,000 to enter every year is Hyung-chan Kim, "Korean Emigrants to the United States, 1959–1969," *Korea Journal* 11, no. 9 (1971): 16–24, 31. The only book-length studies of contemporary Korean immigration are Illsoo Kim, *New Urban Immigrants: The Korean Community in New York* (Princeton: Princeton University Press, 1981); and Won Moo Hurh and Kwang Chung Kim, *Korean Immigrants in America: A Structural Analysis of Ethnic Confinement and Adhesive Adaptation* (Cranbury, N.J.: Associated University Presses, 1984). Illsoo Kim's book (*New Urban Immigrants*); and Hagen Koo and Eui-Young Yu, *Korean Immigration to the United States: Its Demographic Pattern and Social Implications for Both Societies*, Papers of the East-West Population Institute, no. 74 (Honolulu: East-West Center, 1981), offer the most sophisticated analyses of the global context of the current influx. Chang-soo Lee, "The United States Immigration Policy and the Settlement of Koreans in America," *Korean Observer* 6 (1975): 412–51; and Tomoji Ishi, "International Linkage and National Class Conflict: The Migration of Korean Nurses to the United States," *Amerasia Journal* 14, no. 1 (1988): 23–50, also suggest theoretical frameworks for understanding Korean immigration today; while Luciano Mangiafico, *Contemporary American Immigrants: Patterns of Filipino, Korean, and Chinese Settlement in the United States* (New York: Praeger and Co., 1988) discusses the Koreans alongside two other groups.

Though Korean immigrants have been similar in many ways to newcomers from other Asian countries, they differ in one significant aspect: an unusually large proportion of them are Protestant Christians, partly as a result of the active involvement of missionaries in their original exodus. For that reason, churches have played a crucial role in Korean immigrant communities. Studies of the religious life of Korean American Christians include Sang-in Han, "A Study of Social Religious Participation in Relationship to Occupational Mobility and Self-Esteem Among Korean Immigrants in Chicago" (Ph.D. diss., Northwestern University, 1973); Sangho Joseph Kim, *A Study of the Korean Church and Her People in Chicago, Illinois* (San Francisco: R and E Research Associates, 1975); Illsoo Kim, "Problems of Immigrant Society and the Role of the Church with Reference to the Korean Immigrant Community in America," *Korean Observer* 7 (1976): 398–431; Steve S. Shim, *Korean Immigrant Churches in Southern California Today* (San Francisco: R and E Research Associates, 1977); Jang Kyun Park, "A Study of the Growth of the Korean Church in Southern California" (D.Min. diss., School of Theology at Claremont, 1979); Paul Shu Kim, "A Study of Ministry to Second Generation Korean Immigrants in the Church" (D.Min. diss., Drew University, 1980); Woong-Min Kim, "History and Ministerial Role of Korean Churches in the Los Angeles Area" (D.Min. diss., School of Theology at Claremont, 1981); Tai Ki Chung, "Pastoral Care for Korean Immigrants in the United States Experiencing Cross-Cultural Stress" (D.Min. diss., School of Theology at Claremont, 1983); Yong Jai Jun, "A Holistic Evangelization of Korean Churches in the Los Angeles Area" (D.Min. diss., School of Theology at Claremont, 1984); Dae Gee Kim, "Major Factors Conditioning the Acculturation of Korean-Americans with Respect to the Presbyterian Church in America and Its Missionary Obedience" (D.Miss. diss., Fuller Theological Seminary School of World Mission, 1985); Illsoo Kim, "Organizational Patterns of Korean-American Methodist Churches: Denominationalism and Personal Commitment," in *Rethinking Methodist History*, ed. Russell Richey and Kenneth E. Rowe (Nashville, TN: United Methodist Publishing House, 1985), pp. 228–37. See also the articles on Korean churches in America in the anthologies edited by Hyung-chan Kim, Byong-suh Kim et al., and Eui-Young Yu et al.

Observers have also been fascinated by the tendency of contemporary Korean immigrants to enter small businesses. Research on this subject is reported in Hyung-chan Kim, "Ethnic Enterprises Among Korean Immigrants in America," *Journal of Korean Affairs* 6 (1976): 40–58; Edna Bonacich et al., "Koreans in Business," *Society* 14 (1977): 54–59; Edna Bonacich and Tai Hwan Jung, "Korean Immigrant Small Business in Los Angeles," in *Sourcebook on the New Immigration: Implications for the United States and International Community*, ed. Roy Bryce-LaPorte (New Brunswick: Transaction Books, 1979), pp. 167–84; Jin H. Yu, *The Korean Merchants in the Black Community*, Philip Jaisohn Memorial Papers, no. 7 (Elkins Park, PA: Philip Jaisohn Memorial Foundation, 1980); Hyung-ki Jin, *A Survey of the Economic and Managerial Status of Sewing Factories Owned and Operated by Korean Contractors in the Los Angeles Area* (Pomona, CA: Industrial Research Institute for Pacific Nations, California State Polytechnic University, Pomona, 1981); Heeduk Bang, "The Self-Help/Mutual Aid Component in Small Business within the Korean American Community" (D.S.W. diss., University of Pennsylvania, 1983); John Y. Lee, *A Study of the Financial Structure and Operating Programs of Korean Small Businesses in Los Angeles (with Emphasis on the Mid-Wilshire Area)* (Los Angeles: Mid-Wilshire Community Research Center Corp., 1983); David M. Oh, *An Analysis of Korean Firms in the Los Angeles Area* (Los Angeles: Mid-Wilshire Community Research Center Corp., 1983); Moon-Ik Song, "Successful Korean Businesses in the United States: A Study of Excellence" (D.B.A. diss., United States International University, 1983); Pyong Gap Min, "Minority Business Enterprise: A Case Study of Korean Small Business in Atlanta" (Ph.D. diss., Georgia State University, 1983); Philip K. Y. Young, "Family Labor, Sacrifice, and Competition: Korean Greengrocers in New York City," *Amerasia Journal* 10, no. 2 (1983): 53–71; Pyong Gap Min, "From White-Collar Occupations to Small Business: Korean Immigrants' Occupational Adjustment," *Sociological Quarterly* 25 (1984): 333–52; idem, "A Structural Analysis of Korean Business in the United States," *Ethnic Groups* 6 (1984): 1–25; Kwang Chung Kim and Won Moo Hurh, "Ethnic Resource Utilization of Korean Immigrant Entrepreneurs in the Chicago Minority Area," *International Migration Review* 19 (1985): 82–111; Sang Hwan Lee, "Determinant Attributes in the Selection of Financial Institutions by Residents of the Los Angeles Korean Community" (Ph.D. diss., United States International University, 1985); Pyong Gap Min, "Filipino and Korean Immigrants in Small Business: A Comparative Analysis," *Amerasia Journal* 13, no. 1 (1986): 53–71; idem., *Ethnic Business Enterprise: Korean Small Business in Atlanta* (Staten Island, N.Y.: Center for Migration Studies, 1988); and Edna Bonacich and Ivan Light, *Immigrant Entrepreneurs: Koreans in Los Angeles* (Berkeley and Los Angeles: University of California Press, 1988).

Other studies of Korean economic adaptation in the United States include Kwang Chung Kim, "Social and Occupational Assimilation of Korean Immigrants in the United States," *California Sociologist* 3 (1980): 125–42; idem, "Job Information Deprivation in the United States: A Case Study of Korean Immigrants," *Ethnicity* 8 (1981): 219–32; Sookja Paik Kim, "Underemployment of Recent Asian Immigrants: Koreans in Los Angeles" (Ph.D. diss., Virginia Commonwealth University, 1982); Michael Myong O. Seipel, "Occupational Adjustment Patterns of Korean Immigrants in the American Labor Market" (Ph.D. diss., Cornell University, 1982); and Eui Hang Shin and Kyung-Sup Chang, "Peripherization of Immigrant Professionals: The Case of Korean Physicians in the United States," *International Migration Review* 22 (1988): 609–26.

The assimilation and acculturation of Koreans in America are explored in Hyung-chan Kim, "Some Aspects of Social Demography of Korean Americans," *International Migration Review* 8 (1974): 23–42; Marn J. Cha, "Ethnic Political Orientation as Function of Assimilation: With Reference to Koreans in Los Angeles," *Journal of Korean Affairs* 5 (1975): 14–25; Jong Sam Park, "A Three Generational Study: Traditional Korean Value Systems and Psychological Adjustment of Korean Immigrants in Los Angeles" (D.S.W. diss., University of Southern California, 1975); Won Moo Hurh, *Assimilation of the Korean Minority in the United States*, Philip Jaisohn Memorial Papers, no. 1 (Elkins Park, PA: Philip Jaisohn Memorial Foundation, 1977); Jung Shig Ryu, "The Mass Media and the Assimilation Process: A Study of Media Uses by Korean Immigrants" (Ph.D. diss., University of Oregon, 1977); Woo-Hyun Won, "Values and Mass Media Preferences of Korean Immigrants" (Ph.D. diss., Boston University, 1977); Bok-Lim C. Kim, *The Asian Americans: Changing Patterns, Changing Needs* (Montclair, N.J.: Association of Korean Christian Scholars in North America, 1978), pp. 177–211; Won Moo Hurh, "Towards a Korean-American Ethnicity: Some Theoretical Models," *Ethnic and Racial Studies* 4 (1980): 444–63; Kwang Chung Kim and Won Moo Hurh, "Korean Americans and the 'Success' Image: A Critique," *Amerasia Journal* 10, no. 2 (1983): 3–22; David M. Oh, *An*

Analysis of the Korean Community in the Mid-Wilshire Area, pts. 1 and 2 (Los Angeles: Mid-Wilshire Community Research Center Corp., 1983), pp. 3–21; Sun Bin Yim, "Social Networks among Korean Immigrants in the United States" (Ph.D. diss., University of California, Los Angeles, 1984); and Hyo Jin Chang, "A Study of Korean Nurse Immigrants' Adaptation Experience to the Nursing Profession in the Los Angeles Area" (Ph.D. diss., University of Michigan, 1986).

Several researchers have focused on the impact of communication patterns on acculturation: Jin Keon Kim, "Communication Factors in Acculturation: The Case of Korean Immigrants in Southern California" (Ph.D. diss., University of Iowa, 1978); Chong Hyuk Cho, "Communication Modes in Adaptation Process: A Case of Korean Immigrants" (Ph.D. diss., University of Michigan, 1982); Margaret Inglis and William B. Gudykunst, "Institutional Completeness and Communication Acculturation: A Comparison of Korean Immigrants in Chicago and Hartford," *International Journal of Intercultural Relations* 6 (1982): 251–72; and Myong Jim Won-Doornink, "Television Viewing and Acculturation of Korean Immigrants," *Amerasia Journal* 14, no. 1 (1988): 79–92.

Edward Tea Chang, "Korean Community Politics in Los Angeles: The Impact of the Kwangju Uprising," *Amerasia Journal* 14, no. 1 (1988): 51–68, is the only study available of the politics within the contemporary Korean immigrant community. James Chin, "Crime and the Asian American Community—the Los Angeles Response to Koreatown," *Journal of California Law Enforcement* 19 (1985): 52–60, examines some community problems from the point of view of law and order.

For two overviews on Korean women in America during the pioneer period, see Eun Sik Yang, "Korean Women of America: From Subordination to Partnership, 1903–1930," *Amerasia Journal*, 11, no. 2 (1984): 1–28; and Alice Y. Chai, "Korean Women in Hawaii, 1903–1945," in *Asian and Pacific American Experiences: Women's Perspectives*, ed. Nobuya Tsuchida (Minneapolis: Asian/Pacific American Learning Resource Center, University of Minnesota, 1982) pp. 75–87. Alice Y. Chai, "The Life History of an

Early Korean Immigrant Woman in Hawaii," *University of Hawaii Women's Studies Program Working Papers Series* 1 (1978): 50–59; Harold Hakwon Sunoo and Sonia Shinn Sunoo, "The Heritage of the First Korean Women Immigrants in the United States: 1903–1924," *Korean Christian Scholars Journal* 2 (1977): 142–71; and Sonia S. Sunoo, "Korean Women Pioneers of the Pacific Northwest," *Oregon Historical Quarterly* 79 (1978): 51–63; and Sonia Shinn Sunoo, ed., *Korean Kaleidoscope* (Davis, CA.: Korean Oral History Project, Sierra Mission Area, United Presbyterian Church, U.S.A., 1982) based on oral history transcriptions, offer glimpses of individual women, most of them picture brides. Bong-Youn Choy, *Koreans in America*, pp. 308–24, also contains biographical sketches of three women.

Harold Hakwon Sunoo and Dong Soo Kim, eds., *Korean Women in a Struggle for Humanization* (Memphis, TN: The Association of Korean Christian Scholars in North America, 1978); and Eui-Young Yu and Earl H. Phillips, eds., *Korean Women in Transition at Home and Abroad* (Los Angeles: Koryo Research Institute, Center for Korean and Korean-American Studies, California State University, Los Angeles, 1987) contain essays on women in Korea as well as in the United States.

The plight of Korean women who married American military men has captured the attention of social workers. Three pieces by Bok-Lim C. Kim, "Casework with Japanese and Korean Wives of Americans," *Social Casework* 53 (1972): 273–79; "Asian Wives of U.S. Servicemen: Women in Shadows," *Amerasia Journal* 4, no. 1 (1977): 91–116; and *Women in Shadows: A Handbook for Service Providers Working with Asian Wives of U.S. Military Personnel* (La Jolla, CA: National Committee Concerned with Asian Wives of U.S. Servicemen, n.d.); Bascom W. Ratliff et al., "Intercultural Marriage: The Korean American Experience," *Social Casework* 59 (1978): 221–26; Harry H. L. Kitano and Lynn Kyung Chai, "Korean Interracial Marriage," *Marriage and Family Review* 5 (1982): 75–89; and a master's thesis and four Ph.D. dissertations, Dorothy W. Trebilcock, "The Individual Social and Cultural Implications of the Cross-Cultural Marriage: Korean Wives and Their American Husbands in Michigan" (M.A. thesis: Michigan State University, 1973); Sil Dong Kim, "Interracially Married Korean Women Immigrants: A Study in Marginality" (Ph.D. diss., University of Washington, 1979); Daniel B. Lee, "Military Transcultural Marriage: A Study of Marital Adjustment between American Husbands and Korean-born Spouses" (D.S.W., University of Utah, 1980); Brooke Lilla Brewer, "Interracial Marriage: American Men Who Marry Korean Women" (Ph.D. diss., Syracuse University, 1982); and Young In Song, "Battered Korean Women in Urban America: The Relationship of Cultural Conflict to Wife Abuse" (Ph.D. diss., Ohio State University, 1986) contain much useful information analyzed from various perspectives.

The thousands of Korean children, many of them war orphans, who have been adopted by American families since the 1950s have received some scholarly attention. Available studies are Won Moo Hurh, "Marginal Children of War: An Exploratory Study of American-Korean Children," *International Journal of Sociology of the Family* 2 (1972): 10–20; Claude Guilbault, "A Descriptive Study of the Adjustment of Korean Children Adopted by Families in Minnesota" (M.A. thesis, University of Wisconsin, 1972); Minsum Sung Whang, "An Exploratory Descriptive Study of Intercountry Adoption of Korean Children with Korean Parents" (M.A. thesis, University of Hawaii, 1976); Chim Kim and Timothy G. Carroll, "Intercountry Adoption of South Korean Orphans: A Lawyer's Guide," *Journal of Family Law* 14 (1977): 223–53; Dong Soo Kim, "How They Fared in American Homes: A Follow-Up Study of Adopted Korean Children," *Children Today* 6 (1977): 2–6, 31; idem, "Intercountry Adoptions: A Study of Self-Concept of Adolescent Korean Children Who Were Adopted by American Families" (Ph.D. diss., University of Chicago, 1978); Peter Kim, "Behavior Symptoms of Three Transracially Adopted Asian Children: Diagnostic Dilemma," *Child Welfare* 59 (1980): 213–24; Arnold Richard Silverman, "Transracial Adoption in the United States: A Study of Assimilation and Adjustment" (Ph.D. diss., University of Wisconsin, Madison, 1980); and William Feigelman and Arnold R. Silberman, "The Long-Term Effects of Transracial Adoption," *Social Service Review* 58 (1984): 588–602.

T. S. Chang, "The Self-Concept of Children in Ethnic Groups:

Black-Americans and Korean-Americans," *Elementary School Journal* 76 (1975): 52–58; Johng-doo Song, "Educational Problems of Korean Children in the United States," *Korean Observer* 6 (1975): 231–44; Michael G. Fowler, "An Analysis of the Problems of Korean Students in American Secondary Schools as Perceived by Korean Students and Parents and the Teachers in Public Schools" (Ed.D. diss., University of Northern Colorado, 1978); Bok-Lim C. Kim, *Korean-American Child at School and at Home: An Analysis of Interaction and Intervention Through Groups*, Project Report to the Administration for Children, Youth, and Families, U.S. Department of Health, Education, and Welfare (1980); and Suk-ho Jun, "Communication Patterns among Young Korean Immigrants," *International Journal of Intercultural Relations* 8 (1984): 373–389, deal with the children of contemporary immigrants.

The relationship between assimilation and education is analyzed in Eui-Young Yu, "Korean Bilingual Education in Sociological Perspective," *Bilingual Resources* 3 (1980): 4–8; Kenneth Kim et al., *Korean-Americans in Los Angeles: Their Concerns and Language Maintenance* (Los Alamitos, CA: National Center for Bilingual Research, 1981); Dong Ha Lee, "A Descriptive Analysis of Selected Korean Ethnic Schools in the United States" (Ed.D. diss., West Virginia University, 1981); Chung-Hee Park, "Ethnic Identification, Sociocultural Adjustment, and School Achievement of Korean-American Youth in Los Angeles" (Ph.D. diss., University of Southern California, 1981); and Nomyon Pak, "A Survey Study of Korean-American Acculturation, Value System, and Attitudes toward Bilingual Education in Northern California" (Ed.D. diss., University of San Francisco, 1984).

Studies of the elderly include Keum-Young Chung Pang, "Everyday Life, Health, and Illness of the Elderly Korean Immigrants: Cultural Construction of Illness" (Ph.D. diss., Catholic University of America, 1984); Christie Kiefer et al., "Adjustment Problems of Korean American Elderly," *Gerontologist* 25 (1985): 477–82; Paul I. Kurzeja et al., "Ethnic Attitudes of Asian American Elderly: The Korean Immigrants and Japanese Nisei," *Research on Aging* (1986): 110–27; and Jae-Heung Park, "Exchange Resources and Their Effects upon Status in the Family, Health, Adjustment to the Host Society, and Subjective Well-Being: A Case Study of Korean Elderly in New York City" (Ph.D. diss., State University of New York, Buffalo, 1986).

Other aspects of Korean American family life are discussed in Don Chang Lee, "Korean Families in America," *Migration Today* 5 (1977): 13–15; Kwang Chang Kim et al., "Division of Household Tasks in Korean Immigrant Families in the United States," *International Journal of Sociology of the Family* 9 (1979): 161–75; Byung Chul Ahn, "The Determinants of the Husband's Household Task Participation in Korean Immigrant Families" (M.A. thesis, University of Iowa, 1981); Heeja Kim Chang, "Parental Authority as a Factor in Decision Making of Korean-American Youth" (Ph.D. diss., Michigan State University, 1982); George De Vos, "Achievement Motivation and Intra-Family Attitudes in Immigrant Koreans," *Journal of Psychoanalytic Anthropology* 6 (1983): 25–71; Chong Ok Kim, "Korean Immigrant Mothers in the United States: Patterns of Assimilation in Relation to the Perception of Their Children's Behavior" (D.S.W. diss., Adelphi University, 1983); Pyong Gap Min, "An Exploratory Study of Kin Ties Among Korean Immigrant Families in Atlanta," *Journal of Comparative Family Studies* 15 (1984): 59–75; Kwang Yoi Yom, "Adolescent Relationships with Parents as Perceived by Selected Korean-American Early Adolescents and Their Counterparts in Korea" (Ed.D. diss., Temple University, 1985); E. C. Choi, "Unique Aspects of Korean-American Mothers," *Journal of Obstetric, Gynecologic, and Neonatal Nursing* 15 (1986): 394–400; Alice Yun Chai, "Sexual Division of Labor in the Contexts of Nuclear Family and Cultural Ideology Among Korean Student-Couples in Hawaii," *Humboldt Journal of Social Relations* 10 (1986): 153–74; and Kay Kyung-sook Song, "Defining Child Abuse: Korean Community Study" (D.S.W., University of California, Los Angeles, 1986).